A
Flexible
Approach
to
Working Hours

A Flexible Approach to Working Hours

J. CARROLL SWART

amacom

A Division of American Management Associations

To be published by AMACOM: *Alternative Work Schedules,* a research report on flexi-time, compressed workweeks, and permanent part-time employment by Stanley D. Nollen and Virginia H. Martin. The study, which is based on 805 responses from a mail questionnaire survey of managers, describes the extent to which each alternative work schedule is used, where and how they are used, how they were implemented, and what employers' experiences with them are. The reasons for both good and bad experiences are analyzed, and changes that resulted from them over time are identified.

Library of Congress Cataloging in Publication Data
Swart, John Carroll, 1931–
  A flexible approach to working hours.
  Includes index.
  1. Hours of labor, Flexible — United States.
  I. Title.
  HD5109.2.U5S95 331.2′572′0973   77-25074
  ISBN 0-8144-5461-5

Second Printing.

TO DIANE,
AND TO MY PARENTS

Preface

Among the many things that motivated me to write this book—and shored up my confidence—was first and foremost my intense interest in the subject. Secondly, little had been written in book form about flexible working hours in the United States. A third factor was my extensive travel and teaching experiences in Europe, experiences that provided great illumination on the similarities and differences of working life in varied cultures. And lastly, a multidisciplinary academic background plus years of teaching management courses in organizational behavior and personnel administration in universities produced a vital awareness of problems and issues in the world of business organizations.

I owe immeasurable gratitude to my wife, Diane, for her empathy and understanding during the many months of research and writing. Deepest gratitude is also owed to my parents, Julia and Jack Swart, for their quiet reassurance.

Dean J. B. Black and Associate Dean John Hannaford of the Ball State College of Business are two scholars who provided generous support and encouragement. I am equally indebted to Sajjad A. Hashmi, Chairman of the Finance and Management Department. For funding allocations I appreciate very much the efforts of Dr. Joseph Brown and the Bureau of Business Research. Michael A. Murray, a graduate student, gave valuable assistance, and a warm note of thanks goes also to Mary Ann Livovich and Leah Paris, my expert secretaries, who worked those many long hours typing and proofreading the manuscript.

To the various organizations and managers providing me with information that formed the foundation on which this book is constructed, I extend my deep appreciation.

Last, but not least, my gratitude to Eric Valentine, Acquisitions and Planning Editor of the American Management Associations, for his sophisticated guidance and encouragement, and to AMACOM for overall publication support.

College of Business   *J. Carroll Swart*
Ball State University
Muncie, Indiana

Contents

Introduction

"For me, the workday begins at 8:00 A.M. and it ends at 5:00 P.M." For about the past thirty years in the United States, that statement aptly described the typical workday of the average full-time employee. The Fair Labor Standards Act of 1938 established as norms the 5-day workweek, 8 work hours per day, and 40 work hours per week. Those standards have had remarkable staying power—they remain in effect to this day late in 1977. Typically, employees go to work at one fixed time. And there is a fixed morning work break; there is a fixed lunch break; there is a fixed afternoon work break; there is a fixed quitting time. That is all part of a normal workday.

Although the issue of working hours may be perceived as one in which change forces have been relatively inactive, it is apparent that we live in an age in which few things remain sacred—including work schedules. Must all permanent employees in an organization adhere to the same work schedule? Do alternative work patterns exist which would aid employees and organizations in their efforts to attain objectives? With increasing frequency these questions are being answered in the affirmative.

Part-time employment is one alternative. Traditionally, it means regular voluntary employment carried out over a workday distinctly shorter than normal, in which the employment is considered permanent rather than temporary or intermittent. Characteristically one discovers part-time employment opportunities where tasks can be accomplished in less than a full workday. Examples are theater usher, clerk at a retail store that remains open for extended hours, part-time bookkeeper. According to the U.S. Department of Labor, persons

1

employed for fewer than 35 hours per week fall into the category of part-time employees.

A second version of part-time employment concerns "job sharing" (or "twinning"), in which the responsibility for completing one full-time job is divided between two part-time employees. Under job sharing, a company that needs a typist for 8 hours a day can hire two employees to share the daily responsibility of discharging the 8 hours of typing work. Person A might work 4 hours and Person B might work 4 hours, or Person A might work 3 hours and Person B might work 5 hours. Job sharing may become more popular in future years, especially among employees who want to trade income for additional leisure. An interesting job-sharing experiment was under way in Sweden in 1977, where married couples acted as two-person teams.

A second alternative is the *task system*. No set number of hours of work is required. The employee is free to end the workday when the day's job responsibilities are fulfilled. Methods engineers determine a standard work output for 8 hours for a particular position in, for example, a furniture factory. On any particular workday, whenever the employee assigned to that position has accomplished the task responsibilities, he or she is free to leave.

The *compressed workweek* is a third alternative. Under this system a workweek is compressed into fewer than 5 full working days. One version is the $4\frac{1}{2}$-day week, wherein an employee works 8 to 9 hours a day on four days of the week and $\frac{1}{2}$ day on the fifth day. A second model requires a worker to put in 9 to 10 hours a day, 4 days a week. The 4/40 plan (4 workdays per week and 10 hours per day) has been the subject of considerable discussion and controversy over the past few years. The 3-day week is yet another version of the compressed workweek. A person works 12 to 13 hours a day, 3 days per week. Additional variations of compressed workweek models exist, but these are the main ones.

In *group flexibility*, employees decide as a group — sometimes with and sometimes without direct management participation — on a specific work arrival time that remains in effect for one day, or a limited number of days.

Staggered hours is a schedule in which employees arrive at work at different times according to a predetermined master plan. Different interval frames are established for employees to begin the workday. Once an arrival time is established for a particular worker, that time usually remains in effect over many weeks and months.

Flexitour is an alternative work schedule in which the worker selects one interval frame at which to begin work, and remains on the specific schedule until afforded the opportunity to switch to another tour. Depending on the overall plan, another "open season" for selecting a different schedule could be based on each pay period or each quarter, or could be semiannual, seasonal, or annual.

Flexitime ("gliding time") is a working pattern in which an employee can, on a daily basis and within specific limits, start and finish work at his or her discretion, so long as the total number of hours required for a given time period are completed.

This book does not discuss part-time employment or the task system. By indirect reference and for comparison purposes, it does touch upon the 4-day workweek; yet the 4-day workweek is not the central subject either. This book is mainly about group flexibility, staggered hours, flexitour, and flexitime. Where the subject is alternative work schedules, close to 90 percent of the focus is on flexitime.

Flexitime and flexible working hours are aspects of total organizational life and, for that reason, any in-depth examination of these systems must be seen within the larger entity that we call the quality of working life. Part I of this book is addressed to the related topics of the quality of working life, including humanistic management, an approach that has received wide attention. Chapter 1 studies the quality of work life on conceptual and abstract levels. Changes in the ideas about the relative importance of work in an individual's life and about job enrichment are the central topics. Chapter 2 concerns applications of humanistic management in organizations. Humanistic management is rooted in the contention that an organization is more likely to attain hoped-for goals when its employees perceive the organization as a main instrument through which they are able to fulfill their human needs. The discussion of humanistic management is not abstract and philosophical but realistic, with descriptions of actual business situations where, in order to achieve higher levels of work motivation, performance, satisfaction, and morale, modifications were made in work content and in the work environment.

The first section in the book ends on the note that heretofore in the United States most organizations have failed to realize the potential values to be derived through the more flexible utilization of time. This book has as one of its objectives the remedying of such a situation.

Part II, consisting of Chapters 3 through 10, forms the heart of the book. It is in Part II that the reader discovers the intricacies of flexitime and flexible working hours.

Chapter 3 clarifies four alternative work schedules: staggered hours, flexitour, flexitime, and group flexibility. An automatic time-recording instrument often used in conjunction with flexitime is also explained.

Chapter 4 concerns the origins and development of the flexitime system outside the United States. Following a brief sketch relating to historical origins, the remainder of the chapter is devoted to illustrations of flexitime programs in other nations.

Chapter 5 investigates flexitime's growing pains in America. The section reveals particulars concerning three federal laws that affected flexitime. Case examples show applications of those laws in organizational settings. Presented next is a listing of the major reasons why flexitime got off to a slow start in the United States. In section four the views of unions about flexible hours are investigated. A fifth section focuses on jobs and unemployment, and the next section deals with proposals aimed at altering overtime-pay laws. The final section in the chapter surveys legislative proposals in the period 1975–1977 to change overtime-pay requirements and allow for more flexibility in work scheduling.

Chapter 6 shows applications of alternative work schedules in the private sector in the United States. Companies in diversified industries are included in the discussion, and illustrations of group flexibility, staggered hours, flexitour, and flexitime are given. On occasion, indirect references are made to the compressed workweek. Major consideration is devoted to the flexitime concept. Some readers may prefer to read the chapter in its entirety; others may prefer to survey the chapter's contents first and follow up by studying in more detail those companies of particular interest.

Are there organizations outside the private sector using flexible hours? If the answer is yes, what are their experiences? Alternative work schedules outside the private sector is the subject of Chapter 7. A program at a nonprofit association is described. Discussion then turns to alternative work patterns in municipal and federal government agencies. As in Chapter 6, central attention is drawn to flexitime in Chapter 7.

Chapter 8 concentrates on flexitime and on listing the system's limitations. The listing is based both on limitations actually experienced and on those that are viewed in the light of potential drawbacks. As pointed out in the chapter, the drawbacks may or may not occur in an organization that establishes a flexitime program. Some 21 different drawbacks are identified. Immediately following each stated drawback is a brief clarification, including an illustration.

Chapter 9 presents flexitime's advantages. As many as 37 of these are catalogued under five headings: benefits to the community; off-the-job advantages to employees; advantages to employees relating directly to the job; advantages to organizations based on objective measures of productivity; and other benefits to organizations. Similar to the perspective advanced in Chapter 8, the point of view taken in Chapter 9 is that flexitime's advantages are real but not inevitable. The benefits may or may not occur in an organization that establishes a flexitime program.

How to set up a flexitime program in your organization is the subject of Chapter 10. The reader is given a sequential outline of suggested steps to follow, from a determination of flexitime's feasibility to an evaluation of an extensive flexitime program in operation. The chapter contains five major sections: determining the feasibility of flexitime; carrying out a flexitime pilot study; planning and developing an expansive flexitime program; implementation; and evaluating results of an expansive flexitime program.

Part III takes a look into the future. Explored initially in Chapter 11 are three prominent and vital topics that concern us now and that will occupy our thoughts in the future: work, leisure, and productivity. Interwoven amidst the contextual framework is a discussion of the relevancy of flexitime. Near the end of the chapter I present my overall point of view about flexitime in relation to the future.

Part I

Managing Workers in an Age of Turbulence

1

The quality of working life

Some answers—and additional questions

There can be no joy in life without joy in work.
St. Thomas Aquinas

The Industrial Revolution involved not only the mechanization of tasks previously performed by people but also the organization of work on a machine principle. This principle placed the machine in the foreground. A new direction in the individual's relation to his or her work was thereby established; that is, the worker's role was to attend to the needs of machines and to fill in the gaps between the processes carried out by the equipment.

The full implications of this concept were brought out by the founders of the so-called "scientific management school," especially Frederick Winslow Taylor (1856–1917). According to Taylor, not only were the operations of machines to be scientifically engineered, but the operations of each individual were to be planned with detailed precision and exactitude. Applications involved the minute division of tasks among workers. The philosophy achieved its ultimate expression in twentieth-century assembly-line procedures, where a worker frequently may perform operations taking only a few seconds, often with little understanding of the significance of the task to the total operation. In numerous ways scientific management reduced employees' freedom and opportunity to introduce variety into their tasks or into their manner of carrying out those tasks. It was a kind of tech-

9

nological determinism, in which requirements of the technology prescribed the tasks of the worker within very narrow limits.

One must not forget, however, that the "machine approach" to human work has produced tremendous benefits for every level of society. It has made possible a dramatic rise in living standards in all nations that have applied it, together with a shorter workday and increased leisure. It is steadily removing drudgery and fatigue from much human work. In many ways the onward march of technological sophistication exerts a vitally liberating influence on human welfare.

The Changing Concept of Work

The machine approach to human work, however, has come under criticism for its alleged dehumanizing effects on workers. To use Douglas McGregor's terminology, Theory X thinking was part and parcel of scientific management philosophy. The Theory X manager assumes that the average person has an inherent dislike for work and will avoid it whenever possible. People must therefore be coerced and threatened with punishment to get them to exert effort toward the achievement of organizational goals. Furthermore, such workers contrive to avoid responsibility, have little ambition, and want security above all.

Criticisms of scientific management take yet another form. The assertion that "labor is not a commodity" contains an indictment against the machine approach to human labor. This contention implies that the work of a man or a woman is not a product to be judged solely by economic considerations. Instead, each human being has a need and a right to work, not only to survive but also to express his or her own individuality. From the view that labor is not a commodity, it follows that the nature of human work and the conditions under which it is done are not to be determined by economic factors alone; considerations of social justice must also be weighed. This perspective opens the way directly to the premise that an individual's work and the conditions under which it is done should preserve human dignity, and should also give the individual power to influence the nature of his or her life at work and to guarantee that the work environment does not impair the individual's life as a citizen and as a person. In effect, one sees the evolutionary development of a humanistic approach to people as workers.

What is meant by the phrase "humanization of work"? The International Institute for Labor Studies asserts that the concept includes at least six strands of thought. One is the need to protect employees from hazards to health and safety, while providing physical working conditions appropriate to the living and social standards of the time. In effect, this aspect of the concept of humanization of work covers the *physical working environment.*

A second aspect is the *wage-work bargain,* which focuses on such factors as wages, hours, and fringe benefits. Whereas concern with the physical working environment implies that employees should work under "decent" conditions, the wage-work bargain implies that employees should have an "adequate" and "fair" standard of living, negotiated freely by them or their union on equal terms with the employer.

Third, the *protection of workers against hazards of illness and unemployment* is an important objective. Although related to the wage-work-bargain clause, this third strand of thought places primary emphasis on provisions such as employees' compensation insurance, unemployment compensation, and group life, medical, hospital, and disability insurance.

Fourth, concern for the humanization of work also emphasizes the *protection of the worker against the exercise of arbitrary authority* by the employer. Grievance procedures are a tangible expression of this concern.

Fifth, the *protection and extension of human rights in the society,* enabling employees to have their interests represented by their own organizations, is an important element. Rights to establish and strengthen unions represent this feature.

Finally, there is the strand of thought centering attention on *workers' needs for meaningful and satisfying work and for participation in decisions that affect the workers' situation.* McGregor's Theory Y provides an example and reinforces ideas about employee participation in decision making. As explained by McGregor, the average human being does not inherently dislike work. In fact, the expenditure of physical and mental effort in work can be as natural as it is in play or rest. Furthermore, workers will exercise self-direction and self-control in the service of objectives to which they're committed. External control and threats of punishment are not the only means for bringing forth employee effort. And, in terms of obligations, the average worker not only will tolerate and accept responsibility but will actually

seek it. In essence, McGregor asserts in his Theory Y that commitment to objectives is a function of the rewards associated with their
achievement. The most significant of such rewards—more ego and
self-fulfillment satisfactions—can be direct products of efforts toward
organizational goals.

Regarding the humanization of work and the six directions just
identified, a great deal has been done since the early days of the Industrial Revolution. What is new about the current interest in the
humanization of work and the quality of working life is the growing
demand that technology no longer be taken as given. Greater numbers of individuals and groups are insisting that technology and the
organization of work be changed to provide for more meaningful
work and for full participation of workers in all decisions that affect
them. In Germany in 1976, efforts aimed at adding additional
workers to Volkswagen's supervisory board are an example of the
kind of full participation some labor groups want. And in England
and Sweden in 1977, labor unions were similarly engaged in pushing
for legislation designed to place their members on company direc-
torship boards.

The new demands go much further than those of the "human
relations" movement of the 1950s. Then the demands for better
human relations between management and subordinates called for a
degree of participation by workers, but they stopped far short of the
changes in technology, tasks, and organization of work now ad-
vocated.*

No Will to Manage

The changing concept of work can also be viewed from within
the occupational framework of managers and potential managers. Is
there a different concept of work and its purpose among tomorrow's
managers? According to research conducted by Lewis B. Ward and
Anthony G. Athos at the Harvard Business School, major limitations
on the concentration and effectiveness of corporate power and service
may take the form not of legal constraints but rather of slow starva-
tion from lack of future managerial talent.

*Some information discussed in this section was obtained from "Humanization
of Work and the Quality of Working Life—Trends and Issues," by Yves Delamotte and
Kenneth F. Walker, *International Institute for Labor Studies, Bulletin 11* (Geneva, Switzerland: International Institute for Labor Studies, 1974).

Research by John B. Miner* of the University of Georgia indicates a notable shift among students away from the types of motivation characterizing those who typically seek managerial careers in large corporations and succeed in those careers. Six main factors were noted as contributing to the motivation to manage. His measurements in numerous companies led Miner to the conclusion that managers scoring high on the factors tend not only to be rated high on job performance but also to move up in the organization more rapidly than others. In all six factors, managerial groups consistently scored higher than the students. Furthermore, students' managerial motivation scores have moved steadily downward over the past years. What are these managerial motivation characteristics?

1. *Favorable Attitude Toward Authority.* Managers are expected to act in ways that will not provoke negative reactions from their superiors; ideally, positive responses are elicited. Also, managers must be able to exert influence and represent their group upward in the organization. This necessitates a good relationship between managers and their superiors.

2. *Desire to Compete.* A strong competitive element is built into managerial work, at least insofar as peers are concerned. Managers must compete for the available rewards, both for themselves and for those accountable to them. On occasion, a challenge may also come from below, among a manager's own subordinates.

3. *Assertive Motivation.* Managers are expected to take charge, to make decisions, to take such disciplinary action as may be necessary, and to protect members of their group.

4. *Desire to Exercise Power.* Managers must exercise power over their subordinates and direct their actions in a manner consistent with organizational goals. They must tell others what to do when this becomes necessary and back up their words through positive and negative sanctions. The person who finds such behavior difficult and emotionally disturbing, who prefers not to command others or be-

---

*"The Real Crunch in Managerial Manpower," *Harvard Business Review*, November-December, 1973, pp. 146–158.

lieves it is wrong to do so, probably cannot be expected to meet requirements calling for the exercise of power.

5. *Desire for a Distinctive Position.* The managerial job requires that a manager behave differently toward subordinates from the ways subordinates behave toward each other. Such a person must be willing to occupy the center of the stage and assume a position of high visibility. He or she must lead in ways that invite attention and perhaps criticism from others in the group.

6. *A Sense of Responsibility.* The managerial job requires acceptance of task demands and the imperative to get the work out. Things that have to be done must actually be done. A manager must be capable of handling these types of responsibilities and, ideally, of gaining some satisfaction from them.

In spite of the research findings, one might argue that no talent shortage will result because students will be forced into management positions by their need and desire for money, even if they lack all managerial motivation. Once they are on the scene, exposure to managerial work will change their thinking and their managerial motivation scores will soon become similar to those of successful managers of today. Unfortunately, such a turnabout tends not to occur, Miner claims. He has found little evidence indicating that managerial motivation increases in the normal course of events merely because of exposure to the job. Managers in their fifties and sixties have the same scores on the average as those in their thirties and forties.

From what I understand, Miner's recent researches have disclosed no significant trends away from directions set forth in his 1973 *Harvard Business Review* article.

Who Are the Workaholics?

The product slogan "We're Number One" can be appropriately borrowed in referring to the economic power of the United States. America got to be number one for many reasons. Hard work and the Protestant ethic contributed strongly. Traditionally, hard work has been up there with motherhood and apple pie, both as a religious virtue and as a form of patriotism. That leads to the question: If a person regularly and persistently works hard, is he a workaholic?

The verb "to work" causes more confusion than elucidation. In essence, the verb means "to spend or use energy," which says nothing about whether the work is painful or joyful. Historically and implic- itly, to work suggests painful energy expenditure, yet we also use the verb on occasion to describe joyful experiences. If I say "I worked in the yard all weekend," you don't know if you should commiserate or congratulate me. If I enjoyed myself, this verb is inappropriate, but we have no other.

According to Wayne Oates, a behavioral scientist who wrote a book on workaholism, work addicts drop out of the human commu- nity. They're slaves to a set schedule, merciless in their demands on themselves for peak performance. They cannot delegate authority. They're compulsively overcommitted. Oates suggests that such peo- ple are sick.

My own opinion is that reservations must be stated before one labels hard-working people as sick or workaholics. Why are they com- mitted to the work arena? Are they satisfied and, in a sense, in control of their destiny? Do they really enjoy what they're doing? Are they in control of their work pursuits? Or do they feel they're overrun by events and deadlines, many of which they perceive to be devoid of real meaning?

Beverly Sills is one of this nation's leading opera stars. All she does, she says, is work, work, and more work. She is compulsive, maybe even obsessive, about opera. But she is also quick to state that she experiences opera as a joyful art form, not a torturous thing. Ad- vertising executive Mary Wells Lawrence and ABC's newscaster Bar- bara Walters also are deeply absorbed in their work. Yes, it might be appropriate to say that their work is their life. What these three women have in common is a delight in what they do.

Bob Hope is obsessed with work. As he puts it, "It's my bag." This comedian finds gratification and fulfillment in his professional endeavors and in the recognition derived through work. When he's not working, he feels out of sorts. In 1977 he cut short a fishing vaca- tion in British Columbia because, as he says, the fish didn't applaud. Ralph Nader and businessman-inventor Bill Lear are two other ex- amples of work-oriented men.

Appraise the work habits of Beverly Sills, Mary Wells Lawrence, Barbara Walters, Bob Hope, Ralph Nader, and Bill Lear. They pur- sue different careers. Their hours are long, their work is demanding. They're not much for vacations. They seem rushed, even driven. But they're not workaholics. To a significant extent, they control their work destiny; they're not overrun by events. More important, they ap-

pear to be having too good a time. On the other hand, take the salesman who doesn't really enjoy what he's doing, who is not personally
sold on the product he's pushing, who cuts short his vacation because
of a morbid fear that others in the territory might replace him. He
slaves long hours to bring home "a pile of bread." This worker is not
deriving satisfaction through his labors. Essentially, he's not really
having a good time. In my estimation, he's a workaholic.

There are a lot of workaholics. But concepts of work are changing. Years ago there was little discussion of the merits and demerits of
hard work and almost no discussion of workaholism, because for all
practical purposes the word did not exist. We reported on John
Miner's findings, namely, that increasing numbers of students are
questioning whether being a successful manager is worth all the effort. Other studies, notably the surveys of Daniel Yankelovich, reveal
that people over a broad scale are examining the work ethic more and
more closely.

Cultural Trends Transforming the American Work Ethic

Daniel Yankelovich, professor of psychology at New York University, has been measuring attitudes for many years. His findings
also point in the direction of a changing work ethic.* What are some
of the new cultural trends?

The Changing Definition of Success. When reviewing the first two
decades following World War II, one is inclined to conclude that most
Americans shaped their ideas of success around money, occupational
status, possessions, and the social mobility of their children. More
recently, however, thoughts about success have revolved primarily
around various forms of self-fulfillment. The emphasis is on self and
its unrealized potential. Accompanying this change is a corresponding change in ideas about one's moral obligations to family, to
friends and acquaintances, to one's employer, and to the community.
In short, whereas a major motif of the past was "keeping up with the
Joneses," more people are now saying "I have my own life to live." In

*Daniel Yankelovich, "Turbulence in the Working World: Angry Workers,
Happy Grads," *Psychology Today,* December 1974, pp. 81–87.

the climb for success, money, possessions, and a good position are still important, but they must compete with other, less materialistic means of self-fulfillment.

Managers and organizations can no longer assume the automatic loyalty of their employees. The willingness of employees to subordinate their own interests unquestioningly to the company is slowly disappearing. Instead, workers are asking why they should show allegiance, and want to know what satisfactions they can derive from being part of a larger unit.

The Reduced Fear of Economic Insecurity. Inflation and unemployment during the last few years have increased the concern of young people about finding a job. Yet beneath this concern lies a deep-seated assumption, bred in part by the extended period of economic prosperity following World War II, that it is not all that difficult to make a living.

Among working people, the prospect that they might be unable to make a living seems curiously unreal. Although 60 percent of all adults continue to place economic security above all other goals, a large 40 percent announce they are prepared to take economic risks to enhance the quality of their lives. This change in values is new and far reaching, and quite obviously has significant implications for the work world.

The Spreading Psychology of Entitlement. A new psychology of entitlement is ushering in a variety of new "social rights." Wants and desires are being converted into a set of mandatory rights. We're witnessing a move from "I'd like to participate more in decisions that affect my job" to "I have the right to take part in decisions that affect my job." This process is not new, but in recent years it has accelerated.

Disillusionment with the Cult of Efficiency. People are beginning to question the Western passion for efficiency and cost effectiveness. Although the general public tends to be less critical than the cultural radicals about the cult of efficiency, more and more young people are beginning to wonder whether efficiency and rationalization are robbing them of life's excitement and mystery.

According to Yankelovich's surveys, students are not turned off by the thought of hard work. On the other hand, they demand that the hard work center on areas in which more fulfillment is possible. In their view, the problem is that hard work does not pay off in terms of self-fulfillment. In 1967 almost seven out of ten said they thought "hard work always pays off"; by 1973 only four out of ten students held that belief.

Students believe that hard work and fulfillment are more likely combinations in medicine, law, and numerous professions. In 1973 some 87 percent of the respondents ranked self-fulfillment as very important, whereas only 43 percent ranked work as very important. Evidence suggests that while most college students readily accept the necessity for hard work, these same students reject a nose-to-the-grindstone philosophy of life. In other words, they don't want to become workaholics.

But the more optimistic view of the future observed among college-educated people headed for the professions dramatizes the plight of the majority of young people. Seven out of ten young people in the nation do not attend college. The members of this majority recognize that they're less likely to find interesting work. In the past, this was not a crucial matter. People worked mainly for extrinsic rewards. Now, however, ideas about success and fulfillment and interesting work are seeping into the consciousness of all young people. Even those who will never attend college want interesting and challenging work. But as work is now organized, they will not readily find what they seek.

As explained by Yankelovich, because they are less insecure than their parents, these young people take "less crap" on the job. They're not automatically loyal to the organization. They feel free to express their discontent in myriad ways: absenteeism, lateness, insubordination, poor-quality work, and, at times, sabotage of company products and buildings. Moreover, if the work itself is not meaningful, they are more likely to opt for "30 and out" retirement, shorter workweeks, more leisure, and other methods for cutting down on their job commitment.

In summary, as shown by Yankelovich's findings—and as related to the changing concept of work—the definition of success is undergoing transformation. This suggests that increasing stress will be placed on the quality of working life, so that the psychological demands will approximate the desire for an adequate economic payoff. Work will have to pay off in self-fulfillment as well as money.

Job Enrichment: Mixed Reviews

Herzberg and Job Enrichment

Frederick Herzberg is referred to as the contemporary father of job enrichment. During the 1950s and 1960s this psychologist concentrated on studying work satisfaction and work motivation. More recently, at the University of Utah, Herzberg has utilized his earlier findings in plotting profiles of organizational health and illness.* For those readers unfamiliar with Herzberg's motivation-hygiene ideas, a brief explanation is provided.

Motivation-hygiene theory suggests that job dissatisfaction and job satisfaction are produced by different work factors. What makes people satisfied at work relates to the content of their jobs — specifically, achievement, recognition for achievement, increased responsibility, opportunities for growth, interesting work, and advancement. These six factors are known as motivators because, where they are present in appropriate amounts in any organization, they bring about work motivation as a corollary to their creating positive attitudes of job satisfaction.

On the other hand, what makes people unhappy at work is not what they do but how well or poorly they are treated. The dissatisfaction factors are related to the context or environment of the job and not to the content of the work. The main dissatisfiers are company policy and administration practices, interpersonal relationships, supervision, salary, status, security, and working conditions. These factors describe the job context and, in their negative aspects, serve to produce job dissatisfaction. They are referred to by Herzberg as hygiene factors, symbolizing their importance in making up the preventive and environmental conditions of work.

In essence, Herzberg is saying that job satisfaction and motivation are rooted, not in the context or environment of work, but in factors intrinsic to the content of the work itself. Organizations are missing the boat when the reward package focuses almost exclusively on providing workers increasing returns in forms such as more money, better fringe benefits, and better working conditions. According to Herzberg, such hygiene factors prevent worker dissatisfaction, but have little to do with building satisfaction and motivation.

---

*Frederick Herzberg, "Motivation-Hygiene Profiles: Pinpointing What Ails the Organization," *Organizational Dynamics*, Fall 1974, pp. 18–29.

Herzberg's ideas have been used as a foundation for building job enrichment programs. In effect, organizations aiming to enrich jobs study them with the intent of building into them more opportunities for achievement, recognition for achievement, interesting work, increased responsibility, growth, and advancement. Chapter 2 includes a discussion of the work arrangements at a pet-food plant in Kansas; in most essentials, what is described is the planning and implementation of a job enrichment program.

A Government View of the Quality of Working Life

In 1973 came the much publicized book *Work in America,* a special task force report submitted to Elliot L. Richardson, then Secretary of Health, Education and Welfare. The report was prepared under the auspices of the W. E. Upjohn Institute for Employment Research, and was directed by a member of its staff, Dr. Harold L. Sheppard.

According to the researchers, job frustration is intensifying and is finding expression in reduced productivity, the doubling of mandays lost per year through strikes, rising absenteeism, high turnover rates, sabotage, and poor quality of work. The study points to the irony that these symptoms have increased despite general improvements in the physical conditions and monetary rewards for work. The panel report notes that dull, repetitive, seemingly meaningless tasks offering little challenge or worker discretion are causing discontent among employees at all occupational levels. One of the main problems, it is claimed, is that work has not changed fast enough to keep up with the rapid and widespread changes in employee values, attitudes, and aspirations.

The study favorably cites research studies showing that productivity increased and social problems decreased when workers participated in decisions. The project group asserts that the discontent of women, minorities, youth, and blue-collar workers would be considerably less were these Americans to have an even more active voice in making the decisions that most directly affect their lives in their workplace.

Some Academics Criticize Job Enrichment

Many college professors are sympathetic to assertions that considerable alienation exists in the workforce and that job enrichment is the key to job satisfaction. On the other hand, many people in

academia do not support such views. Irving Kristol, New York University professor of urban values, wrote a biting commentary on the conclusions of *Work in America.* In a feature article in *The Wall Street Journal,* Kristol debunks the idea that the American worker is alienated. In his view, the HEW project group falls prey to a belief that the system dehumanizes its workers because it forces them to sell their labor as a commodity. Since the assertion is assumed to be a fact, and since it is further assumed (quite reasonably) that no one likes to be dehumanized, the project group is quick to discover discontent where others might have trouble finding it.

Kristol cites a report showing that more than 75 percent of American workers, when asked if they are satisfied with their jobs, answer in the affirmative. It would therefore seem that *Work in America* is trying to show that these people don't mean what they say. Thus, if a telephone operator tells an interviewer that she finds her work satisfying, but also says that she'd like to switch her job for something better, the HEW task force concludes that she's not really satisfied with, but is rather really alienated from, her work. If blue-collar workers state that they're not as fascinated with their daily tasks as doctors and lawyers are, this too is taken as an unmistakable sign of alienation. Kristol goes on to say that it's utopian to expect ordinary working people to be as content with their jobs as the most successful lawyer or surgeon.

In Kristol's judgment, the following is a realistic perspective. First, many of the commentators who talk about worker alienation have little firsthand knowledge of the world of work that is inhabited by ordinary people. Second, when contemplating the assembly line and the possibility that many of those who work there might be alienated, one should realize that less than 5 percent of all persons in the labor force actually work on assembly lines. Third, undue attention devoted to Detroit and the automobile industry makes for gross distortion. General Motors is not a typical firm and the automobile industry is not a typical industry. More typical is the Bendix Corporation, in which less than 10 percent of the 60,000 employees are on the assembly line, while 50 percent are white-collar workers and 30 percent are professional and technical staff. Fourth, the average employee in the United States does not work for a manufacturing firm. More and more, as the American economy advances further into its post-industrial, service-oriented phase, fewer people are engaged in blue-collar work of any kind.

Charles L. Hulin, University of Washington psychology professor, has some provocative thoughts on the subject of alienation and the need for job enrichment. As he explains, enrichment efforts are based on a faulty view of human nature. The assumption behind job enrichment is that all workers can be made to think that their job is their life. That simply is not the case. The job enrichment philosophy now current resembles earlier single-variable notions that also promised to solve motivation problems in industry. Late in the nineteenth century and early in the twentieth century, there were the economic-man model and the propositions of Frederick W. Taylor that assumed that rational working people would work for little else than money. Later, Harvard researcher Elton Mayo conducted the Hawthorne studies and asserted that man was motivated by social needs. Time has discredited the hopes that either Taylorism or Mayoism would be panaceas, and time will also lessen the zeal of those who crusade on behalf of job enrichment and its theory that man is motivated primarily by self-actualization needs.

According to Hulin, job enrichment shares the same failings that weakened the notions of Taylor and Mayo, in that all these approaches consider the industrial environment and its inhabitants as less complex than they are. Job enrichers have devised schemes that presuppose the widespread acceptance of their own middle-class values, with the emphasis on job satisfaction and self-actualization. Hulin suggests that there are profound differences between worker subgroups; the values and attitudes toward work found among these subgroups vary as drastically as they do among certain primitive tribes.

Consider the Tikopians of Oceania and the Siriono of the Amazon Basin. As Hulin describes them, the Tikopians view idleness as akin to a religious offense; every day they begin work early, take few breaks, and even compete among themselves to get things done. By contrast, the Siriono see work as a necessary evil. They work only to obtain food and immediately take their ease once the food is in hand. In attitudes toward work, Hulin's theory is that our own labor force may be part Tikopian and part Siriono. He concludes that work is likely to be perceived as a means to an economic end by the unskilled worker, whereas it has intrinsic meaning for the white-collar worker.

George Strauss is a professor of business administration at the University of California in Berkeley. He supports a number of job enrichment ideas, but also holds certain reservations. As basic needs are largely fulfilled, workers may be in a position to demand satisfaction for their egoistic and self-actualization needs. If so, such employees are less likely to settle for apathy or even for a job that offers high income and a rich social life but no intrinsic satisfaction. For such workers, money alone may have declining marginal utility and may no longer motivate them. On the other hand, it is also true that today's luxuries become tomorrow's necessities. Wants grow at least as fast as paychecks, and Strauss doubts if economic motivation will atrophy as fast as some psychologists suggest.

Strauss concludes that job dissatisfaction can be caused as much by low pay, job insecurity, inadequate fringe benefits, or inferior supervision as by lack of ego-fulfilling possibilities. For employees at all levels — even managers and professionals — lack of challenge is much less oppressive than lack of income. Workers as a whole are willing to tolerate large doses of boredom if they are paid enough. Strauss believes that intrinsic motivation factors are not to be ignored. Yet he tends to agree with those union leaders who argue that economic conditions are a greater cause of dissatisfaction than any intrinsic sterility on the job.

Additional skepticism exists. David Sirota, a management professor at the University of Pennsylvania's Wharton School, does not doubt the value of redesigning jobs. But he is disturbed that consultants prescribe it so indiscriminately. In his words: "Selling job enrichment like soap is bound to create a high failure rate." And the view is shared by Harry Levinson, president of the Levinson Institute in Cambridge, Massachusetts, and, on occasion, visiting professor at the Harvard Business School. He observes that job enrichment, worker teams, and participative management programs often provide relief that is more temporary than permanent.

Unions Eye Job Enrichment

To most unions and union leaders, job enrichment is bad news. In general, organized labor sees job enrichment as a scheme for getting more work out of fewer workers. It appears that job enrichment is clashing with what has long been a primary goal of unionism: negotiating standardized wage scales, seniority rights, and working conditions to ensure that everyone gets "a fair day's pay for a fair day's work."

According to William Winpisinger, a vice president of the International Association of Machinists, job enrichment is nothing more than a stopwatch in sheep's clothing. It is another attempt to divide workers and their union. This labor official is credited with the resounding statement: "If you want to enrich the job, enrich the paycheck. The better the wage, the greater the job satisfaction. There is no better cure for the blue-collar blues." Thus, he argues that the real ways to enrich jobs are those that trade unions have always pursued: higher wages, reduction of the workweek, earlier retirement, efforts to combat noise and heat, and so forth. In Winpisinger's view, job enrichment, as managers understand it, is above all a new means of increasing productivity, just as time and motion studies once were, with the sociologist's questionnaire now replacing the stopwatch.

As unions view it, the management decisions that workers resent, and that really cause alienation, are those that rearrange job assignments or upset existing work schedules without reference to the rights of the workforce. Unions fear that job enrichment will cost jobs. They conclude that substituting the questionnaire for the stopwatch is likely to result in no gain for workers.

According to a noted labor historian, job enrichment programs have been just as effective in reducing jobs as automation and stopwatches. And the rewards of productivity are not always equitably shared. Concerning the latter point, oftentimes an enriched job also means a job with increased responsibility. Employees of course believe that increased pay should go along with an expansion of responsibility; this point about increased pay coinciding with increased responsibility does pose a problem. In the words of a labor relations manager at a major glass company, "People expect money to follow naturally from deeper involvement in their work. We'll have to do something to bring pay along or we'll get into trouble."

In 1977 Leonard Woodcock resigned as president of the United Auto Workers. A few months prior to his resignation he asserted that job enrichment is the plaything of elitist academics writing a lot of nonsense. Woodcock agrees that work is monotonous and dull in many ways. "But if it is useful, the people who do it are entitled to be honored and not degraded, which is what's going on in this day and time." While Woodcock was putting down job enrichment, a UAW vice president was offering a different point of view, saying that the blue-collar blues are indeed a problem and that an intensive search for answers is necessary.

Finally, there's a life-and-death reason why most union leaders oppose job enrichment plans. In situations where employers faced with disruptive and costly employee discontent are forced to sincerely and honestly commit themselves to making disagreeable jobs more agreeable, unions will be faced with a major test of their ability to respond to a new situation and survive. For if the employer does manage actually to enrich a job, it seems inevitable that the employees involved will begin to question the need for paying union dues.

Further Observations

As explained, some people suggest that work alienation and the need to enrich jobs are mere inventions by intellectuals who see a problem where none exists. The views of respondents representing the International Institute for Labor Studies are of particular interest at this point in the discussion. Four basic arguments are advanced by these analysts.

> *Production workers are much more easily able to put up with monotonous, fragmentary, and repetitive jobs than intellectuals imagine.*

Supporters of the argument assert that inquiries among employees performing such jobs show no widespread dissatisfactions or particular frustrations. Also, when it is suggested to workers that they might try out new and more stimulating ways to do their jobs, they frequently show no enthusiasm and prefer to stick to the old system.

This argument and the observations introduced in its support are not convincing. Responses given to such questions as "Would you say you're satisfied with your present job?" are not significant. A simple psychological process may explain the frequency of affirmative responses to this type of question. Most production workers know they don't have much chance of finding different types of jobs offering substantially higher pay. Under such circumstances the best thing is to put up with the job one has. Satisfaction thus appears as the result of a process of adaptation that may take several years. It is probable that if these same workers were asked, "Would you want your son to perform the same job as you when he grows up?" significantly fewer of them would reply in the affirmative.

The fact that workers often display little enthusiasm for trying out more stimulating methods of production should not mislead anyone: this is a perfectly normal reaction for employees who have found a balance between what they get out of the enterprise and what they give to it, and who at the same time feel an instinctive mistrust of new initiatives on the part of the company. Do these reactions constitute a justification of the status quo? What seems more illuminating is that production workers who have participated in the numerous experiments dealing with the redesigning of jobs seldom have wanted to return to the old system. In short, when an opportunity is presented to workers to demonstrate their attitude to the traditional system and to their usual jobs, either by encouraging them to try out the new plan or by asking them whether they would like their children to do those jobs, the workers are more critical of the jobs they currently occupy or have occupied.

The need for achievement and participation does not
exist among most production workers. Needs and values
that are not really theirs are foisted on them.

Persons advancing this argument refer to the results of certain empirical studies and interviews, but one must determine what type of participation such information relates to. If participation is defined as the possibility of exerting an influence on one's immediate environment and of making certain decisions oneself with regard to matters of greater concern, then the reactions of workers will probably be more positive than if reference is to ineffective and perfunctory participation with a management group that is perceived as insincere, distant, and remote. All things considered, personal and concrete participation appears to be the more effective antidote to powerlessness.

In summary, the line of argument based on observation of workers' attitudes or on replies given in interviews is liable to uphold the status quo.

It is probable that workers will discover jobs
suitable for them and adapted to their personalities
either in their present enterprise or elsewhere.

This argument generally maintains that many workers prefer a life that is not too demanding, that they can put up with monotony and dullness, and that their true interests are off the job. By contrast, the production worker who really does aspire to achievement and greater independence is likely to find an appropriate job either in the organization of his or her employment or elsewhere.

This line of thought postulates a preestablished harmony between types of workers and types of jobs. Such a view of the world, however, appears far too optimistic and is refuted by the facts, particularly the high rates of absenteeism and quitting among young people in so many of today's industrial organizations.

Employees who want more satisfying work are not willing to give up traditional claims such as higher pay, better working conditions, and job security in exchange for work satisfaction.

This proposition—expressed most clearly in the statement: "If you want to enrich the job, increase the paycheck"—maintains that changes in the organization of work to make it more satisfying may result in raising costs and perhaps impairing the capacity of the organization to provide higher wages or provide better working conditions. In these circumstances, most employees confronted with a choice between job satisfaction and other benefits will choose those other benefits.

Although the above argument is valid in many instances, it does not eliminate the possibility that certain types of employees may define a good job as one that not only pays well but also provides on-the-job satisfaction. Naturally, the possibility that a demand for such jobs might materialize depends on many factors, including the state of the labor market. Some employees may have to forgo job satisfaction in exchange for better wages or job security. In fact, some may voluntarily choose to do so. Yet others may sacrifice economic gains in return for jobs they prefer on grounds of job satisfaction.

Of particular significance in this connection is the proportion of workers who would continue to work even if they had no need of money. One survey, for example, found that approximately 80 percent of employed men would continue to work, the proportion rising higher in occupations requiring training and skills and falling to 58 percent among unskilled workers. For these people, at least, work held greater significance than as a mere means to survival or to a higher income.

The Future Outlook

Will the present widespread interest in humanized forms of work fade into oblivion, or is it an indication of an enduring trend in industrial society? Of importance here is the extent to which the search for humanized work is driven by the need organization managers feel to solve practical problems surrounding their everyday basic business functions. To the extent that these managers perceive the question to be of practical significance, interest in the humanization of work may be expected to continue and even to grow.

Humanizing innovations in work are undoubtedly made by management for various reasons, including those based on practicality and expediency. In some instances the goal is to achieve more flexibility in order to cope more effectively with a variable economic environment. In other cases the objectives are to resolve certain personnel problems such as absenteeism, turnover, difficulties in recruitment and hiring, and unsatisfactory levels of work performance. To the degree that such problems persist or become more serious, managers of organizations will continue to be driven to search for solutions.

Of course, the humanization of work is not exclusively a concern of management trying to cope with practical problems. It is also an objective for workers. Here the question is the relative importance attached by workers to various rewards of working life and the concrete goals they seek at any given time.*

While it may be premature to give a definite answer to the multiple problems considered in this chapter, it is abundantly clear that the humanization of work is far from being a consensus issue. On the contrary, it suggests serious practical problems, including potential conflicts of interests between management and employees, between various types and groups of workers, and between business organizations and the community. It also may have wider economic and social implications and repercussions.

*Information in this section and the one preceding was obtained mainly from Delamotte and Walker, "Humanization of Work and the Quality of Working Life — Trends and Issues."

2

Humanistic management:

Applications in organizations

> *If you have a Mickey Mouse job and you*
> *put a good man in it, the odds are that*
> *you'll end up with a Mickey Mouse man.*
> ANONYMOUS

In 1922 Henry Ford said, "The average worker wants a job in which he does not have to put much physical effort. Above all, he wants a job in which he does not have to think." Henry Ford was a giant in the auto industry's early years, and a number of his ideas are valid to this day. On the other hand, very many executives today believe that Ford's philosophy is no longer valid. A growing number of business leaders have modified their attitudes concerning the relative importance of employee needs and values, and think that the behaviorists may have something when they talk about upgrading the workforce and giving people a greater sense of responsibility. To use the vernacular, "We've come a long way, baby."

The preceding chapter was essentially conceptual and abstract. We saw there that the concept of work is undergoing a metamorphosis, new ideas and values are evolving, and managers are witnessing the development of a humanistic management philosophy covering many aspects of the business environment. The contention is that an organization is more likely to attain hoped-for goals when its employees perceive that the organization itself is a main instrument through which they are able to fulfill higher-level as well as lower-level human needs.

In this chapter, humanistic management will be described in actual business situations where modifications were made in work content and in the work environment — with higher levels of work motivation, performance, satisfaction, and morale as the targets. Although job enrichment is proving to be an important means for achieving these four goals, it is not the only way.

Basically, job enrichment means letting workers plan and control more of their work. Or, expressed another way, it essentially means vertical job enlargement or job loading. By contrast, horizontal job enlargement involves adding somewhat similar tasks to a job without increasing planning and control responsibilities. Defining what job enrichment is in words is no problem, but I'm sure many managers and nonmanagement-level employees will agree that it's not always easy to know precisely when job enrichment is being used in particular on-the-job applications. In modifying jobs one is not always able to identify the precise point at which vertical job enlargement ends and horizontal enlargement begins. A point on which most of us might agree, however, is that job enrichment is a part of that larger subject identified as humanistic management.

Because business leaders as well as behavioral scientists are not in unanimous agreement on what job enrichment encompasses in actual job situations, I shall avoid semantic quicksands and, instead, discuss the human element in organizations mainly within a framework labeled humanistic management. Meanwhile, throughout our discussions of job enrichment, the reader should bear in mind our contractual arrangement, namely, that job enrichment is but one tool among others in humanistic management.

In the concrete examples of humanistic management innovations offered here, the reader is asked to answer for himself or herself the question: What applications of humanistic management, if any, might be appropriate in the organization where I work? No pious value judgments are intended by the author.

Two Examples: Logical or Bizarre?

At a large home-appliance firm in Japan, the battery division contains "self-control rooms," where many male workers attempt to relieve themselves of pent-up tensions. On approaching the control area, the worker first looks into a number of concave and convex mirrors. The immediate reaction to the sight of his own distorted image may be laughter. Next the worker enters a gymnasium equipped with punching bags and an assortment of exercise equipment, a place where he warms up for the main attractions.

He then moves to the central control room containing life-size dummies seated on knee-high platforms. He is provided with a bamboo stave and, yelling and cursing, clubs, swats, and slashes a life-size dummy to his heart's content, keeping in mind the individual (probably a boss) who is the object of his blows.

After his aggressive behavior is spent, he listens to one of a series of tape-recorded speeches by the board chairman himself, urging harmony and meaningful relationships. If these activities fail to satisfy the employee, a counselor is standing by in an adjacent room to talk with him.

The innovative employer also might want to consider applying lunar cycle theory to his workforce. A Japanese firm in the transportation industry takes into account each worker's lunar cycle, the few days each month when, according to some physiologists, the employee functions below par, as a woman during her menstrual period might. To keep depressed workers clear of danger, the company assigns them to nonhazardous jobs during their lunar cycle. The firm claims a 30 percent drop in its accident rate since the program went into effect.

Most readers probably feel that the two illustrations are ludicrous and far-fetched methods for improving employee work motivation, performance, satisfaction, and morale. I suggest that you keep an open mind about these methods. If, after a complete reading of this chapter, all other methods discussed seem bland and unworkable by comparison, then in aiming to improve the lot of workers in your organization you may want to try the Japanese style.

White-Collar Applications

A Banking Firm. A New York bank deliberately made a number of jobs more complicated. Targets were higher worker satisfaction and greater productivity. The bank previously had established a production-line setup for a segment of its check-sorting operations. One group of women took checks out of envelopes, another encoded the checks, another put entries in proper accounts, another stapled checks, and the last group enclosed checks in envelopes to be returned to customers.

A decision was made to abolish the production-line procedure. Individual employees were given responsibilities for handling a series of tasks from start to finish for specified accounts. In effect, each woman knew what accounts she was working on. In turn, clients of the bank, in this case commercial banks, knew — or could find out — which employee was handling their business. The result was that the women handled more total volume more efficiently than they had before.

As a specific example, Mary, a bank clerk, had the job of pulling invoices and checks out of envelopes and stacking them into three piles: one, under $10; another, between $10 and $25; and a third, over $25. She would then pass the piles on to the next person. After two months she was so bored she was ready to quit.

After the bank applied job enlargement concepts, Mary handled all the processing for 22 corporate accounts, from crediting payments to returning unsigned checks. She said that handling her own accounts was a lot more interesting and gave her feelings of accomplishment. In the four years prior to job enrichment, turnover in Mary's department averaged 59 percent a year, nearly double the bank's overall rate of 31 percent. After job changes were introduced, the turnover rate in the department plummeted to 24 percent. According to an assistant vice president, the impact of boredom on productivity had outweighed the benefits of extreme specialization.

An Insurance Company. Account supervisors at an insurance firm formerly spent about 35 percent of their time answering questions from subordinates and 45 percent doing production work — essentially handling clerical tasks when clerks ran into snags. With the application of humanistic management, clerks were delegated more authority and were encouraged to solve more problems on their own. In consequence, the two functions together consumed only 25 percent of the account supervisors' total time; the clerks felt greater satisfaction with their jobs; and account supervisors were able to devote more time to planning and budgeting.

A Brokerage Firm. Following work modifications in one office in a large brokerage firm, 17 clerks were able to do the work that a year earlier had required 25 employees. In addition, the worker error rate was reduced from 4 percent to 1 percent. Improvements were accomplished mainly by stimulating interest and making fuller use of potential. Previously, the clerical supervisor was spending 4 hours a day on the phone answering questions from brokers. The processing of stock certificates was broken down into so many tiny tasks that only the clerical supervisor could handle a question about end results.

After job tasks and relationships were reorganized, each clerk was assigned to handle all the office work on a certificate and to take responsibility for it. In processing stock certificates, each clerk was now required to sign her name and indicate her phone extension on the paperwork. Also, the company specified that clerks had to be able to handle incoming phone calls from brokers, and convey to them the accurate stock certificate information. One effect was that the clerical supervisor's phone time with brokers was reduced by 70 percent. The company found that overall results were positive in terms of employee satisfaction and productivity.

A Private Utility Company. Utilization managers for the American Telephone and Telegraph Company, at the urging of the personnel director for manpower, initiated job improvement programs at some 400 locations. In the capital city of a midwestern state, female employees once compiled telephone books by working on specific information pieces. Now that job enlargement concepts are being applied, employees have the responsibility of putting together all the white pages of a phone book, for example, for a specific city in the state. If a city is large, the phone book for that city is assembled by a team.

As another example within the AT&T system, the manager of the commercial division in a western state increased the service representatives' responsibilities and their authority to make decisions. The results were better customer service, more job satisfaction, and higher productivity. Turnover was reduced from 62 percent to 48 percent. The company saved $3,800 in training costs for each service representative who was retained instead of replaced.

In brief, the job enrichment program at AT&T contains four basic ingredients. First, the "work module" must be identified. In the company's terminology, the work module means a slice of work that gives an employee a "thing of my own." Slices of work are accumulated until one of three entities is created for the worker: a customer (usually someone outside the business), a client (usually someone inside the business, helping the employee serve the customer), or a task (in the manufacturing end of the business, for example, where, ideally, individual employees produce complete items). Second, the module must be controlled. That is, with management support the employee learns how best to handle an increase in responsibilities. The third essential ingredient is feedback. Defining a module and controlling it are exercises in futility unless the results of the employee's efforts are discernible. These results are beamed directly to where they will nurture motivation, that is, to the employee. The fourth aspect goes beyond individual job enrichment and takes in the idea of "job nesting." In other words, related jobs are pulled together and different individual work units are formed. What evolves are cohesive, coordinated teams.

A Commercial Airline. In a midwestern city, one of the nation's largest airlines improved the commitment and morale of 20 of its agents who handle flight boarding. Two agents had been assigned to each flight, under the direction of a supervisor. In the redesign of the relationships of responsibility and authority, one of the agents was designated as flight coordinator and given the responsibility for getting the flight off the ground. It was necessary for him to clear only the most unusual decisions.

In one instance a flight coordinator delayed a takeoff to accommodate 20 passengers from a competing airline that had canceled its flight. In the coordinator's judgment the additional revenues would justify the delay.

A Sales Division. In Washington, West Virginia, the Marbon Division of Borg-Warner Corporation applied job enrichment ideas to the sales force. The plastic products division recently assigned its more productive sales personnel to plan the national sales meeting, develop a training program, and even develop marketing plans for a given product.

The division also is considering reducing each salesman's paperwork and expanding his authority to arrange prices. The manager of markets for the division is trying to make the sales job rewarding enough in its own right so that people will look at it as a career rather than as a stepping-stone.

Gripes from Sales People. Managers must give sales people a larger role in decision making and in planning and controlling their own work, according to a consulting firm. As reported in *The Wall Street Journal* in December 1976, the consulting firm surveyed some 1,800 sales people in different organizations and concluded that the biggest gripes were focused on the cutting of sales territories, on the proliferation of paperwork, and on preimposed sales priorities.

Most survey participants favor a stronger role in establishing their sales goals and in determining marketing strategies. They want larger and tougher territories and demand that they be "treated like pros" by their managers. One of their pet peeves is that they're required to do the legwork to grab a big order and then must watch the boss step in at the last minute to close the deal.

An Electronics Plant. Humanistic management is also incorporated in management training programs. At one of the nation's biggest firms, about 2,000 foremen and supervisors have participated in role-playing sessions. The program encourages managers to use alternative ways to deal with workers.

A foreman playing the role of a worker may act out a situation in which a worker is called in by his superior to discuss a problem — anything from absenteeism to poor work habits. The action is videotaped and shown to supervisors, who engage in lively discussions and critical analyses concerning the particular role-playing exercise. According to a personnel research executive, most men who have gone through the sessions go away feeling that they can be more effective in their jobs if they put aside their tough-guy image.

In one electronic components plant a group of supervisors went through the training. Ten weeks later, the workers they were supervising were performing at a level of production efficiency that was 20 percent higher than before the training. A research officer said, "We're not trying to change a foreman's behavior with a lot of theory. We're saying there's more to his job than just clobbering people when they get out of line, which is the way a shop has traditionally been run."

A Footwear Manufacturer. The R. G. Barry Corporation, a shoe manufacturer in Columbus, Ohio, has been attempting to measure the human element through human resource accounting. Working with researchers from the University of Michigan, the firm is one of a handful of enterprises trying to assess, in an unconventional way, how effectively their investments in human resources are being used.

Barry has incorporated human resource measures in its annual reports to stockholders, side by side with conventional accounting measures. The firm calculates the investment it makes in hiring and training new managers and in developing the abilities of existing managers. Then it amortizes this investment over appropriate periods.

A recent Barry Corporation balance sheet—in the column *Conventional and Human Resources*—provides an example. Under *Assets,* a financial figure indicates "New investments in human resources" ($1,561,264). Under *Liabilities,* "Deferred federal income taxes based upon full tax deduction for human resource costs" ($780,632) is listed. And under *Stockholders Equity,* one entry reads "Retained Earnings: Human Resources" ($780,632).

Robert N. Anthony, a faculty member in the Harvard Business School, believes that human resource measures may be extremely important for service and professional businesses such as accounting and law firms, consultants, and medical clinics. In these types of enterprises, he asserts, return on investment makes no sense, either as a basis for pricing or as a method of measuring performance. He concludes that the resource is not the amount of capital involved but rather the skill of the professionals the firm has hired, trained, organized, and motivated.

Perhaps many readers assess human resource accounting as an ambiguous and fragmented system that will never go beyond the experimental stage. Such an assessment may be correct. On the other hand, many persons view the Barry Corporation's conventional and human resource balance sheet as indicative of that firm's sensitivity to the human element and of its open-minded approach to ways in which it might be measured.

Inland Division of General Motors. As reported in a 1976 issue of *Business Week,* for the last few years Inland has been running a participatory management system designed to keep the division's 600 line managers from getting lost in the corporate shuffle. The general manager claims—and most of his managers agree—that the system provides the division with a quicker response to annual model changes.

Teams of 25 to 75 members function internally as individual firms and are responsible for one or more of Inland's product lines, which range from ball joints to foam seats. The role of team chief is rotated among specialists in product engineering, manufacturing, or production engineering; each specialist serves as boss for four months each year when the product cycle is especially demanding of his or her expertise. A nine-member division staff acts as a "board of directors" for each team, reviewing progress at quarterly "board meetings" at which up to 12 members of a single team may discuss problems such as manufacturing performance and quality control.

For example, before the new system was instituted, a quality control inspector might have given little concern for a production manager's problems. Now, managers incorporate their individual job responsibilities within the larger framework of team responsibilities and work on problems in a cohesive manner. If something doesn't work right, all managers on the team are in the same boat. Under the team system problems become mutual. Decision making is more likely to emphasize "we" instead of "I."

Thus far at Inland, the team concept has been applied mainly at the manager level. As of 1977 the division had made little headway in attempts to involve hourly employees. Only a handful of the division's 5,500 hourly workers were included in the team arrangement.

Applications in the Factory

Salary and Time Clocks

For most employees, more status is associated with salary than with wages. "Guaranteed" annual income suggests more regularity in the pay checks received and, in turn, promotes greater feelings of security. In the late 1970s and early 1980s, companies might anticipate that more contract talks with unions would include demands for income regularity — either through salary or a guaranteed annual wage (recall the United Steelworkers' efforts in 1977 to win a guaranteed annual "wage").

In France, Renault agreed in 1973 to give monthly pay status to workers. Following Renault's lead, the Patronat, the French employers association, reached an agreement with unions in 1975, with the result that a larger number of French industrial workers were given the status of monthly personnel. It was suggested that the change would go a long way toward ending the working class stigma felt by French employees who were paid on an hourly basis.

Closely allied to the salary issue are company policies on the use of time clocks. Although atypical in this regard, some firms have removed time clocks. A number of these companies retained the wage form of compensation, whereas others initiated salary pay. Examples of firms that have either done away with time clocks altogether or placed less emphasis on them are Corning Glass, Texas Instruments, Alcan Aluminum, Donnelly Mirrors, Motorola, Eaton Yale & Towne, and R. G. Barry. According to a spokesperson at one corporation, taking out the time clocks was a sign that the company wanted to treat employees like adults, not control them like children or mechanical devices. As Frederick Herzberg puts it: "How motivated would you be if your job consisted of tightening five bolts with a torque wrench a thousand times a day, and if, in addition, mechanical devices called time clocks and whistles told you when to work, when to eat, when to stretch your legs, and when to use the bathroom."

Herzberg's contention is that most production jobs provide so little satisfaction that they should be automated out of existence. Or, where such a transformation is not economically feasible, an honor system that eliminates time clocks will help improve worker motivation and satisfaction.

Redesigning Jobs and Building Teamwork

A Glass Factory. This eastern plant employs about 300 people and primarily manufactures sophisticated scientific instruments. With absenteeism and turnover running at high rates, the company decided to make some major changes. Privileged parking spots for executives were removed, jobs were redesigned to make them more interesting and challenging, and employees were given a greater voice in setting and meeting their own work schedules. Increased responsibilities enabled the plant to operate with two fewer managers.

Today, employees meet monthly with department heads to discuss production goals, and twice a month teams of employees confer with the plant manager in sessions officially called "coffee with the boss." The workers participate in decision making. When an inventory buildup occurred recently, the majority of workers suggested that the firm go temporarily on a three-week month to slow production and avoid having to lay anyone off. After considering the proposal, the plant manager agreed with it.

The following illustrates job enrichment applications. Women employees who previously worked assembly-line fashion in putting together laboratory hot plates were trained to assemble the entire unit from start to finish. The pilot experiment was so successful in increasing worker satisfaction and efficiency that jobs in other departments at the plant were scrutinized and, where applicable, job cycles were expanded. Another change: Each employee attaches his or her name to the finished product. The "brag tag" has had good results in encouraging pride of workmanship and improving product quality.

A Manufacturer of Auto Accessories. The company's president believes that people will do any job—under two conditions. They must feel that the way the job is being performed is the best way to do it, and they must be genuinely respected by management. Company philosophy preaches that every person is creative. To the question, "Which side do you want the creativity on?" the answer is: "If it's not working for you, it's working against you."

The firm's 450 employees are all on salary and belong to task-oriented teams supervised by foremen who in turn are members of teams of foremen. In addition to their salary, workers are paid a bonus that is tied to production. They can decide how large a salary increase they will receive; however, they must find ways to pay for it through higher productivity, cost reduction, and elimination of needless jobs. Quality is also a factor in calculating the amount of the bonus.

Production workers decide how fast the assembly lines will run and how often they will take breaks. Teams of supervisors work out coordination problems between various departments. If a new process is being considered, the employees involved are consulted on how to implement it. When new machines are needed, the employees who will run them participate in their selection. Workers are free to recommend that their own jobs be eliminated, and they often do just that. Where displacement occurs, workers are assured of no change in pay for at least six months or until a new job opportunity develops. The company claims that some other job invariably does develop—and often a better one—before the six months are exhausted.

In 1967, time clocks were removed and workers were put on salary. Since profit sharing was instituted, production per worker has more than doubled, return on investment has more than tripled, and the company's principal product sells for about 25 percent less than it did 20 years ago. Over the past ten years workers have received monthly bonuses averaging 12 percent, and have voted themselves wage increases in excess of $1,000,000. Operating costs have been reduced by some $2,000,000. In a survey conducted by a major university, 97 percent of the workers said they were satisfied with the company and with their jobs. At this particular corporation, participative management is the key to the company's success.

A Manufacturer of Aluminum Products. At the corporation's rolling mill in an eastern state automation prompted plant officials to think about ways to improve morale, Some of the problems at this $90 million installation with a workforce exceeding 600 people were especially costly. When a bored or disgruntled worker pulled a wrong lever somewhere along the 600-foot-long hot rolling mill, often the entire mill had to be shut down for repairs.

The plant removed time clocks and took steps to permit employees to determine their own work breaks and lunch times. Job rotation was also introduced. With appropriate training, workers began relieving each other until most of them knew one or two jobs in addition to their own. For example, a cutting machine operator also learns to drive a forklift truck, and the forklift truck driver becomes competent in running an overhead crane. As a result, when a man becomes eligible for a better job, he probably has already done it. In effect, the versatile worker is in a better position to know if he wants a particular job on a permanent basis. Because some employees can do several jobs, total employment at the facility is as much as 100 men fewer than under standard union job definitions.

The company guarantees full pay for time taken off for urgent business — with one day's notice. An employee idled by layoff is also eligible to receive full salary for up to 26 weeks. On days when no production is scheduled, workers pull out brooms or paint brushes for plant cleaning.

The plant is the only nonunionized facility in the area despite a pay scale slightly lower than the industry average. Absenteeism runs at about 2.5 percent, compared with an industry average of about 10 percent. According to one employee, it's a lot easier getting up in the morning to go to work at this rolling mill location.

A Conglomerate. This midwest-based firm has used a heavy dose of job enrichment with both salaried and hourly workers in attempting to create a climate in which workers can share their ideas and make them operational throughout the system. In the words of a top executive: "We're convinced that in terms of productivity, the man who is most productive is the one who has a real piece of the action.

He's in a job where he has control and influence, and one where he is measured on results."

In one of its manufacturing plants a few years ago, the corporation created the semi-autonomous work team. Workers were given the responsibility of assembling a product as a team rather than being asked to perform assembly-line tasks separately. According to officials, productivity went up 15 percent.

General Electric. GE is included in a list of firms aiming to incorporate the team concept and make work more interesting. According to the company, what is important is to identify a task and then assign a group of 5 to 15 people to handle it. The key is to give the group as much responsibility as possible.

In a fabricating plant, for example, 12 welders were given responsibility for planning and scheduling their own workload. They determined how much time it would take to meet specifications on any items requiring special welding techniques, a job formerly done by a methods and standards engineer. The welders were experienced enough to decide which one of them would perform a specific job within what time frame. The company's interpretation was that the responsibility meant the men had a bigger say in how they did their jobs. They became more committed to the work because of their status as team members.

How did the engineers feel about the change? They were freed to work on new-product models while the welders decided how the daily work was going to be done. Overall, both the efficiency and the quality of work improved.

An Automobile Manufacturer. In an attempt to involve production employees in the entire production process, the management of one Detroit parts plant asked its workers to reevaluate the entire manufacturing operation. As a result, one department was rearranged and the workers thereby displaced were reassigned to jobs where they were needed elsewhere in the plant. The company's conviction is that top management must win back the allegiance of workers and lower-level supervisors, and that the firm must let responsibility extend down to its lowest practical level and give authority to go along with that responsibility.

At an axle plant, in a section long plagued by worker turmoil, 2,700 workers were grouped into three independent units to create the effect of three small plants instead of one huge impersonal outfit.

The company claims that the changes brought about improved communication within the facility and improved workers' attitudes.

To further acquaint managers with its new ideas, the company
frequently arranges to have them spend several days holed up in a
Detroit hotel engaged in lengthy soul-searching sessions on how to
improve the dignity and responsibility of jobs. Several task forces
have been established. Their aim is to figure out ways to enrich jobs at
lower levels.

The firm also put into effect a "career ladders" program at two
of its plants in the midwest. The object is to identify routes of employee advancement from even the most menial jobs — jobs that once
were considered dead ends. Counselors help employees use skills they
already have and advise them on how to achieve job mobility. For example, the company has discovered people with college degrees working on assembly lines; they applied for the work without stating their
college experience because they needed the job. This type of situation
creates a greater need for rational understanding of upward mobility
possibilities.*

A Total System

With few exceptions, humanistic management has been applied
on a piecemeal basis. Examples cited in this chapter depict behavioral
ideas applied mainly to departments, offices, and particular jobs. At
one firm in particular, however, behavioral concepts have been
applied over a total system. Because of the uniqueness of the application, this section is devoted exclusively to a discussion of that company's experiences.†

A few years ago, General Foods Corporation decided to build a
new pet-food plant in Topeka, Kansas. In planning the overall

---

*A great deal of job enrichment experimentation in the auto industry has taken
place in Sweden during the 1970s. For example, at Volvo's new plant at Kalmar the
conventional assembly line has been abolished. Automobiles are assembled by work
teams of 15 to 25 persons each, with members exchanging jobs as well as changing
teams. Overall results include higher satisfaction and morale, better quality of work,
and reduced absenteeism. Also, Volvo's 1976 sales and profits figures were higher than
in 1975. For details, see "Battling Boredom: Auto Plant in Sweden Scores With Worker
Teams," *The Wall Street Journal*, March 1, 1977, p. 1; and Pehr G. Gyllenhammar, "How
Volvo Adapts Work to People," *Harvard Business Review*, July-August, 1977, pp. 102–
113.

†Richard E. Walton, "How to Counter Alienation in the Plant," *Harvard Business
Review*, November-December, 1972, pp. 70–81.

design, the company sought to incorporate and apply knowledge developed by the behavioral sciences. A number of key managers were selected. For more than two years the appointed group met with behavioral science experts and visited industrial plants that were experimenting with innovative organizational methods. Recommendations of this management group were instrumental in the preparation of the overall design of the Topeka plant. Key features of the company's systems approach are discussed below.

Autonomous Work Groups. The total workforce of approximately 70 employees is organized into six teams. Three teams are at work on any one shift, each team covering an entire phase of the plant's operation: processing from the raw materials to the end product, packaging and shipping, and office work. A team comprises from 7 to 14 members (called *operators*) and a team leader. Which individuals work at which sets of tasks is subject to team consensus. Although each operator has primary responsibility for a set of tasks at any given time, some tasks can be shared by several operators. In addition, tasks can be redefined by the team on the basis of individual interests and capabilities.

Other issues that fall within the scope of team recommendation or decision making include: temporarily redistributing tasks where some workers are absent, studying manufacturing problems that develop within or between the teams' areas of responsibilities, selecting team workers to serve on plantwide task forces or committees, screening and selecting individuals to replace departing team members, and counseling employees who do not meet team standards.

Integrated Support Functions. Most staff units are eliminated. Activities typically performed by quality control, maintenance, custodial, industrial engineering, and personnel units are built into an operating team's responsibilities. Complicated electrical maintenance is one exception. Team members maintain the equipment, "housekeep" their areas, perform quality tests and ensure quality standards, and screen job applicants.

Challenging Job Assignments. Every set of tasks is designed to include functions that require definite responsibilities and specialized abilities. The integrated support functions provide an important source of job enrichment. Also, plant technology is designed to eliminate dull jobs as much as possible. Innovative approaches are used to compensate for nonchallenging, yet basic, tasks. For example, in many respects the forklift truck operation does not require higher-order human abilities. Consequently, the team operator having that responsibility is assigned other, more mentally demanding tasks, such as planning warehouse space utilization and shipping activities.

Job Mobility and Rewards for Learning. Because all sets of jobs are purposely designed to be equally challenging—even though each set comprises unique skill demands—a single job classification, covering all operators, has been established. Increases in pay are geared to an operator's mastery of an increasing proportion of jobs, first in the team and then in the total plant.

Thus, team members are paid for learning more and more aspects of the total manufacturing system. Because there are no limits on the number of workers who can qualify for higher pay brackets, operators are encouraged to teach each other. The old plant, in contrast, featured numerous job classifications, with pay increases based on progress up the classification hierarchy.

Facilitative Leadership. Team leaders are selected from foreman-level talent and are largely responsible for group decision making and team development. The new system is in sharp contrast to the old plant's use of supervisors to plan, direct, and control subordinates' work. The company believes that the teams might eventually be self-directed. If so, the formal team leader position might not be required.

Self-Government. Before the new plant started operating, the organization refrained from formulating any plant rules in advance. The firm is committed to letting these rules evolve from collective experience.

Congruent Physical and Social Context. Differential status symbols characterizing traditional work organizations are minimized in the new plant. There is a single entrance for both office and plant personnel, an open parking lot, and a common decor throughout the reception area, locker rooms, cafeteria, and offices.

In many ways, the Topeka plant is a working laboratory for testing behavioral theories about employee motivation, productivity, satisfaction, and morale. What were results after the first 18 months of operations? Using standard data, industrial engineers originally projected that 110 employees would be needed to run the plant; the actual average workforce employed at Topeka, however, was 70. The safety record was one of the best in the company. Turnover was far below average. The plant's fixed overhead rate was 33 percent lower than in the old plant.

Reductions in variable manufacturing costs, an absenteeism rate 9 percent below the industry norm, and 92 percent fewer quality rejects resulted in annual savings of $600,000. Operators, managers, and team leaders became more involved in their work and derived higher satisfaction from it.*

Conclusion

When considering the systems approach as applied at the General Foods plant in Topeka, it's doubtful that we'll witness large numbers of organizations implementing humanistic management concepts in such a vigorous and adventuresome manner in the immediate future. That's my opinion. On the other hand, some organizational behavior specialists believe that over a longer period of time the opposite phenomenon will occur. In fact, one noted management consultant—and events may prove him to be correct—comments in words similar to these: A company where teams of workers perform without supervision, where many decisions are determined on the basis of employee consensus, and where most staff functions are assigned to line operators—how likely is it that such an organization will become the norm? Very likely, because such innovations are part of the emerging answer to alienation in the workplace.

The purpose of this chapter is to illustrate company approaches to humanistic management. I repeat a request made in the introductory words of the chapter, that each reader ask himself or herself the

---

*As of 1977 there were conflicting stories about how things were working out at General Foods' Topeka plant. According to some reports, GF has applied a similar system at a second dog-food plant in Topeka and at a coffee plant in New Jersey. A former top manager concluded that the system was a success from the standpoint of humanistic working life and economic results. As of 1977 unit costs were 5 percent less than under a traditional factory system, resulting in savings of about $1 million a year. Also, turnover was only 8 percent. On the negative side of the ledger, however, the system apparently provoked a power struggle, and was too threatening to too many people— mainly managers. For a good update on the GF Topeka story, see "Stonewalling Plant Democracy: Manager Resistance Spells Grief for General Foods' Worker Participation Plan," *Business Week,* March 28, 1977, pp. 78–82.

question: What applications of humanistic management, if any, might be appropriate in the organization where I work?

As demonstrated, top managers are increasingly aware of and sensitive to issues of worker motivation, satisfaction, and morale. They also show a keen interest in studying intricacies of human behavior in the workforce. In the immediate future, we shall undoubtedly read that a number of humanistic work designs survived the test of time. In all likelihood, we shall also read that many designs that proved to be costly and unworkable were abolished.

What is an important purpose of humanistic management? In the words of Frederick Herzberg, "Managers must get more men going home to their wives saying, 'Honey, do you know what I did today?' instead of 'Honey, do you know what they did to me today?' "

Information given in Part I is useful in developing additional awareness of the multiple challenges that organizations must meet in their attempts to manage workers effectively in an age of turbulence. But has every aspect of the problem been discussed? Is some issue conspicuous because of its absence? The answer is a ringing "Yes!" All working people go to their jobs at various *times*. All are variously involved during certain *times* of the workday (as we know, not all are actually working). They all take lunch and coffee breaks at various *times* during the workday. Many look forward to and concentrate on the *time* when they can leave work and go home, and all of them do depart at various *times* during the workday. Conspicuous because of its absence in Part I is the issue of *time*.

If "time is of the essence," then organizations should develop greater awareness and appreciation of the ways in which time can be used as an asset. This factor can be focused on in different ways. One way is in terms of its flexibility.

Most American organizations fail to realize the potential benefits to be derived through the more flexible utilization of time. The concept of flexible working hours is a most useful tool in the humanistic manager's carpentry box — because it has a lot to do with worker motivation, satisfaction, morale, efficiency, and productivity. After all, aren't these factors close to, and don't they contribute to, that all-important bottom line? So let's get on with it and talk about that valuable and often hidden asset of time. The remainder of this book is devoted to the study of alternative work schedules, with a focus on flexible working hours.

Part II

Alternative Work Schedules

3

Four
alternative
work schedules

Worker discontent spells trouble. It manifests itself in many ways—
tardiness and high absenteeism, marginal motivation to work, low satisfaction and morale, static or decreased productivity, and high turnover. In the view of some experts in human behavior, a worker's discontent arises in part from a lack of personal identification with and a
perceived absence of control over his or her environment.

Coupled with problems of alienation are difficulties experienced
in getting to and from work. As one person phrases it, "As our urban
population grows, a worker is squeezed fender to fender with his
fellow commuters, arriving at work frustrated and irritated with
nothing to look forward to at the end of the day but a rerun of the
same misadventure."

Are such problems rampant in organizations? What are possible
causes of worker disenchantment? What actions should organizations
take to reduce the harmful effects of these problems?

The main thrust of this book concerns the subject of time. Our
goal is to see more vividly how time spent in work situations can be expanded, contracted, chiseled, and sculptured in ways that will be received with appreciation and applause by employees and employers
alike.

In many respects, people's activities run in different directions.
Some are ecstatic about boating; others prefer golf, tennis, fishing, or

building racing cars. But whatever their particular enthusiasms, all people, both on and off the job, are keenly interested in time. How to save it. How to spend it. The issue of time has universal appeal.

For a moment, let us transfer this universal appeal of time to the workforce and come up with some figures that will dramatize the significance and potential value of the time factor. According to U.S. Labor Department statistics for 1974, 82 percent of all full-time employees worked 5 days per week on their sole or primary job, 16 percent worked 5½ to 7 days, and 2 percent worked 3 to 4½ days. The vast majority working 5 days per week worked 40 hours. In 1977 *The Wall Street Journal* reported on a more recent Labor Department study showing that 83 percent of the workforce was on a 5-day workweek in 1976 (up from 82 percent in 1974).

What is to be gained by laying out these statistics? First of all, the labor force consists of a great many people, all of whom are interested in the time pattern of their workday. Even those who are less interested in doing their job than in pursuing off-the-job kicks are interested in their working pattern. In fact, in some ways they're more concerned with time—with looking at the clock while at work—than the others. Each sweep of the second hand—for them a painfully slow sweep—brings these employees that much closer to ending the agony of a workday.

Over the past few years we've heard much about the 4-day workweek, and especially the 4/40 plan—4 workdays per week and 10 hours per day. In actuality, only 1.2 percent of the labor force was on a 4-day week in 1976 (down from 1975 figures). Interestingly, more Americans worked 7 days a week than worked 4 days. Also, only about 10 percent of the 4-day people worked 10 hours per day. In reality, those who worked 10-hour days were most likely to work 5 days per week (a good 60 percent of all 10-hour-day workers), or 6 days per week (close to 25 percent of all 10-hour-day workers). "No industry or occupation showed extensive use of 4-day workweeks in 1976, nor a substantial increase since 1973," said the Labor Department.

We thus have a second reason for presenting these statistics: the need to build flexibility into the basic 5-day workweek. The statistics lend support to the argument that it makes hard sense to talk about working time patterns and flexibility principally over a 5-day period.

While our attention focuses mainly on a 5-day workweek and its structure, at the same time we must prepare intelligent and tentative working time patterns for future years. This matter will be examined in depth in the final chapter of this book. Briefly, this nation will in all probability move in the direction of the 4½-day, and even the 4-day, workweek, using highly adaptable flexible hours systems in a variety of workweek patterns.

The reasons *why* most people are now on a 5-day workweek—the "mold," as its detractors term it—need not concern us at this point. The question is relevant to the subject of flexible hours, and is discussed more appropriately in a subsequent chapter.

I have already attempted to accomplish one purpose in this chapter, namely, to explain why the factor of time is worthy of a probing analysis, and why it makes considerable sense to discuss intricacies of a 5-day workweek. A second purpose is to clarify—with both definitions and discussion—four alternative work schedules. A third purpose is to explain the workings of an automatic time-recording instrument often used in combination with that schedule offering the greatest degree of working time flexibility, namely, flexitime.

Four Different Systems

The four different alternative work schedules to be examined in this book are staggered hours, flexitour, flexitime, and group flexibility. No lengthy discussion of their relative advantages or disadvantages is attempted in this chapter. Such discussion, especially in regard to flexitime, is brought out in considerable detail in subsequent chapters.

Staggered Hours
Staggered hours is a working-time pattern whereby individuals and groups within an urban area—or within a firm—do their work within different time frames according to a master plan. The system is also referred to as "multiple reporting times." Here are two variations.

In the first example, the workweek is 37½ hours, the workday is 7½ hours, and the lunch break is ½ hour:

I	Start time 8:00 A.M.	End time 4:00 P.M.
II	Start time 8:30 A.M.	End time 4:30 P.M.
III	Start time 9:00 A.M.	End time 5:00 P.M.

In the second example, the workweek is 40 hours, the workday is 8 hours, and the lunch break is ½ hour or 1 hour:

I	Start time 7:00 A.M.	End time 3:30 P.M.	(½-hour lunch break)
II	Start time 7:00 A.M.	End time 4:00 P.M.	(1-hour lunch break)
III	Start time 7:30 A.M.	End time 4:30 P.M.	(1-hour lunch break)
IV	Start time 8:00 A.M.	End time 5:00 P.M.	(1-hour lunch break)
V	Start time 8:30 A.M.	End time 5:30 P.M.	(1-hour lunch break)
VI	Start time 9:00 A.M.	End time 5:30 P.M.	(½-hour lunch break)
VII	Start time 9:00 A.M.	End time 6:00 P.M.	(1-hour lunch break)

In the majority of staggered hours schedules it is mainly management that draws up a master plan containing numerous "interval frames" (intervals between the arrival times of the different groups, or 30 minutes in both examples above). The amount of employee input and participation in drawing up interval frames and start and end times depends on the company, its functions, and its philosophy. For example, in one company the first-line supervisory unit establishes interval frames and start and end times. This unit is defined as a supervisor and the employees report to him or her. In some other firm, employee input and participation in drawing up a master plan are minimal.

In a majority of the plans, most participants are "nonexempt" workers — that is, wage and salary earners qualifying for overtime pay on the basis of laws and/or contractual agreements. In some plans, both nonexempt and "exempt" employees participate -- the latter defined as executives, professional employees, supervisors, and salespersons not qualifying for overtime pay on the basis of laws and/or contractual agreements.

Once starting and ending times are established, they apply to all employees participating in the plan, and no deviation in these times is permitted from day to day. In all plans, although employees have the right to state their preferences as to start and end times, management has veto power over those preferences. The main reason is that management is responsible for ensuring that sufficient work coverage is provided at each reporting time. Merit, seniority, order of signing up, business requirements, and various combinations of factors are used in determining an employee's specific start and end times.

In some plans, all members of a particular job category make a joint decision with management on a preferred "time frame" (for example, time frame III in Case 2 above). Then all members are bound by that majority decision to start work at the same time. In other programs, where adequate work coverage is provided for, different individuals within the same job category are able to select different time frames for starting work. In either instance, however, the arrival time selected remains in effect over a considerable time span—typically, over many weeks and months.

Flexitour

Flexitour is a working-time pattern whereby an employee selects a starting time from an established listing of numerous time frames, and works according to that specific schedule each day until the opportunity becomes available for selecting a different starting time.

Essentially, the main difference between flexitour and staggered hours is that the former system permits workers to choose their own starting time rather than assigning them to a particular schedule. Starting-time changes might be permitted each pay period, each month, each quarter, semiannually, seasonally, or annually. There are two common variations of the basic flexitour model.

Under the first modification an employee selects a starting time as under the basic flexitour model, but is permitted a degree of deviation on either side of the selected arrival time. In most cases the maximum deviation allowed is 15 minutes. For example, if a schedule of 8:30 A.M. is selected, the employee might be permitted a 15-minute deviation on either side of that time. In this model, if a worker began as early as 8:15 A.M., that would become the individual's starting time for that day and that quarter hour would count toward the completion of that 8-hour day. Conversely, the employee who arrived at 8:45 A.M. would not be considered tardy. However, it would be understood that the basic schedule was 8:30 A.M. and under normal circumstances the worker would be expected to adhere to that tour. Deviation would be expected to occur only on an occasional basis. If the employee should deviate frequently from the selected tour, consideration would be given to establishing a new tour.

Under the second modification, the individual also preselects a starting time from the established listing of numerous time frames; however, the schedule may be modified with prior notification to and approval by the supervisor. Such prior notification and authorization would typically be required one day in advance.

Flexitime (Gliding Time)

Flexitime (gliding time) is a working-time pattern whereby an employee can, on a daily basis and within specific limits, start and finish work at his or her discretion, as long as the person completes the total number of hours required for a given time period. The reader should become familiar with the following terms.

Core time — A designated time period during which all employees must be on the job. The term is also referred to as "block time."

Flexible starting time — A time band within which an employee is able to begin work at his or her discretion. In this book, flexible starting time is frequently referred to as "FST."

Flexible quitting time — A time band within which an employee is able to end the workday at his or her discretion. In this book, flexible quitting time is frequently referred to as "FQT."

Midday flexibility — A time band in the middle of a workday during which an employee is able to exercise options at his or her discretion: to work, to take lunch, to engage in off-the-job activities.

Bandwidth — The entire workday, from the beginning of the flexible-starting-time band through the end of the flexible-quitting-time band.

Two examples, shown graphically, should lend clarification to the terms and depict basic ways in which the factors are used in conjunction with one another. In both examples, the workday is considered to be 8 hours long.

FST	CORE TIME (excluding lunch break)	FQT
6:30 A.M.	9:30 A.M. 3:00 P.M.	6:00 P.M.

Here the core-time band extends from 9:30 A.M. to 3:00 P.M.. A ½-hour lunch break is to be taken at some time within the established core-time band. On either side of this band there are flexible time bands of 3 hours. Flexible starting time is any time between 6:30 and 9:30 in the morning, and flexible quitting time is any time between 3:00 and 6:00 in the afternoon. Thus an employee might come to work at 6:30 A.M. and leave as early as 3:00 P.M. Alternatively, the employee might start the workday as late as 9:30 A.M. and leave at 6:00

P.M. All employees, in other words, begin the workday at any time between 6:30 and 9:30 A.M. and quit working 8½ hours later.

The following plan offers additional features.

FST	CORE TIME	MIDDAY FLEX	CORE TIME	FQT

6:30 A.M.	9:00 A.M.	11:00 A.M.	1:00 P.M.	3:00 P.M.	5:30 P.M.

This plan differs from the former one in two major respects. The first difference is the split core time, and the second difference is the midday flexibility and options available to the employee between core times. An employee might decide to take ½ hour for lunch and work straight through 8 hours. However, the employee might instead take advantage of the midday 2-hour flexible band for shopping, personal business, a long lunch, or a luncheon meeting. A ½-hour period within this midday-flex band is allocated for lunch.

An additional comment about terminology is called for here. Throughout the book it is intended that a number of terms have precisely the same meaning. For example, the following terms are synonymous and interchangeable: "flextime," "flexitime," "gliding time," "gliding hours," "sliding time," "sliding hours," "adaptable hours," "variable hours," and "individual flexibility." All suggest a system whereby starting- and quitting-time flexibility is afforded to the *individual* employee. Of the terms just listed, "flexitime" and "gliding time" are those used most frequently in describing this particular flexible hours schedule.

In the private sector the term "flextime" tends to be used frequently while "flexitime" is preferred in government circles and in publications alluding to government organizations. Some people suggest that "variable hours" should refer to a system in which there is starting-time flexibility, quitting-time flexibility, and *no core hours*. Such a differentiation appears unnecessary. Not only is it confusing, but many organizations currently use the term "variable hours" in ways that make it clearly synonymous with all others just listed.

What benefits might employees derive from gliding hours? A formal display of numerous benefits, accompanied by appropriate discussion, appears later in this book; just now the question may be asked: Is there a simple way to describe what flexitime is all about—in terms of the flexibility it offers? In poring over the assortment of solicited materials sent to me by organizations, what caught my eye was a simple yet illuminating description in a booklet published by Hewlett-Packard Corporation. The company has granted me permission to share the following "short story" with you.

> Meet Howard Johnson, an assembler of pocket calculators at Hewlett-Packard Corporation in California. Howard is 37 years old and has been with the company for 9 years. He is a husband and a father of 2 young boys. He commutes 15 minutes to work each day.
>
> *Monday* — 8:00 A.M. until 4:30 P.M. was Howard's workday. Why? Bright and early at 7:00 A.M. Monday morning, Howie strolled out his front door, ready to begin a new week — and there sat his car with a flat tire. After a few words and 45 minutes, he had the tire changed and was on his way once again.
>
> *Tuesday* — 6:30 A.M. until 3:00 P.M. was Howard's workday. Why? One of Howie's sons had a Little League game at 3:30 and being an interested father and devoted baseball fan, Howie wanted to attend the game. He began work at 6:30 so that he could leave work early in the afternoon.
>
> *Wednesday* — 7:00 A.M. until 4:30 P.M. was Howard's workday. Why? One of Howie's co-workers was retiring after 25 years with the company, and the department was holding a special 1½-hour luncheon in his honor.
>
> *Thursday* — 8:30 A.M. until 5:00 P.M. was Howard's workday. Why? Howie awakened at 6:30 with a toothache and headed off for an early morning visit to the family dentist. He arrived at work at 8:30 A.M..
>
> *Friday* — 6:30 A.M. until 3:00 P.M. was Howard's workday. Why? Howie and his family planned to go to the mountains for the weekend and Howie wanted to beat the afternoon traffic.

The story portrays one workweek in the life of Howard Johnson. He had quite a workweek, didn't he? The days were very different from the standard 8:00 to 5:00 workdays so many people experience. Howard did his job, but because of flexitime he was also able to do his own thing.

Group Flexibility

Group flexibility is a working-time pattern whereby employees, acting as a group — sometimes with and sometimes without direct management partici-

pation — decide on a specific work arrival time that remains in effect for one day or a limited number of days.

How does this differ from flexitime? Under group flexibility the individual worker is not able to select daily, at his or her discretion, starting and quitting times. Although individual workers contribute to the group decision, they subordinate their personal preferences and adhere to the group's judgment. "Floating as a team" often describes this system.

How does group flexibility differ from staggered hours, given that predetermined arrival times are required in both systems? There are two major differences. Formalized interval frames with different arrival-time slots are not built into the group flexibility plan. Also, under group flexibility, the group-determined arrival time is likely to remain in effect for only one day, or for a limited number of days.

One example of group flexibility is in reference to the sanitation department in a midwestern city. The city operates a fleet of trucks used in the collection of trash and garbage. Three-person teams are assigned to each truck. Workers manning the trucks have the right to begin workdays any time between 7:00 A.M. and 8:30 A.M. On any given day, team members on each truck decide *as a group* exactly when they'll begin the next workday.

A New Mechanical Time Recorder

Organizations use various methods to record work time under gliding hours. A "manual time-recording method" sometimes is used, such as the honor system, a checklist, a sign-in sheet, or a log. Also frequently employed is a "traditional mechanical method," namely, the punch or time clock. Meanwhile, a relatively new mechanical device is experiencing a rapid growth in popularity. Because the instrument is referred to frequently throughout this book, it is appropriate at this point to explain exactly what it is.

The device is called the "Flextime Machine"* (also referred to as

*The term FLEXTIME® is a registered trademark of Hecon Corporation — Flextime Division. The word "flextime," used as a concept or idea, has been popularized in the literature over the past few years; but now that the term is a registered trademark, it is predicted that it will be used infrequently to denote a concept or idea. Instead, the term "Flextime" will be employed mainly (and legally) where it is directly associated with equipment manufactured by Hecon Corporation — Flextime Division.

the "Flextime Mechanical Time Recorder," or "Flextime Time Ac-
cumulator"), and it features an automatic time meter. The specific
machine being described is patented, manufactured, and sold by J.
Hengstler KG—Gleitzeit Division of West Germany and by the firm's
American subsidiary, Hecon Corporation—Flextime Division. (A
somewhat similar machine is manufactured by the Hasler Corporation in Switzerland. These two firms, Hengstler and Hasler, dominate
the field.)

A Flextime Machine is about the size of a clock radio. Built into
each machine are a number of *automatic time totalizers* (in multiples of
8) that record net hours worked. Each employee is assigned his or her
own totalizer (a totalizer is about the size of a thin paperback book)
and an individually coded *activator key.* An activator key is quite similar
in appearance to a plastic identification card—or may indeed be the
employee's plastic identification card. At one end of the key is the employee's picture (in many firms the key doubles as a security pass).
The other end of the key is notched in a particular way and fits only
the employee's assigned totalizer.

Time recording begins when the employee inserts the activator
key into the totalizer, and time accumulates automatically as long as
the key remains inserted. When the employee's time counter (totalizer) is activated, a little light comes on, and remains on as long as
the key remains inserted. Thus, the key is used by a worker both to
start and to stop his or her personal accumulation of time on starting
or finishing work. On the Flextime Machine and adjacent to each individual's name is a small window frame. In each window frame the
employee's total work-time accumulation is displayed.

By contrast, some Flextime models feature bi-stable activators
that are activated on insertion of the key, and deactivated on reinser-
tion of the key. Thus, with the bi-stable model, for work time to accumulate it is not required that the activator key remain inserted in
the machine.

The Flextime Machine is quite different from a time clock. A
time clock "clocks" an employee in and out, that is, notes the time the
worker arrives at and departs from work. The Flextime Machine does
not record exact arrival and departure times. It accumulates and
displays the total number of hours worked during whatever the accumulation period may be—one week, two weeks, or even a month.

If a worker forgets to pull the key at the end of the day, won't
the totalizer continue to accumulate hours? No. The machine is set to

count time each day only within the bandwidth. On days when over-time is worked — and the bandwidth has been appropriately expanded — the machine will automatically stop counting time at the end of the overtime period.

The John Hancock Mutual Life Insurance Company installed automatic time totalizers. In the company's judgment time accumula-tors have two distinct advantages: They aid in the administration of a highly flexible program, and they guarantee to management that the total weekly number of hours required of the worker are in fact being fulfilled.

The use of time accumulators in programs with little or no flexi-bility is an irritant to employees, the insurance firm claims. Their use in programs where the flexibility varies greatly may initially be slightly irritating to employees, but, the company claims, the recorders will be accepted because employees are able to see their necessity.

It does make considerable sense to think seriously about using automatic time recording equipment in a work arrangement permit-ting numerous options. Consider the following possibility. An em-ployee flexes in at 7:16, flexes out at 7:32 for breakfast, flexes back in at 8:16, flexes out at 11:33 for lunch, flexes back in at 1:40, flexes out at 3:32, and leaves for the day. Computing the hours worked during time on the job might require the addition of some clerical personnel; however, the machines perform the task of accumulating these hours.

The Sun Oil Company has a number of years' experience with adaptable hours. The firm recommends the use of automatic time re-corders for all employees using flexible hours. Yet the firm believes that the decision should be left to the individual managers who decide to install flexitime.

At Sun Oil, the concept of "tracking" work hours seemed con-troversial at the time when an experiment with Flextime time record-ers was initiated in the Engineering Division. Would employees feel that the use of time-recording devices was a form of negative control? Could it be expected that exempt employees would interpret the use of such devices as "putting them back on the time clock," and thus as taking away their professional status? Actually, in a questionnaire sur-vey it was found that both exempt and nonexempt employees reacted positively to working with automatic time recording, when they com-pared this to their experience with the manual system used pre-viously.

The petroleum firm believes that how the employee perceives

automatic time recording prior to its installation has much to do with his or her acceptance or rejection of the system. The firm's psychological approach takes this form: The time-accumulating device is *only* for the employee's use. On any day of the week it helps the employee identify the exact number of work hours accumulated. At any given moment, a glance at the recorder's window frame conveys specific information about total number of hours worked. The device is not there for management inspection purposes.

The oil company also conducted a cost study of the financial feasibility of automatic time totalizers. According to the company's figures, the cost for purchasing electronic time recorders is approximately $50 per employee. Another approach is lease/purchase for about $19 per employee per year. Using the engineering department as a model, the $19 is worth about 2 hours of an average engineer's time. The firm concluded that it is completely reasonable to expect to recover the lease expense per employee over a year's time.

As already mentioned, one drawback to the automatic time recorder is that it does not record exact starting and quitting times. Also, the device operates as a running meter and records the total number of hours worked, but does not distinguish between the optional hours and the compulsory core time during which all employees have to be at work; this represents a second limitation. Third, since meters (automatic time totalizers) have to be provided for each individual, installation costs per head do not markedly fall as numbers covered rise. A fourth limitation is that the automatic time recorder is not always "computer compatible"; that is, the recorder device may not be compatible with a firm's existing computer equipment.

The most sophisticated time-recording method is "computer based and centralized." Companies like Hengstler, Olivetti, and ARC Europa offer recording equipment that is exclusively electronics based. Installing or modifying a computer-based system for time-recording purposes can be costly, at least in the short run. But for medium-size and large organizations, a computer-based system often is feasible.

As indicated in this section, there are numerous ways to record working time: manual, the traditional mechanical or time clock, the automatic time recorder, and a computer-based method. As the saying goes: "You pays your money and you takes your choice."

In a firm that has a dedicated workforce and a program with limited flexibility — meaning no multiple flex ins and outs during a workday, no flexible lunch break, no split core-time bands — either the manual or the time-clock method may be appropriate. But in a large firm where a time plan offers a great degree of flexibility and numerous options, it is recommended that serious consideration be given to installing either automatic time recording or a computer-based system.

As pointed out early in the chapter, during any given week the majority of employees work 5 days and 40 hours. Concerning the four alternative work schedules presented, the reader should bear in mind that, from the standpoint of the *individual* employee, the work schedule offering the least flexibility is staggered hours. In fact, some people believe the system offers no flexibility at all. By contrast, flexitour is definitely a flexible hours schedule, and flexitime offers individual employees opportunities for the greatest amount of flexibility. In short, as relating to the individual employee, the direction from the least to the greatest amount of flexibility is: staggered hours, flexitour, flexitime.

Group flexibility allows for variations in group-determined working hours. Various organizations, including the National Council for Alternative Work Patterns, are rendering valuable contributions in the form of identifying and clarifying various alternative work schedules; but for reasons unknown to me, group flexibility is seldom included in their listings of alternative work schedules. In my opinion, it definitely should be included. In the first instance, because group flexibility provides groups of employees with work-hours options, it is not a fixed work-hours schedule. Second, one group that favors humanistic management preaches the advantages of attacking organizational problems through the use of small and cohesive work groups. Group flexibility, as relating to working hours, fits into such a framework.

This is a brief but important chapter. Having become familiar with alternative work schedules, the appropriate definitions, and the concept of automatic time recording, we're prepared to advance to the intricacies and excitement of flexitime — the alternative work schedule receiving central attention in this book.

4

Gliding time outside the United States

My main purpose in writing this book is to explore flexible working hours in the United States, with central focus on flexitime. It might therefore seem natural for some readers to assume that the idea of flexitime originated someplace in America and that most plans currently are in operation in this country. The opposite is true. Gliding time originated in Europe. Some historical comments are appropriate here.

The Origins of Gliding Time

Gliding time is a product of West German industry. Some scholars credit its invention to a West German woman, Christel Kammerer. Kammerer, a political economist and management consultant, published in the mid-1960s the basic explanation of core time and flexible work periods.

Original credit for installing the gliding time system is generally given to Messerschmitt-Bolkow-Blohm, a German aerospace firm. The company's research and development center is located at Ottobrunn, near Munich. In the mid-1960s, because of the inadequacy of the roads leading to the plant and a rapid increase in the number of cars driven by employees attempting to meet the 7:00 A.M. starting time, the firm experienced major problems of employee lateness and absenteeism.

The firm therefore hired Christel Kammerer, with the hope that new ideas suggested by a noncompany person might lead to a workable solution. Kammerer studied the company's operations and then suggested *gleitende arbeitzeit*—gliding work time—as the answer. The company introduced gliding time to its 2,000 Ottobrunn employees in 1967. Top management was gratified when the change produced the desired improvement in traffic flow, but it was positively surprised to discover numerous side-effects: absenteeism declined by about 40 percent, overtime dropped by 50 percent, employee turnover was reduced, tardiness disappeared, and morale rose sharply.

Major credit must also go to the J. Hengstler Corporation, a West German manufacturer of high-performance electromechanical counters and controls. Realizing gliding time's potential, the company developed an automatic time recorder for timekeeping purposes. Through the firm's Hengstler-Gleitzeit Division, the Flextime Machine was produced and marketed throughout the world. This new piece of equipment went hand-in-hand with the spread of the gliding time concept.

The Spread of Gliding Time

Accurate statistics on the subject are hard to come by. Figures reported in various newspapers, magazine articles, and government documents are far from consistent in what they tell us. On the basis of information at my disposal, and through averaging out some conflicting statistics, I assessed the situation as follows for the year 1977.

In *West Germany*, 30 percent of the total labor force was working under gliding time. Although the origins of gliding time are traced to West Germany, the Swiss adopted it in the most rapid manner. Approximately 40 percent of the total labor force in *Switzerland* was on gliding time in 1977. In *France*, the system covered more than 20 percent of the workforce. The idea was also being adopted at a rapid rate in the *Scandinavian* nations. Although no specific figures are available on flexitime's growth in *Canada*, it appeared that the idea was catching on quickly there. Two illustrations of gliding time in Canada are offered later in this chapter.

For reasons unknown to me, *Great Britain* was relatively slow to adopt flexitime. The first British experiments with flexible working hours began as late as 1971. The Wiggins Teape Company claims the honor of being the first major UK company off the starting line. The Hengstler Corporation says that three times as many Flextime Machines were sold in France as in England in 1975; nevertheless, in 1976 there were about 250,000 British employees monitored by the equipment of the specialist companies in addition to an unspecified number who might have tried out the idea "on a pencil and paper basis," without buying recording hardware.

I estimate that less than 10 percent of the British workforce was on gliding time in 1977. Yet the idea was being adopted by an increasing number of firms. The British Department of Manpower claims: "Given the range of organizations into which flexible hours have already been successfully introduced, the current occupational and industrial structure of the UK labour force, and growth both in white-collar work and in the service sector, it seems likely that flexible working hours could feasibly become a feature of employment for up to 50 percent of all employees."

Some illustrations of flexible hours programs as established outside the United States are now presented.

Omega Watch Company

The Omega Watch Company, located in Switzerland, has a gliding time arrangement covering 90 percent of its 2,500 employees. A normal workday at this firm is 8½ hours, and a normal workweek is 42½ hours. The company's time plan is set up in this way:

FST	CORE TIME	MIDDAY FLEX	CORE TIME	FQT

| 6:30 A.M. | 8:30 A.M. | 11:30 A.M. | 2:00 P.M. | 4:00 P.M. | 6:00 P.M. |

—The schedule features a very wide bandwidth extending 11½ hours, from 6:30 A.M. until 6:00 P.M. FST falls within the 6:30 to 8:30 morning segment, and FQT is from 4:00 to 6:00 in the afternoon. There is a generous 2½-hour midday-flex period. Morning core time extends from 8:30 A.M. until 11:30 A.M., and afternoon core time is from 2:00 P.M. until 4:00 P.M. What this all means, of course, is that workers on gliding time must be on the job from 8:30 to 11:30 in the morning and from 2 to 4 each afternoon. Employees can complete the rest of the workday—the other 3 hours and 30 minutes—at any time the plant is open, from 6:30 A.M. to 6:00 P.M.

Gliding Time on the Assembly Line

It is interesting to learn that gliding time has been applied successfully to many of Omega's assembly-line operations. This is quite atypical. As shown in subsequent chapters, assembly-line operations in numerous industries frequently rule out the use of individual flexibility (gliding time). And when assembly-line operations occur in conjunction with different work shifts, installing a workable gliding time program is even more difficult.

So how does Omega do it? The assembly-line coordination problem has been solved by building up a "buffer stock" at each point along the line. Since installing gliding time, Omega officials report that production has dropped slightly but quality has improved substantially enough to cause a net gain. Of course, one realizes that an assembly line in the watch industry is substantially different from an assembly line in numerous other industries. In the former instance, many workers are able to exercise some discretion in determining exactly when they wish to turn out a day's production. Frequently the individual production worker is able to "hand over" batches of in-process components on which his or her job duties have been performed. Typically in the watch industry, a line of in-process units does not move in monotonous and regular rhythm in front of the workers, demanding their attention, deciding precisely when they are to be at work, and dictating the speed at which they must work.

Sulzer Frères

The firm is Switzerland's largest builder of machines and pumps. Gliding time (the term used at the company) covers more than 8,000 employees, about 90 percent of the payroll. A company official reports that Sulzer extended flexible hours progressively over practically the entire workforce. Pressure came from workers against fixed hours once they learned of the satisfaction of a pilot group working under individual flexibility.

The company solved one of its toughest problems—how to

apply flexible hours to the foundry, where teams of men operate large furnaces—by specifying that each team must "float" as a group. Before leaving work each day, team members agree on the next day's starting time. In this particular foundry work situation, gliding time is not in effect—the individual worker is not able to select daily starting and quitting times at his own discretion. He subordinates his personal preferences and adheres to the *group's* decision.

On the other hand, the group is not forced to work—for consecutive weeks or months—precisely within the same time frame. Acting in conjunction with other groups, a group makes decisions each day on the starting and quitting times that are to be effective on the subsequent day. Thus, the Sulzer Frères program is not one of staggered hours in its foundry. In staggered hours procedures, arrival and departure times, once determined, remain in effect for at least one week. In fact, as previously explained, in most cases specific arrival times remain in effect for many consecutive weeks or months.

In short, the alternative work schedule in Sulzer's foundry operations is neither a pure gliding time arrangement nor a staggered hours procedure. It is appropriately described as "group flexibility."

Friedrich Uhde Corporation

The Friedrich Uhde Corporation, founded in 1921, is a West German engineering firm. It is 100 percent owned by Hoechst AG of Frankfurt, West Germany. From its head offices at Dortmund, Uhde Corporation engages in the design and construction of plants for the chemicals and allied industries. For example, it has built breweries, petroleum refining facilities, factories for reprocessing irradiated nuclear fuels, and plants for the production of carbide, powdered paints, carbon monoxide, phosphorus, plastics, sealing compounds, synthetic rubber, solvents, and pharmaceutical packaging.

The firm's workforce consists of approximately 2,700 employees, of whom about 2,200 are technical specialists. Members of Uhde's engineering and commercial divisions work on all five continents. To date, the company has assisted in the design and construction of plants in some 50 countries. Its major American subsidiary is the Hoechst-Uhde Corporation of Englewood Cliffs, New Jersey.

In its European operations as well as in its American subsidiary, "sliding time" (the firm's preferred designation) is used. In 1976 a top corporate official at Dortmund sent me this message:

> It is gratifying to note that a professor in the States is interested in "sliding time" and is writing a book on the subject.
>
> Sliding time is not really an invention of the sixties or seventies, but is a further development of the staggered working hours practiced in Germany as early as the twenties and thirties.
>
> The background circumstances for introducing both staggered hours and, later, sliding time are indeed manifold. From the physiological point of view, the work rhythm of the employees varies and should not be left unconsidered. Moreover, more humane working conditions are desirable in that every person should be able to choose his "come" and "go" times individually, thus assuming more responsibility and, consequently, obviating the need to supervise people's punctuality. A further point is that no two persons follow the same life rhythm — that is to say, an individual's behavior differs widely in the morning and in the evening, since it partly depends on the size of his family, his style of living, and his personal interests — and sliding time is thus an ideal opportunity to adapt the working hours to one's personal habits.
>
> A major factor that affects both the employer and employee alike is the traffic situation which is becoming more and more precarious as time goes on and seriously impedes the way to and from work. The rush-hour problem, which is as serious in the States as it is in Europe, is overcome to a large extent by the sliding time system.
>
> We initially introduced sliding time as a 6-month trial in one department only. Having heard the opinions of superiors and employees, the system was found to work and, in addition, people seemed to like the idea. We then proceeded with the formalities of coming to an agreement with the employees' representatives (Work Council), since German legislation stipulates that this body must be consulted with regard to working hours and duration of work.
>
> As time went on, ever more German firms examined and adopted the sliding time system. Manufacturers, on the other hand, do not as a rule use sliding time: They can at best stagger their hours, since most of them work in shifts. Exceptions prove the rule, of course, and Siemag Corporation of Hilchenbach, for instance, introduced sliding time in its production plant. And of course Messerschmidt-Bolkow-Blohm GmbH of Ottobrunn near Munich was one of the major pacemakers in the sixties. Incidentally, due in large part to its early experience with sliding time, this latter firm now sells sliding time systems (hardware and software) as a sideline.
>
> Widely varying equipment is now available for every practicable

sliding time system. Different companies compete with each other, the main point of issue being the expectations placed on the hardware. Uhde is currently in the process of converting from simple mechanical control clocks with punch cards to more sophisticated equipment compatible with electronic data processing.

One last point. For psychological reasons it is of utmost importance that everyone, from the president to the last employee, take part in the time control, since it constitutes a check on oneself, and every superior should set an example.

On the basis of materials received, at least as of 1976, the Friedrich Uhde Corporation had very good experiences with sliding time.

Qantas Airways Limited

Qantas is Australia's main overseas airline. The headquarters office is in Sydney, Australia. A flexible hours program began at various Australian locations in 1973, and was extended to the San Francisco regional headquarters in April 1976. Some hard data are available concerning the airline's Australian program.

Before the flexible hours system was installed, the normal workday for most employees at the Sydney headquarters office was 8:45 A.M. until 5:15 P.M. At a main branch at Mascot, most persons worked a 9:00 to 5:00 schedule. The firm was mainly interested in extending gliding time (the term in use at the airline) to as many employees as possible. For employees not able to work under that flexible hours system, staggered hours was to be used.

The company defines gliding time as "the ability to vary on a daily basis starting, lunch, and finishing times according to your own personal requirements." And it defines staggered hours as "starting and finishing work and taking lunch breaks at fixed times either each day or according to a regular pattern, as required by your department."

Qantas installed gliding time in November 1973. The experiment was conducted only in those areas where work commenced or finished between the hours of 8:00 A.M. and 6:00 P.M. As mentioned, although the company wanted to include as many persons as possible in the new system, employees doing certain jobs had to be excluded.

For example, because of the work requirements of various departments and a need to meet computer input or clearing house deadlines, affected workers were put on staggered hours. Thus, in some cases, fixed starting, luncheon, and finishing times were established according to a regular pattern as required by departmental needs.

Similarly, most shift workers were excluded, as Qantas was not able to resolve problems peculiar to areas involving double shifts or round-the-clock operations. The areas concerned were maintenance and overhaul, customer service and passenger handling units at the Sydney Airport, and information services operations at a different center. In short, where meeting public contact requirements and maintaining production levels and equipment during flexible periods outside core times were major obstacles, staggered hours was the alternative used. (In 1973 and 1974 Qantas sought shift-work information from Lufthansa Airlines at Cologne, Germany.)

In the company's view, the handling of passenger ticket sales at Sydney's "Booking Mall" provides an example of the need for staggered hours. There, because of the need to extend working hours from 8:00 A.M. to 9:00 P.M. and because a sufficient number of ticket sales officers must be on duty to meet passenger requirements — which peak during the luncheon period — it was necessary that affected employees work under staggered hours.

At Qantas Airways, as of November 1973, approximately 1,850 nonmanagement employees and more than 100 supervisors began working under either gliding time (more than 80 percent of the total) or staggered hours.

For employees on gliding time the arrangement takes this form:

FST	CORE TIME	MIDDAY FLEX	CORE TIME	FQT

8:00 A.M.	9:30 A.M.	12:00 P.M.	2:00 P.M.	4:00 P.M.	6:00 P.M.

Employees commence work at any time between 8:00 and 9:30 in the morning and end work at any time between 4:00 and 6:00 in the afternoon. Morning core time runs from 9:30 to noon, and afternoon core time spans the 2:00 to 4:00 period. A minimum ½-hour lunch break is taken during the midday-flex band. In this plan the midday-flex period has the effect of splitting core time into two separate segments.

During 1974 a program evaluation was made through two questionnaires, one completed by all employees (including supervisors), the other completed by supervisors only. Because the questionnaires involved a large number of employees, and because interesting particulars are revealed, we'll now look closely at the respective questionnaire findings.

Questionnaire to All Employees

Data in Table 1 pertain to the questionnaire completed by all employees, including supervisors. What does one get out of the data? Specifically, they show that gliding time was the main system used; workers' arrival and departure times were earlier; communication was about the same in terms of ease or difficulty; completion of daily work requirements was not affected in an adverse way; there was no significant change in supervisory availability; advantages were cited much more frequently than disadvantages; and only one percent wanted flexible hours discontinued. Some 44 percent wanted flexible hours continued. In fact, some 48 percent desired opportunities for even more work-hours flexibility.

Questionnaire to All Supervisors

Now let us turn our attention to the results of the other questionnaire. Table 2 shows what Qantas supervisors said about flexible hours, in contrast to the fixed hours schedule previously in use. Specifically, the responses show that planning and distributing work was about the same in terms of ease or difficulty; deadlines were still met in about the same way (with more ease in some cases); the amount of overtime, and the time allocated to employees and their problems, remained at about the same levels; supervisors were hesitant to report ways in which flexible hours made the job of supervision more difficult, but appeared eager to confirm ways in which the job was made easier; the quality of work remained about the same (with improvement in some cases); absenteeism remained at about the same level (and was even reduced in some instances). Finally, more than 50 percent of the supervisors thought that the flexible hours program in effect at the time was a good idea, and 40 percent wanted the program to incorporate even more flexibility.

Table 1

QUESTION AREA	%
1. Employees working under:	
Staggered hours	16
Gliding hours	81
No response	3
2. Arrival time was:	
Earlier	45
Later	7
Same time	32
No set pattern	12
No response	4
3. Departure time was:	
Earlier	50
Later	6
Same time	26
No set pattern	14
No response	4
4. Communication both within and outside the department was:	
Easier	8
More difficult	8
No different	80
No response	4
5. Completion of daily work requirements was:	
Easier	31
More difficult	2
No change	63
No response	4

QUESTION AREA	%
6. Supervisor availability:	
More available than before	4
Less available than before	4
No change	88
No response	4
7. Advantages of flexible work hours:	
Able to attend to private arrangements	66
Able to travel more easily	61
Able to take more rest after overtime	11
Working atmosphere is more relaxed	25
Able to work more efficiently	36
Other	8
No advantage	8
(In some cases, more than one answer was given.)	
8. Disadvantages of flexible work hours:	
Transportation not readily available	5
Communication with colleagues more difficult	3
More controlled by time than before	3
Other	3
No disadvantage	82
No response	4
9. Recommendations:	
Flexible hours is a good idea — continue	44
A good idea, but add more flexibility	48
Flexible hours — not worth the effort	2
Makes no difference	1
Discontinue flexible hours	1
No response	4

Table 2

QUESTION AREA	%
1. Planning and distribution of work are:	
Easier	12
Harder	3
Same	83
No response	2
2. Deadlines are met:	
More easily	18
Less easily	6
Same	75
No response	1
3. Overtime has:	
Increased	2
Decreased	8
Not varied greatly	68
Not applicable	13
No response	9
4. Flexible hours system permits you to allocate:	
More time to your employees than before	16
Less time	6
About the same time	75
No response	3
5. Supervision is harder because:	
It is not known when staff will arrive	9
More time is spent to see if people are working	3
Own attendance patterns differ from those of workers	1
Other	8
No change	5
No response	74

QUESTION AREA	%
6. Supervision is easier because:	
Communications are better	15
Morale is higher	74
Employees are more responsible	42
Employees are available for longer periods	19
Productivity appears to be higher	22
Other	4
No change	6
No response	3
(In some cases more than one answer was given.)	
7. Quality of work has:	
Improved	21
Suffered	1
Not changed	77
No response	1
8. Absenteeism is:	
Reduced	27
Increased	0
Not changed	71
No response	2
9. Recommendations:	
Flexible hours is a good idea—continue	54
A good idea, but add more flexibility	40
Flexible hours—not worth the effort	1
Makes no difference	1
Discontinue flexible hours	1
No response	3

Summary Comment

Generally, the concept of gliding time has been well received at Qantas Airways. Employees enjoy their added responsibility and their sense of being trusted to work part of the day unsupervised. Their attitude toward work has improved, and in many areas morale has increased. The majority of employees agree that the ability to vary work times is beneficial and should be continued.

Gliding time is used by a number of airline companies, and over different continents. Among the flexible hours programs described in this book are those of Qantas Airways, Lufthansa German Airlines–Europe Division, Lufthansa German Airlines–North and Central American Division, and Eastern Airlines. The reader is invited to look for similarities and differences in gliding time programs among firms within this industry.

Gulf Oil–Canada

Gulf Oil–Canada has experimented with gliding time at the company's Toronto and Montreal data centers. At both locations the firm was interested in comparing the operating results obtained in January-February-March 1974 (during which there was no flexitime) with the operating results obtained in January-February-March 1975 (during which there was flexitime). To make the comparison more meaningful, as many as possible of the 1975 employees who worked at the firm during the first three months of 1974 were participants in the study.

The company's program includes the opportunity for employees to "bank" hours. Workers are allowed to put in extra hours—at regular pay rates—and bank a maximum of 10 hours. In conjunction with this option is a "flex-day" privilege. That is, an employee is able to compensate for extra hours worked by working a shorter day, or by taking an extra full day off with pay.

As mentioned, sites for the study were Toronto and Montreal. However, since most of the materials available to me relate to the Toronto study, flexitime at Toronto is the main focus. The Toronto Data Center includes at least five "units" (departments).

Objective Measures at the Toronto Data Center

Sickness and Paid Absence. During the first three months of 1974 —when employees worked a standard workday—there were 423 days of paid absence among five units. During the first three months of 1975, when working under flexitime, there were 328 days of paid absence among these units. Thus, absenteeism was reduced by more than 20 percent.

Commenting on the performance of a unit where absenteeism totaled 204 days during the first three months of 1974 and only 143 days one year later, the manager of the unit says: "There is no way of proving this is as a result of flexitime, but in our opinion some of the credit must go to flexitime. It is our feeling that some of the 'flex-days' taken would have been sick-leave days if not for flexitime."

Overtime. Overtime comparisons were based on a six-month period in 1974 (January through June) versus the same period in 1975. Among five units, overtime totaled some 12,000 hours in 1974 and 6,600 hours in 1975. Overtime was reduced by close to 45 percent. In reflecting on the difference, one unit manager comments:

> Overtime has been greatly reduced, and while we cannot credit it all to flexitime, it is noticeable in areas where work flow is uneven. Some employees will work longer hours on peak days and shorter hours on nonpeak days. A good example is in the _____ unit where Mondays and days after a holiday result in heavy volumes. It is a fact that more employees work longer hours on peak days and shorter hours on non-peak days. Prior to flexitime we would have required overtime.

Productivity. One unit manager reports: "As you can appreciate, productivity in groups such as ours is very difficult to measure. However, there has been no noticeable reduction in output." A manager of a different unit says: "We are unable to quantify any benefits relative to productivity." A third unit manager reports: "It is difficult to assess the productivity aspect in most units although the reduction in overtime suggests better productivity."

A fourth unit did establish what was felt to be a meaningful measure of productivity. The number of cards keypunched per hour was measured.

	1974	1975
January	579	716
February	613	718
March	665	742

In reference to the 1975 increase in cards keypunched per hour, the unit manager says: "There is a marked increase in productivity which we feel is directly related to flexitime. It could be argued that the increased productivity is due to less staff turnover and therefore more experienced operators, but the smaller turnover could be attributed to the happier environment due to flexitime."

Overall Assessment of Flexitime at the Toronto Data Center

In my possession is a top manager's report summarizing major findings at Toronto.

Without exception, the unit supervisors strongly supported flexitime to the point that it was necessary to reassure them that this review was not an indication that consideration was being given to its discontinuance. I have summarized their main comments to avoid the necessity of your perusing their written submissions which are available should you desire them.

Time lost due to late arrival, extended hours, and early departure has been eliminated. In addition, fewer requests have been received for time off for personal appointments. In some instances, employees with accumulated hours in excess of the ten maximum for carry-forward have sacrificed the excess time. The combined effect of these factors is to provide more production hours but we are unable to quantify this gain.

The pressures of rigid deadlines combined with flexible working hours have made employees more conscious of the need to effectively manage their time, and increased their sense of responsibility toward their job. Employees are aware of the timing of peak periods with the knowledge that they can compensate for these extra hours by working shorter days or taking a flex-day in less demanding periods.

Flexitime provides a buffer to the pressures of critical deadlines, thereby reducing tensions.

Flexitime has had a definite positive effect on employee morale. Employees have more latitude in planning their business and social activities and are happier working in a less structured environment. Restrictive changes to flexitime would not be received graciously by employees.

Supervisors can concentrate on getting the job done with less concern for the hour the employee arrives or leaves, thereby eliminating an irritant between supervisors and staff as confrontations caused by tardiness or early departure no longer exist.

Most unit supervisors feel that flexitime has contributed to the reduction of paid overtime. It is my personal opinion that the number of flex-days taken by nonexempt employees is the best indicator of the

overtime hours saved as they represent hours taken off in relatively
slack periods in compensation for hours required in busier periods.

None of the Unit Supervisors noted any decrease in productivity, while many expressed the opinion that productivity had in fact
increased—although they were unable to provide supporting data.

Montreal Data Center Appraises Flexitime

Information from Montreal is more sparse. It appears, however,
that gliding time is a very useful tool there. According to reports, employees are happy with the system for a number of reasons: "They
have work-hours autonomy as responsible employees should . . . the
atmosphere is more relaxed . . . it provides flexibility for off-the-job
activities . . . the guilty feeling of lateness disappears . . . [and] they can
accumulate hours for flex-day."

Supervisors have noticed no decrease in productivity during
core hours. In fact, some supervisors believe that productivity has increased. Absenteeism and "sickness" have decreased or remained the
same, and overtime has not gone up.

A top manager concludes his report by saying: "So, in summary,
it appears that the Montreal Data Center is not paying dearly for flexitime, and the employees refer to flexitime as 'the greatest thing that
has happened since sliced bread.' "

I have no information on the number of employees at Gulf Oil–
Canada who are working under flexitime. It is known, though, that
flexitime is in operation in a number of departments, and that the
success of the system is considerable. The company welcomes the new
working-time pattern. A top manager at Gulf Oil–Canada wrote the
following to me in 1976: "We have concluded that the overall results
are positive and therefore we are not conducting any formal assessment program at the present time."

Firestone Corporation–Canada

Firestone's Canadian headquarters is at Hamilton, Ontario. This
installation began flexitime use in December 1974. The normal workday here is 7½ hours, and company policy stipulates that at month's
end the total accumulated hours should average 7½ hours per working day. The company offers its Canadian employees the option

whereby each of them is able to bank a total of 5 hours per month. Specifically, a debit or credit of up to 5 hours is allowed, but must be accordingly compensated for during the following month. For time-recording purposes Firestone of Canada uses the Flextime Machine.

A Pilot Program

In December 1974, Firestone initiated a Flextime pilot program for its Hamilton headquarters office employees for a six-month trial period. During the pilot run a cross section of 11 departments participated. Involved were some 91 employees, or approximately 23 percent of the headquarters office workforce.

The specific time plan was this:

FST	CORE TIME	MIDDAY FLEX	CORE TIME	FQT
7:30 A.M.	9:30 A.M.	12:00 P.M.	2:00 P.M.	3:30 P.M.	6:00 P.M.

As one sees, arrival time is any time between 7:30 and 9:30 in the morning, and departure time falls between 3:30 and 6:00 in the afternoon. There is a midday-flex band of 2 hours, and two separate core-time bands—in the morning from 9:30 until noon and in the afternoon from 2:00 until 3:30. (Incidentally, the company still uses this specific time plan.)

In establishing the program, Firestone was primarily interested in determining flexitime effects on employee travel to and from work, on-job and off-job interface, punctuality, absenteeism, organizational climate, and productivity.

At the end of the trial period the company surveyed employees by questionnaire and, to get management feedback, held meetings attended by the 11 department managers. Also, objective measurements of operations were made throughout the trial months.

The Questionnaire Survey

The form contained 35 questions. A number of the questions were peculiar to the firm and are not of direct concern to us. Instead, our inquiry will focus on the areas of greatest interest and information value. Nineteen question areas from Firestone's employee survey are listed.

1. Do you like to work under flexitime?
   97%   Yes
    3%   Not sure
    0%   No

2. How do you feel about our flexitime program?
   35%   Very satisfied
   51%   Satisfied
    2%   Uncertain
   12%   A little dissatisfied
    0%   Greatly dissatisfied

3. Using the Flextime Machine daily has been:
    0%   Upsetting
   30%   A bit bothersome
   70%   No trouble at all

4. How do you feel about the debit or credit of up to 5 hours?
   65%   Reasonable
   30%   Should be increased
    3%   Should be decreased
    2%   Not sure

5. Do you think flexitime has improved employee cooperation?
   53%   Yes
   26%   No
   21%   Uncertain

6. Under flexitime, morale:
   71%   Is increased
   19%   Is the same
    3%   Is decreased
    7%   Don't know

7. If others are working and are all caught up in the work, how do you feel about leaving before they do?
    9%   Guilty
   73%   Not guilty
   18%   Indifferent

8. If you mentioned flexitime to non-flexitime Firestone employees:
   92%   They showed interest
    6%   They showed no interest
    1%   They thought another system was better
    1%   I don't know any non-flexitime employees

9. If you mentioned flexitime to someone other than a Firestone employee:
   93%   They showed interest

6% They showed no interest
1% They thought another system was better

10. Has flexitime given you more time for your home life?
64% Yes
12% No
23% Still the same
1% Uncertain

11. Under flexitime, my daily work output:
22% Has increased
78% Is still the same
0% Has decreased

12. Are busy or slack periods more easily accommodated within a flexitime system?
66% Yes
7% No
24% Same as before
3% Not sure

13. Under flexitime, my traveling time to and from work is:
13% A lot shorter
32% A bit shorter
55% About the same
0% A bit longer
0% A lot longer

14. With flexitime, efficiency within the department:
29% Has increased
61% Has remained the same
1% Has decreased
9% Uncertain

15. Service to other departments, especially to those *not* on flexitime:
10% Has been affected
66% Has not been affected
24% Not sure

16. Do you feel there has been an overall change in your department's productivity since incorporating flexitime?
22% Yes
43% No
35% Not sure

17. Is it annoying to you when someone you wish to see has left for the day?
14% Yes
86% No

18. Flexitime should be fully incorporated into Firestone after the experimental phase is over.
    91%   Yes
    1%   No
    8%   Uncertain

19. In my opinion, flexitime is *more* beneficial to:
    22%   The employee
    38%   The company
    3%   Uncertain
    37%   Both employee and employer

A study of the questionnaire responses shows that flexitime was received by employees with enthusiasm. Specifically, the vast majority liked working under flexitime, were very satisfied or satisfied with it, believed that cooperation and morale had increased under it, and thought that the new working-time pattern was beneficial to both employee and employer. Employees also said that travel time to and from work was reduced. In terms of performance measures, most employees thought there was no decrease in personal efficiency and daily output. Similarly, the majority believed that departmental productivity did not decrease.

Feedback from Management, and Objective Measurements

Management meetings plus objective measurements supplemented the questionnaire survey of employees. From top management comes the following report on the six-month trial of flexitime.

1. Desired objectives as outlined were being met.
   (a) Efficiency and productivity *have not* decreased.
   (b) Employees feel that less pressure is exerted on them because of the individual's ability to choose hours (that is, appointments, tardiness, and the like, are no longer on company time).
   (c) To some extent traveling to and from work has become more convenient.
   (d) An overwhelming majority (90.9 percent) of flexitime employees, as well as many who were not on the program, expressed a desire to have flexitime permanently incorporated.

2. A study undertaken revealed that one-day absenteeism declined by 12 percent as compared with a similar period the preceding year.

3. All managers were of the opinion that flexitime is a much more advantageous system than that previously in use.

4. Feedback received indicates that flexitime is an incentive that increases employee morale.

Summary Comment

Flexitime was fully incorporated at Firestone's Canada head-quarters office in July 1975. All eligible employees in all 11 departments now participate in the system. From all indications, flexitime is well received at the company.

Lufthansa German Airlines–Europe Division

Lufthansa, Germany's principal airline, is a nationalized firm. It is an international carrier with headquarters at Cologne, West Germany. The firm has more than seven years of experience with gliding time, and claims to be the first air carrier in the world to incorporate the gliding time concept.

How the Lufthansa System Operates

Lufthansa's employees in Germany are on a 5-day workweek, with 8½ hours as a normal workday. (A 42½-hour week is quite common in that nation.) Here is what the specific time plan looks like:

FST	CORE TIME (excluding lunch break)	FQT
7:00 A.M. 9:30 A.M.	3:30 P.M.	7:00 P.M.

The bandwidth is 12 hours, extending from 7:00 A.M. until 7:00 P.M. The core time covers a 6-hour span from 9:30 in the morning until 3:30 in the afternoon, interrupted only by a ½-hour lunch break. As noted, the plan does not have a midday-flex band built into it. Workers can arrive at any time they like between 7 and 9:30 in the morning and can leave at any time after 3:30 in the afternoon. In other words, employees have 2½ hours of leeway in the morning and 3½ hours of flexibility in the afternoon. In effect, from 9:30 A.M. until

3:30 P.M., everyone should either be at work or be on a ½-hour lunch break to be taken between 12:00 and 2:00.

In accordance with the program, no extra pay is given for extra hours on the job unless an employee is asked to work overtime. (The "no extra pay" policy is quite common in Germany.) This company program also offers the option of debiting and crediting working hours. Thus, the Lufthansa plan includes the banking-of-hours idea. Extra hours worked by an employee are classified as "plus" hours; a short workday results in "minus" hours. A total of 10 plus hours or 10 minus hours may be carried to the next month. Where plus hours are accumulated, persons may apply those hours for extra days or parts of days off in the subsequent month.

Workers on gliding time still punch the time card and make their own calculations on how much time they put in on the job. Management spot-checks worker time calculations.

It should be explained that Lufthansa does not use the system where workforce and speed are dictated precisely by the production process. For example, stewardesses, pilots, and other essential flying staff are excluded from this time system. In addition, Lufthansa discovered that it's not easy to apply gliding time to offices where the public is served (customers do not like unattended counters). Yet a limited gliding time format is applied in offices and at ticket counters in various cities, with the understanding that employees make their own group arrangements to keep the counters staffed efficiently.

Summary Comment

When it has applied the system in appropriate work situations, Lufthansa has experienced good success with gliding time in Germany. Productivity has not decreased, and job satisfaction and morale levels have increased. In a Lufthansa poll of workers on gliding time, 95 percent responded that the system was a great help and convenience.

5

Flexitime's growing pains in America

Having examined the birth, growth, and current popularity of the flexitime system of flexible hours in other countries, we now focus on its growing pains in the United States.

Federal Laws Affecting Flexitime Innovation

The Walsh-Healey Act (1936) was directed at companies having contracts with the federal government. As originally written, the Act established minimum wage rates and maximum hours, and prohibited the use of child labor by government contractors. The Act applied to government contracts exceeding $10,000, and to instances where contract provisions called for the manufacturing or furnishing of materials and supplies. Firms covered were required to pay nonexempt employees a minimum of 1½ times the basic hourly rates for time worked in excess of 8 hours a day or 40 hours a week. The latter provision, in particular, is relevant to the subject of flexible hours.

The Fair Labor Standards Act (1938) had wider coverage than the Walsh-Healey Act. In addition to adding provisions outlawing the use of child labor, the FLSA established minimum wages and maximum hours for employers engaged in interstate commerce or in the production of goods for interstate commerce. An 8-hour workday and a 40-hour workweek were other standards established, with time-and-a-half pay for work exceeding 40 hours a week. Congress progressively expanded coverage over the years. For example, the FLSA as amended in 1974 extended minimum wage and overtime requirements to federal, state, and municipal employees. During 1976, however, the Supreme Court invalidated the 1974 wage-and-hour statute as pertaining to state and municipal workers. According to the Supreme Court verdict, an attribute of state sovereignty is the power of each state to determine wages and hours of work within its own agencies, as well as overtime-compensation rates.

The Contract Work Hours and Safety Standards Act (1962) covered business firms engaged in federal government construction projects, and required that the companies pay nonexempt employees (for example, construction workers building barracks on an army base) a minimum of 1½ times the basic hourly rates for time worked in excess of 8 hours a day or 40 hours a week.

Among the various states there exist different statutes setting forth overtime pay particulars. Furthermore, many different contractual arrangements between organizations and unions spell out a variety of overtime-pay details. Obviously, an exploration into the multitude of overtime-pay requirements would not add to this book's central purpose. My main intention at this point is to discuss intricacies of overtime pay within a framework of major federal legislation, and explain how that legislation has affected flexitime's provisions for debiting and crediting work hours. It is accurate to say that, as of 1977, the three Acts just outlined illustrated principal federal legislation concerning overtime-pay requirements.

Case Examples

The Walsh-Healey Act and the Fair Labor Standards Act, in addition to strengthening laws prohibiting child labor abuse, were legislative responses to demands calling for a shorter workday and workweek, higher pay, and work sharing as a cure for the unemployment of the 1930s. The laws provided for overtime premiums, and were designed to encourage employers to hire more employees when there was a need for labor in excess of 40 hours a week. In 1977 a number of thinkers were of the opinion that employer and employee needs and aspirations had undergone change since the 1930s, and that certain laws may act as a deterrent to employees and employers desiring more flexible work-hours arrangements.

Attention here will focus on certain employment situations in which legislation on the books in 1977 caused restrictions in the use of flexitime. Two laws in particular—the Walsh-Healey Act and the Contract Work Hours and Safety Standards Act—also caused restrictions in the use of the 4/40 compressed workweek. Because the main theme of this book is flexitime and not the compressed workweek, however, I shall confine my remarks and illustrations to the former alternative work schedule.

A majority of flexitime programs in operation in the United States were concerned with discretionary ways in which 8 hours of work were distributed over a workday. Where employees worked 8 hours a day and 40 hours a week—or where the workday and workweek consisted of fewer hours—federal legislation was not a major obstacle. It was in other kinds of flexitime arrangements that trouble was encountered.

Case 1
An east coast company using flexitime was engaged in interstate commerce and was covered by the Fair Labor Standards Act. The firm had negotiated no federal government contracts. The normal schedule called for a $7\frac{1}{2}$-hour workday and a $37\frac{1}{2}$-hour workweek. There was a provision whereby an employee could put in, at regular pay, an extra $2\frac{1}{2}$ hours a week—so long as the workweek did not exceed 40 hours. When this latter option was exercised the employee banked $2\frac{1}{2}$ hours for his or her future discretionary use—to be taken in the form of compensatory time off. In effect, on any workday an employee was able to work in excess of $7\frac{1}{2}$ hours—so long as the workweek did not exceed 40 hours.

The problem of overtime pay was therefore neatly managed within legal restrictions in this case. In the following cases, however, complications arise concerning overtime-pay requirements.

Case 2
A different east coast company using flexitime was engaged in interstate commerce and was covered by the Fair Labor Standards Act. The company had not engaged in any contractual arrangements with the federal government. Its regular workweek was $37\frac{1}{2}$ hours. Here, as in the program just described, employees were offered a credit and debit option. A worker was able to work 35 hours one week and owe the firm $2\frac{1}{2}$ hours of extra time during the future week. By

contrast, the worker could bank hours by working 40 hours and taking 2½ hours of compensatory time off in the future. In short, employees had the option of working in excess of 7½ hours on any workday — so long as the workweek did not exceed 40 hours.

The program was in operation about one year. Overall results were beneficial to both the company and its employees. More recently, however, employee representatives said they were strongly in favor of a plan to liberalize the debit-credit option. Specifically, they proposed that the option be extended from 2½ hours to 4 hours. Management claimed that such a change could be accommodated from an operations standpoint but not from a legal standpoint. The employees' plan would have allowed a workweek of 41½ hours on some occasions, thus requiring 1½ hours of overtime pay as prescribed in the FLSA. The firm was not prepared to absorb overtime costs and turned down the proposal, much to the disappointment of all concerned.

Case 3

A midwestern firm manufactured auditorium seats, bus seats, and chairs and desks for classrooms and offices. It operated on a fixed hours schedule, and the normal workweek was 40 hours. About 10 percent of the company's business was with the federal government. Recently, employee representatives proposed that the company adopt flexitime. In calling for retention of the 40-hour week, the advocates proposed a debit and credit option. Because of the nature of its business, the company was covered by all three laws described in this chapter. The firm turned down the employees' recommendation, stating that additional overtime pay — for time in excess of 8 hours on any given workday — would be required under both the Walsh-Healey Act and the Contract Work Hours and Safety Standards Act.

Case 4

A west coast electronics firm had a flexitime program that included debit and credit options. Although the company's main business was with other firms in the private sector, it also did business with the federal government. Consequently, provisions in the Walsh-Healey Act as well as in the FLSA applied to this organization. As the reader recalls, for work done under government contracts, as of 1977 the Walsh-Healey Act still required overtime pay for work time in excess of 8 hours a day. When engaged in competitive bidding for government contracts the corporation included overtime and associated costs in its contract prices.

Recently, when competing with other companies for a government contract, the firm submitted a contract bid that included projected overtime-pay costs of about $300,000. The organization lost the award — because, in management's view, its competitors did not have either flexitime or debit and credit options and so could avoid overtime-pay costs. The firm believes that it lost more than one government contract award because of this very reason, namely, overtime-pay requirements after 8 work hours on any given workday.

Case 5

This example concerns an Ohio firm with a flexitime program that included debit and credit options. The company did both government and nongovernment work and, as a consequence, was covered by the Walsh-Healey Act and the Fair Labor Standards Act. What follows is a development that occurred in 1977 when the firm was working on a government contract.

Because of the Walsh-Healey overtime-pay requirements, employees doing work under a government contract received overtime pay for time worked in excess of 8 hours a day. However, other employees not doing such work were paid at their basic hourly rates for time worked in excess of 8 hours a day. Organization officials report that the overtime-pay requirements had resulted in extra costs to the government (and therefore to the taxpayers) and had caused resentment among the organization's employees because those doing similar work received different rates of pay.

Our examination of the three laws affecting flexitime and our five case studies lead to the following conclusions: The Fair Labor Standards Act, which applied to employers doing work under either government or nongovernment contracts, provided that overtime premiums be paid whenever employees worked more than 40 hours a week. The Walsh-Healey Act and the Contract Work Hours and Safety Standards Act, which were limited to government contractors, required payment of overtime rates for time worked in excess of 8 hours a day or 40 hours a week. Together, these three acts restricted employee flexibility to bank and borrow time when desired.

Stated another way, where one or more of the laws were applicable, overtime pay entered the picture. Consider the situation in which a firm was covered by the Fair Labor Standards Act and in which overtime-pay rates went into effect after 40 hours. A company program offering options to work 45 hours in week one and 35 hours in week two would have required overtime-pay rates during week one — even though the work schedule over the two weeks would have resulted in an average workweek of 40 hours. Or consider the situation in which a firm was covered by the Walsh-Healey Act and the Contract Work Hours and Safety Standards Act and in which overtime pay was required after 8 hours. A company program offering options to work 10 hours on Monday and 6 hours on Tuesday would have necessitated overtime-pay rates on Monday — even though the work schedule over the two days would have produced an average workday of 8 hours.

Reasons for Flexitime's Growing Pains

Why, over the past decade in America, has flexitime not been pushed as a meaningful alternative to the fixed hours schedule? As already noted, written discussions of alternatives to fixed working hours were oriented mainly toward the 4-day, 40-hour workweek. Numerous articles recorded that plan's growth and its effects on organizations incorporating the system.

A second reason is legislation that in effect established the 8-hour workday and the 40-hour workweek as standards. Also, laws specifying overtime-pay requirements discouraged tampering with the fixed hours system.

Third, attitudes toward work and leisure are partly responsible for the submergence of an earlier interest in flexitime. In other words, some thinkers believe that in contrast to Europeans, Americans are more interested in off-the-job satisfactions and pay less attention to schedules aimed at accommodating and linking work and leisure pursuits. The question of cultural mores as mirrored in attitudes about work and leisure is addressed in more detail in the final chapter of this book.

A fourth reason is that during the latter part of the 1960s, when flexitime experienced its initial development and expansion in Europe, American management was apathetic toward the concept and quietly disregarded work-schedule developments taking place in other nations. It goes without saying, however, that such a posture of indifference no longer exists.

Lack of union support is a fifth reason. Unions in the United States did not overtly and concertedly push the flexitime idea.

A sixth reason is the federal government's attitude in the earlier years. This was neither hostile nor favorable to the concept, but mainly indifferent. More recently, however, the government has demonstrated vigorous interest in flexitime, as information to be presented shortly will confirm.

A seventh reason for the lagging interest shown in earlier years is the scarcity of detailed information about flexitime programs. Granted, numerous inserts and articles about the system were scattered among magazines and journals—including my article entitled "What Time Shall I Go to Work Today?" that appeared in *Business Horizons* in October 1974—but in virtually all instances, flexitime entered the American consciousness in bits and pieces. Confirming this statement is information contained in a letter I received in 1976 from Janice Hedges, a senior economist at the U.S. Department of Labor. It reads in part: "We do not have data on the number of firms with flexible work schedules." In short, until recently, the subject area has received little attention from a research standpoint.

U.S. Government: General Accounting Office. In 1974, under the auspices of the U.S. Comptroller General, GAO surveyed 33 organizations that were using work schedules different from a fixed hours format. Sixteen were operating under flexible hours, whereas the others were using a compressed hours arrangement. The survey documented the objectives of the organizations using flexible hours, as well as the results they obtained.

The overall conclusions were that alternative work schedules were advantageous to management and employees in many situations. Although the organizations surveyed generally found flexible hours beneficial to their operations, many could not quantify the advantages and disadvantages. As explained by GAO, managers generally do not analyze schedule changes the way they would a major equipment acquisition. Changes in work schedules require little or no capital expenditures. If the change does not succeed, the organization can quickly return to the old schedule. Finally, in a small number of organizations, GAO did not discern any pattern of success or failure on the basis of organization or type of industry.

University of Pennsylvania. Harriet Faye Goldberg published a doctoral dissertation in 1975 entitled *A Comparison of Three Alternative*

Work Schedules: Flexible Work Hours, Compact Work Week, and Staggered Hours. Her report was centered on 81 organizations in the United States and Canada that responded to a questionnaire survey. Identified were different work-hour schedules and reasons for their development, along with a number of advantages and disadvantages experienced by the organizations. Among the firms Goldberg studied, 57 had used compressed schedules and 24 had used flexible schedules. Only one had discontinued using flexible hours programs, but 17 of the 57 organizations that installed compressed schedules had discontinued their usage.

Business and Professional Women's Foundation. In 1975 Virginia H. Martin published a research report entitled *Hours of Work When Workers Can Choose: The Experience of 59 Organizations with Employee-Chosen Staggered Hours and Flexitime.* Of the organizations studied, 40 had incorporated flexitime and 19 had installed staggered schedules. Listed were major objectives given for establishing the programs along with an enumeration of some benefits derived by employers and employees. A basic conclusion was that technology alone has less potential for increasing productivity than technology coupled with other innovations, including flexible work scheduling.

Ball State University. Financially aided by a grant provided by the Ball State University Bureau of Business Research, in 1975 a colleague and I published a report entitled *The Banking Industry's Appraisal of Flexitime.* By questionnaire, 300 of the nation's largest banks were studied. The investigation was aimed at determining the number of banks that used flexitime among nonmanagerial-level employees, the kinds of results obtained through use of the system, and top management's predictions of trends in flexitime usage in the banking industry through 1980. (Basic results of this study are given in Chapter 11 in this book, in conjunction with the discussion about flexitime's possible application in future years.)

U.S. Environmental Protection Agency. In 1975 the Agency published *Impacts of Energy Conservation Measures Applied to Commuter Travel.* The Agency assessed, among other things, the impact of alternative work schedules on energy consumption by commuters in urban areas. A basic finding was that both compressed and flexible schedules could result in reduced energy consumption by vehicles because of less engine idling time and fewer stops and starts. In short, there would be reduced energy consumption through improved and smoother traffic flow.

U.S. Government: General Accounting Office. In 1976 GAO published findings about 20 organizations that used flexible hours or a compressed workweek. Among flexitime users the advantages of the system far outnumbered the disadvantages.

GAO also asked officials of 44 government contractors whether they had used, or had considered using, alternative work schedules. A few of them used flexitime among some administrative employees exempt from overtime-pay requirements. On the other hand, none of them used flexitime for their production employees. The main reasons were that most firms were not knowledgeable about the system, and those that did demonstrate awareness and interest believed that active consideration of the system might open the door to employee demands for an arrangement for debiting and crediting work hours, which in turn would obligate the firms to pay additional premiums for overtime.

University of Oklahoma. In 1976 Ruby A. Tripp completed a doctoral dissertation entitled *A Study of Potential Benefits of Flexible Working Hours for White-Collar Employees at a State University.* The study sought to investigate whether flexitime's effects on nonacademic white-collar personnel at a state university in the United States were somewhat similar to effects reported at comparable institutions in Europe. Do flexitime's benefits tend to be applicable over the different cultures and environments? A questionnaire was distributed to 300 university employees holding jobs comparable to those for which successful European use of the system had been reported. Altogether, 263 completed questionnaires were returned. One overall conclusion was that flexitime benefited nonacademic white-collar personnel at an American state university, and the positive effects were quite similar to those reported at comparable institutions in Europe.

Unions and Flexitime

Unions in Europe, as in the United States, are interested in reducing working time. In 1977 some 20 percent of Germany's labor force put in 45 hours a week on a job. German unions want 40 hours established as a standard workweek. A similar movement calling for a reduction in the workweek was promoted in Switzerland. For example, in 1976 Switzerland's Trades Union Federation began a public campaign for a generalized 40-hour workweek. A minimum of 50,000 signatures are required under Swiss law to force a national referendum on an issue; the Federation leaders collected the necessary signatures, and a national referendum was undertaken in December 1976. Surprisingly, 78 percent voted against the proposal to cut the workweek to 40 hours.

Although European unions are interested in achieving reductions in work time through a redefinition of the standard workweek, they're also interested in measures leading to redistribution of work time. Their perspective is not one of adamant opposition to flexible hours. In fact, over the past decade the rapid spread of gliding time in Europe is attributable in part to their basic tolerance and acceptance of the flexible hours concept. On the other hand, it's also true that European unions believe strongly in establishing guidelines for negotiating the introduction of gliding time. For example, the German Union of Administrative Employees aims to establish some of the more rigid "guidelines," namely, that employees be compensated for additional output that accrues to firms from the introduction of flexible hours.

In the early months of 1977 the attitude of unions in the United States toward flexitime was still unclear because their opinions on the subject had not been widely publicized. It appeared that most of them would accept the idea, especially where the redistribution of work hours would result in greater employee satisfaction coupled with no loss in pay. But it also seemed likely that most unions across the nation would oppose any tampering with laws requiring premium pay after 8 hours of work per day or 40 hours of work per week.

It is known that in the early part of the 1970s the AFL-CIO Executive Council went on record as rejecting proposals that would have had the effect of dropping the requirement of time-and-one-half pay for over 8 hours of work a day on government contracts.

During the mid-1970s the U.S. General Accounting Office sought out the views of a few unions. At the time of the survey, the United Auto Workers (UAW) reported that it had not studied the matter sufficiently and therefore had no position on flexible hours. A Teamsters Union local expressed the same view. The International Ladies Garment Workers Union (ILGWU) likewise told GAO that no flexible schedules were provided for in its bargaining agreements and that the union had not formally studied the matter. The American

Federation of Labor and Congress of Industrial Organizations (AFL-CIO) stated that it believed that all work in excess of 8 hours a day should require overtime premium pay to employees regardless of the type of work schedule.

In 1977 it appeared that the AFL-CIO was maintaining its position of opposition to that aspect of flexitime dealing with the borrowing and banking of hours. According to an AFL-CIO representative who spoke at the National Conference on Alternative Work Schedules, the union did not want overtime-pay laws relaxed. The spokesperson believed that changing the laws to accommodate the 10-hour workday would make the Department of Labor's enforcement of time standards virtually impossible.

In the spring of 1977 I directed a study of union leaders' views on two alternative work schedules (4-day workweek and flexitime), and on overtime-pay requirements. Using the 1976 issue of *Who's Who in Labor* as a reference, colleague Robert A. Quakenbush and I surveyed 197 national unions by questionnaire (using four questions only). There was about an equal distribution between AFL-CIO and independent unions. Anonymity was guaranteed to all respondents. As part of the "Instructions," it was mentioned that the focus was to be placed on the typical nonexempt worker in the American civilian labor force. Would-be respondents were also told that all references to time worked implied nonweekend and nonholiday dates, that shift-work differential pay would not be affected, and that provisions in any existing contract would not be affected.

Questionnaires were returned by 42 of the 197 unions surveyed (23 AFL-CIO unions, 19 independent unions), a return rate of about 21 percent. Although various factors doubtless contributed to this low return rate, one main reason was that the subject was highly controversial and numerous unions thought it expedient to play it safe and not return the questionnaire — even though anonymity had been guaranteed. The major findings of the survey are these:

Concerning a 4-day workweek, in which overtime pay would apply only to hours worked in excess of 10 hours per day or in excess of 40 hours per week, about 74 percent of the AFL-CIO leadership (17 unions) were in opposition to the proposal. Interestingly, 63 percent of the independents (12 unions) were neutral toward the proposal.

Concerning a flexitime schedule containing the option of debiting and crediting work hours, with the provision that the employee may voluntarily choose to work extra hours so as to use the banked time in the form of time off on a future workday, and with the further provision that overtime pay be required of the employer only for excess hours officially ordered in advance by said employer, about 65 percent of the AFL-CIO leadership (15 unions) opposed the proposal, whereas 47 percent of the independents (9 unions) actually supported the proposal.

Concerning a flexitime schedule not containing debiting and crediting options and in which overtime-pay requirements would not be relaxed, 39 percent of AFL-CIO officials (9 unions) were neutral, while 35 percent (8 unions) were in opposition. Among the independents, 47 percent were neutral (9 unions) and 53 percent (10 unions) supported the proposal.

In brief, the major findings of the study were that, (1) because the questionnaires returned represented only about 21 percent of the total number of unions contacted, conclusions had to be viewed with considerable caution; (2) given the limited framework of the data on the questionnaires, it nonetheless seemed clear that in some ways union leadership was not a monolithic force and that considerable differences of opinion existed among unions, depending in large part on the source of affiliation; and (3) somewhat more importance was attached to the AFL-CIO responses, because in the real world most unions are affiliated with the AFL-CIO.

Reminders from the Past

In the United States, only recently have fresh ideas surfaced and given impetus to both the compressed workweek and flexitime. For example, various proposals have been made to allow nonexempt workers, under designated circumstances, to work in excess of 8 hours per day and 40 hours per week without receiving overtime pay. However, as mentioned earlier, at least three pieces of federal legislation have had the effect of stifling those flexitime innovations that take the form of debit and credit work scheduling. As of late 1977, the proposals for change remained suspended in a state of limbo. Neither the 94th nor the 95th Congress was disposed to pass new laws or to amend previous legislation relating specifically to alternative work schedules.

Before outlining the recent proposals that favor a policy of flexible working hours, I'd like to give a background of relevant historical data pertaining to public policy and labor unions in this country during the 1930s. The shadow of those hard times explains in part why ideas affecting flexitime bogged down in Washington.

From the late 1700s to 1977, employee working hours were reduced from a 6-day workweek of 72 hours to a 5-day workweek of about 40 hours. The reduction in work hours resulted from mechanization, the industrial and technological revolutions, the labor movement, and legislation. The gains were made over these two hundred years by the efforts of individuals, groups, and various organizations.

Large numbers of workers experienced great suffering as they helped carve out the difficult pathway leading to today's working-time standards. Labor unions will not let us forget the bleak economic situation of the 1930s. Unemployment was the overriding fact of life through most of the decade. The government did not systematically collect statistics on joblessness at that time, but the Bureau of Labor Statistics later estimated that close to 13 million people were out of work in 1933, the worst year of the Great Depression. This constituted about 25 percent of a civilian labor force of 51 million. Massive unemployment had a profound social and emotional impact on millions of American workers and their families. In the words of Irving Bernstein, professor of political science at the University of California at Los Angeles: "The great population movement of the thirties was transiency — the worker adrift in a sea of unemployment."

Unemployment remained high throughout the New Deal era. By 1935 about 20 percent of the labor force was still out of work. A burst of recovery occurred between 1935 and 1937. In the latter year, in fact, industrial production exceeded the level reached in 1929. But increased productivity was coupled with a growing labor force, and 7,700,000 persons remained unemployed. That number exceeded 10 million in the recession of 1937–1939. The year 1939 yielded only a modest improvement. As the abysmal decade approached its end there remained almost 10 million persons out of work, over 17 percent of the civilian workforce. It was out of such economic quicksands that the Walsh-Healey Act and the Fair Labor Standards Act surfaced — legislation that established requirements for overtime pay.

The economic malaise of the 1930s and the massive unemployment rates of that decade were soberly recalled in the mid-1970s when unemployment figures were compared with those of the earlier period. Over the past few years we've heard the refrain repeatedly:

"We're experiencing the highest unemployment since the Great Depression." The economic issues of too few jobs, high unemployment rates, and runaway inflation — constantly drummed into the public consciousness — were among the main reasons why Jimmy Carter was catapulted into the White House in 1976.

These bits and pieces of economic history have a great deal to do with recent proposals aimed at overturning overtime-pay requirements. Workers and their unions have memories of past events. They don't want to be exploited. They don't want to be taken in by what some consider to be a clever management plot to reduce costs — through a diversionary propaganda campaign suggesting that changes in overtime-pay requirements will be accompanied by greater job satisfaction among employees.

The road leading to the 8-hour workday and the 40-hour workweek was long and difficult. Many unions and job seekers are determined to preserve and strengthen laws that protect their job security. Where plans are offered to modify overtime-pay statutes, the content and phraseology of those plans are likely to be weighed against a twentieth-century economic experience that produced growth and affluence and comforts for the nation as a whole, but economic adversity of long duration for some.

In the United States, countless numbers of salaried employees have experienced economic advancement and social mobility levels that would have been impossible of attainment in different societies around the globe. To many of these successful persons a discussion of overtime-pay requirements is not directly relevant because so many of them occupy positions that are exempt from overtime-pay regulations. On the other hand, individuals who have experienced hard times are likely to look with disfavor on proposals suggesting a loosening of the laws on overtime pay. Many of these job holders and job seekers are classified as nonexempt employees. Because of provisions in current overtime-pay laws, many in this category believe they have even more compelling reasons for supporting legislation that upholds and strengthens premium-pay requirements.

Proposals to Alter Overtime-Pay Requirements

The discussion so far in this chapter has doubtless convinced many readers that proposals aimed at altering overtime-pay requirements touch on sensitive areas. Where employees would work in excess of 8 hours per day and 40 hours per week without receiving premium overtime pay—in exchange for flexitime debit and credit work-hours entitlements—would the work arrangement constitute a step forward or a step backward? Indeed, in most situations the problem is difficult and all solutions suggested to date have been steeped in controversy.

There is no overtime-pay dilemma where an organization considers installing flexitime among a workforce made up entirely of exempt employees. Thousands of organizations, especially small and non-union, may consist of a workforce that is almost entirely exempt from overtime-pay requirements. In such a workforce the major considerations are whether it is expedient to install flexitime from an operations standpoint and whether employees would like working under an appropriately structured flexitime system. Here, questions of overtime pay are not that germane. A small number of clerical, custodial, and security personnel might work under a fixed hours arrangement—in which overtime-pay laws might apply—whereas all other employees might be plugged into flexitime. Employees in the latter category might fit snugly in a debit and credit flexitime program, with options to work more or less than 8 hours a day and more or less than 40 hours per week. The result could well be smooth operations and satisfied workers.

In work situations where overtime pay does not enter the picture, at least that one thorny issue can be disregarded by management. But in most work situations organizational life is more complex. Substantially more than half of the nation's 1977 workforce fell under the rule of one or more of the three laws discussed in this chapter. Consequently, overtime-pay regulations were, and are, highly pertinent to most organizations.

Many reasons can be cited for formulating and floating proposals to alter overtime-pay statutes. A central reason may well be management's wish to use flexitime's debit and credit options as a smokescreen to camouflage other intentions, such as strengthening the overall position of the organization while weakening the economic posture of employees. Such is likely to be the view of employee spokespersons who believe that all management proposals concerning employer-employee relationships must have as their prime purposes the manipulation, exploitation, and subjugation of workers. But such a view is surely simplistic. The vast majority of persons, groups, and organizations advocating change are not motivated by a desire to put the screws to the worker. In general, proponents of change have honorable intentions.

There are organizations that would maintain or improve productivity if its labor force were able to borrow and bank work hours. There are employees on 40-hour weekly schedules who would prefer on some occasions to work 9 hours one day and 7 hours the next day, and 45 hours one week and 35 hours during a following week. Each of these parties would like these entitlements without recourse to overtime-pay rates. But our discussion has made it abundantly clear that organizations and employees cannot eat their cake and have it too. Not under the statutes still in effect in 1977. And a further question that compounds the problem: How frequently, if at all, should employees work in excess of 8 hours per day and 40 hours per week without receiving overtime pay?

Concerning work-hours and overtime-pay requirements, it is important to include federal government workers in the areas under discussion for at least two reasons. In the first place, the federal civilian workforce numbers about 3 million, almost all of whom are full-time employees. Second, during the 1975–1977 period some legislative proposals dealing with flexible hours and overtime-pay requirements pertained mainly to federal employees.

Before we examine specific legislative proposals, it will be helpful to be reminded of basic requirements affecting federal employees as of late 1977. The Fair Labor Standards Act as amended in 1974 required that nonexempt federal employees be paid overtime for work exceeding 40 hours a week. Also affecting government workers was Title 5 of the U.S. Pay Code (not discussed previously in this chapter because of its exclusive preoccupation with government employees). Briefly, Title 5 specified that the basic 40-hour workweek shall be scheduled on 5 days, Monday through Friday, where possible. It also provided that working hours during the workweek shall be the same, and the basic nonovertime workday shall not exceed 8 hours. Concerning federal employees, therefore, one observes that these laws have stifled the development of flexitime debit and credit programs, as well as compressed workweek schedules.

H.R. 5451 (Flexible Hours Act)

Introduced in March 1975, the Act authorizes federal agencies to establish flexible work-hours programs. The legislation was introduced in Congress by then Representative Bella Abzug of New York.

H.R. 9043 (Federal Employees Flexible and Compressed Work Schedules Act)

The Act was introduced in Congress in July 1975. *Title I* (General Provisions) establishes the overall framework, namely, that controlled experimentation with a variety of workday and workweek configurations shall be conducted by the Civil Service Commission for a three-year period, and that the programs shall provide for testing the impact of various schedules on such factors as productivity, mass transit facilities, and full- and part-time employment. Furthermore, it was stated that provisions of the Act shall not be construed to affect in any way the terms of any negotiated contract between government agencies and government employees' unions.

Title II (Flexible Work Schedules) authorizes the Civil Service Commission to approve proposals for the establishment of experimental flexible work schedules submitted by government agencies. Also, the Act prohibits the payment of premium pay for credit hours worked by decision of an employee. Overtime pay shall be required of the employer, however, for credit hours officially ordered in advance. The Act also contains provisions for the payment of night-shift differential pay to employees on flexible schedules.

Title III (Compressed Work Schedules) specifies that the term "compressed work schedule" shall mean, for full-time employees, a basic 80-hour biweekly schedule in which employees work less than 10 days. Also, the Act contains regulations with respect to overtime-pay requirements.

S. 517 (Federal Employees Flexible and Compressed Work Schedules Act of 1977)

In its essentials, this Act is the Senate version of H.R. 9043 which was introduced in the 94th Congress, passed the House of Representatives in May 1976, but was stalled in the Senate. S. 517 was introduced in the 95th Congress in January 1977 by Senator Gaylord Nelson of Wisconsin.

The bill authorizes the U.S. Civil Service Commission to administer and implement compressed and flexible hours schedules, during a three-year experimental period, in all federal agencies willing to participate in the program. The legislation would amend the Fair

Labor Standards Act and Title 5 of the U.S. Pay Code so as to permit federal employees to accumulate up to 10 credit hours biweekly without premium pay, so long as work time averaged 8 hours a day and 40 hours a week. Similarly, employees in a compressed workweek schedule could choose to work a condensed workweek such as a 4-day, 40-hour week.

H.R. 2732 (Federal Employees Flexible and Compressed Work Schedules Act of 1977)

This bill, introduced in January 1977 by Representative Stephen Solarz of New York, is quite similar to legislation introduced in the Senate by Senator Nelson. The main difference from the Nelson bill is that H.R. 2732 would require participation by all federal agencies in the compressed workweek and flexible hours schedules. The Civil Service Commission could exempt an agency from mandatory participation if it determined that implementation would not be in the best interest of the agency, the government, or the public.

H.R. 2930 (Federal Employees Flexible and Compressed Work Schedules Act of 1977)

Congresswoman Gladys Spellman of Maryland introduced this legislation in February 1977. The Act is identical to H.R. 9043. Representative Spellman's bill, like Senator Nelson's, provides for voluntary participation by federal agencies in compressed workweek and flexible hours schedules.

In 1976 the General Accounting Office, under the auspices of the U.S. Comptroller General, issued a publication concerning alternative work schedules and overtime-pay requirements. GAO's assessment and philosophy were set forth in the Comptroller General's Report to Congress in April 1976. Part of that report reads as follows:

> Many persons believe that overtime premiums should be paid for all time worked in excess of 8 hours a day and 40 hours a week. Some persons would like to see current legislative requirements remain unchanged, and others would like to see legislation enacted to reduce the number of hours in a workday or in a workweek. However, a growing number of others believe that payment of overtime premiums should not be required for work in excess of 8 hours a day or 40 hours a week when employees desire to alter their work schedules to work at times more convenient to their needs and desires. Also many persons

believe that overtime payment requirements should be revised to permit additional use of compressed schedules.

We found that adherence to fixed, 5-day work schedules was not always best for employees and employers. For persons desiring changes to certain altered work schedules, the current overtime payment requirements do not always work to their best advantage. Therefore we believe the Congress should revise the current laws to permit greater use of altered work schedules.

Since the need remains to protect the health and safety of employees, however, we believe the revisions made should continue to protect employees from long hours of labor that could be detrimental to their well-being. Also, since many employees and employers are satisfied with their current schedule arrangements, care should be taken not to place these persons and organizations at a disadvantage.

On the basis of this overall assessment, GAO submitted a number of recommendations to Congress in 1976. Some of the recommendations related exclusively to the compressed workweek. Concerning flexible hours the following recommendations were submitted:

Permit government contractors to use flexible work schedules, allowing employees to bank and borrow time by working more or less than 8 hours a day at the employees' convenience without the contractors' being required to pay overtime premiums for the hours worked in excess of 8 a day or 40 hours a week. To maintain the integrity of the 40-hour workweek provided for in these acts, a provision should be included requiring that the number of hours worked without payment of overtime premiums not average more than 40 hours a week over a specified period, possibly a month or several months. This would also require exempting the government contractors involved from the 40-hour workweek requirement of the Fair Labor Standards Act or changing that act to allow employees to bank or borrow time.

The above recommendations concern the overtime payment requirements that apply to government contractors. Although their adoption would give government contractors additional opportunities to use altered work schedules, separate overtime payment requirements for government contractors still exist.

GAO believes more uniformity in federal overtime requirements may be desirable so that employees are not under one policy when they work on government contracts and another policy for their other work. Uniformity would eliminate differences in pay between persons working on government contracts.

Therefore GAO also recommends that the Congress consider, as a long-range objective, establishing more uniform federal policies on overtime requirements in view of the advantages of altered work schedules cited in this report.*

As the reader notes, these recommendations were in reference to laws regulating government contractors (the Walsh-Healey Act and the Contract Work Hours and Safety Standards Act) as well as to the Fair Labor Standards Act with its more inclusive coverage provisions.

In the next two chapters, the reader will study a variety of alternative work programs operating in organizations in the private and public sectors. Where the emphasis is on flexitime, some readers will wonder why more companies in the United States failed to incorporate debit and credit options in their flexitime programs. Information given in this chapter should help the reader understand why debit and credit options were noticeably absent from most flexitime programs in this country, especially where a 40-hour workweek was part of the contractual arrangement with employees.

*Report to the Congress by the Comptroller General of the United States: Contractors' Use of Altered Work Schedules for their Employees — How is it Working? (Washington, D.C.: U.S. Government Printing Office, 1976), pp. 20–24.

6

Alternative work schedules in the United States— in the private sector

Obtaining details about company programs on alternative work schedules has proved to be very difficult. It does little good to identify an organization if there is little to say about it. Some firms did not reply to my inquiries; others stated only that they did or did not use flexible hours. First, then, the companies discussed in this chapter are those that use some form or other of alternative work schedule. I looked especially for flexitime programs because, as mentioned previously, this book is primarily about such programs. Second, the companies included appeared to be making some effort to measure results. Third, they supplied me with helpful particulars, in addition to granting me permission rights to describe their experiences.

United Vintners

United Vintners is in the wine industry. Its main western location is San Francisco, and its principal business is growing grapes and bottling, distributing, and selling wine and related beverages. The Heublein Wines Group is also part of this firm.

The United Vintners program centers on staggered hours. The company first tried the idea in 1974 at the San Francisco location. Flexibility relates mainly to starting times. Offices open at 7:30 A.M., and various departments schedule employees to start at half-hour intervals between 7:30 and 9:00 A.M. Whatever the starting time chosen, employees are supposed to end the workday not later than 5:00 P.M.

The staggered hours arrangement is built around a 7½-hour workday, not a total workweek, and once the schedule is established employees must work the same hours each day. The company pays time and a half for work in excess of 7½ hours a day. As stated in the company's literature, all scheduling must be at the convenience of the department.

The firm has found the plan to be "very successful." With its earlier starting times the company has increased the available business hours to communicate with its east coast corporate headquarters and regional sales offices in other time zones. Furthermore, the company appraises the system as "a great morale booster, allowing for greater independence and less structure."

General Radio Company

General Radio Company has its central location in Concord, Massachusetts. The firm initiated a flexitime system in 1974. Under the plan employees could come to work at any time between 7:00 and 9:00 in the morning and leave at any time between 3:30 and 5:30 in the afternoon, as long as they worked a total of 8 hours per day. "This proved to be ineffective since appropriate supervision was difficult if not impossible," claims a manager with whom I corresponded.

In March 1975 the company abandoned its flexitime program and in its place substituted a most interesting arrangement.

Policies

A. Each first-line supervisory unit will establish its starting time between the hours of 7:00 A.M. and 9:00 A.M. Similarly, each unit will establish its ending time between the hours of 3:30 P.M. and 5:30 P.M. A first-line supervisory unit is defined as a supervisor and the employees who report to him.

B. Considerations in establishing the starting and ending times involve the types and periods of services the supervisory unit provides to its internal and external users and the personal preferences of the employees involved.

C. Once the starting and ending times have been established, those times will apply to all employees within the supervisory unit. Employees may start work any time within 15 minutes before or after the designated starting time but not before 7:00 A.M. or after 9:00 A.M. Similarly, employees may stop work any time within 15 minutes before or after the designated ending time but not before 3:30 P.M. or after 5:30 P.M., as long as they spend a total of 8½ hours at their site.

D. In certain supervisory units it is necessary to provide coverage outside of the established hours. In these cases, the supervisor will select employees to work a different schedule in order to provide such coverage.

E. In hardship cases employees may be permitted to work hours different from those of the supervisory unit, if approved by the supervisor and the next higher level of management. The supervisor may grant exceptions to the normal supervisory unit starting and ending times if employees need to take care of personal business and will be making up the time within that same day.

F. The supervisory units may change their established starting and ending times as often as they wish, subject to the approval of the supervisor and the next higher level of management.

Summary Comment

A first-line supervisory unit — defined as a supervisor and the employees who report to him or her — determines starting and ending times. In effect, one notes a practical application of humanistic management in the form of active participation by the group in establishing starting and ending times.

The system described above is not a fixed hours schedule. Nor does it center on a staggered hours arrangement, although elements of the staggered hours concept are contained in the schedule described. What one observes in essence is a flexitour arrangement, with employees having considerable input in the designation of starting and ending times. Furthermore, employees are permitted to start work any time within 15 minutes before or after the designated starting time.

General Radio Company's experiences with alternative work schedules are of particular interest from another standpoint, namely, the company's abandonment of flexitime is the one and only case that I know of where such has occurred.

Eastern Air Lines

Eastern Air Lines is one of the nation's larger commercial airlines. Corporate headquarters is located at International Airport, Miami, Florida. The company has four working-time patterns in operation: fixed hours, staggered hours, group flexibility, and flexitime. Let us look at the four systems as they are used in conjunction with one another, reserving most of our discussion for flexitime.

The fixed hours system is in effect both in operational (line) and nonoperational (staff) departments. At Eastern, a normal workweek is $37\frac{1}{2}$ hours and a normal workday is $7\frac{1}{2}$ hours. The workday begins at 8:30 A.M. and ends at 5:00 P.M., with a one-hour lunch break. As the reader might suspect, the nature of an airlines business necessitates rather strict work scheduling in many departments, based on operational demands. Consequently, fixed hours as a working-time pattern continues to receive strong emphasis at Eastern Air Lines.

The staggered hours system (the company's designated term is "multiple reporting times") is in effect in a number of operational and nonoperational departments. For example, some employees report at 8:00 A.M., some at 8:30 A.M., and some at 9:00 A.M. The number of employees reporting at a specific time is based on operational requirements and employee preference. Where the staggered hours alternative is selected, management is responsible for ensuring that sufficient work coverage is provided at each reporting time.

Another schedule alternative allows for a reduction in the length of the lunch break. If work demands allow this possibility, then employees in a department are able to make a group decision as to lunch-break duration. Here one observes group flexibility in operation. By reducing the length of the lunch period from one hour to 45 minutes or 30 minutes, a department may implement a departure from the standard 8:30 A.M. reporting time. For example, if the length of the lunch period is reduced to 45 minutes or 30 minutes, then all employees would report to work at 8:45 or 9:00 A.M., respectively, and leave in both cases at 5:00 P.M.

The Flexitime Plan

In addition to fixed hours, staggered hours, and group flexibility, there is individual flexibility. The system is optional with Eastern's nonoperational — or "administrative office" — departments, where the norm previously was a basic 8:30 A.M. to 5:00 P.M. workday and a $37\frac{1}{2}$-hour workweek.

Flexitime was offered to nonoperational departments at Eastern in 1974. The basic schedule drawn up at that time remains in effect today. Flexitime was first introduced in the corporation's accounting department, and that department remains one of the strongest users of the gliding hours system. The basic time plan used there takes this form:

FST	CORE TIME (excluding 1-hour lunch break)	FQT
7:00 A.M. 10:00 A.M.	3:30 P.M.	6:30 P.M.

As we see, FST falls within the 7:00 to 10:00 range, and FQT is between 3:30 and 6:30 in the afternoon. Core time, excluding the lunch break, runs from 10:00 A.M. until 3:30 P.M. The plan does not offer midday-flexibility options. In short, a person comes to work within the FST period and ends the workday 8½ hours later (7½ work hours plus an hour for lunch). An employee reporting to work after the designated starting period (10:00 A.M.) is considered tardy, and supervisory follow-up is required.

Numerous departments at Eastern Air Lines continue to appraise flexitime's possibilities. The company has developed a concise yet functional guide to assist departments in studying the system.

Guidelines for Evaluating the Feasibility of Flexitime

In evaluating the feasibility of flexitime in your department, the following factors should be carefully evaluated:

1. *Impact on the department's internal and external work flow.* Consider: Possible disruptions in work flow and conflicts in the use of equipment, machines, and facilities, particularly where there are second and third work shifts; exchange of communications with external units which provide input or use output.

2. *Reaction of first- and second-level management.* This is particularly important since implementation could lead to longer hours for some supervisors and/or prescheduled reporting and quitting times for others.

3. *Reaction of employees within your department and in other departments where flexitime is not feasible.*

4. *Availability of reliable and clearly defined measures of productivity.* This information must be available in order to assess the impact of flexible working hours on the units involved.

Approval Method

If flexitime appears feasible within your department, it is suggested that it be implemented for a 90-day trial period, with the approval of your division/department head.

Criteria for Long-Range Acceptance

After the conclusion of the trial period, the long-range desirability of flexible working hours should be evaluated, considering whether:

1. Productivity remained at least constant, if it did not improve.
2. Expense due to tardiness, absenteeism, turnover, and so forth, was reduced.
3. All internal and external conflicts were satisfactorily resolved.
4. Employees involved, for the most part, are in favor of flexible working hours.

If, at the end of the trial period, the four statements above can be answered affirmatively, then it will be clear that flexible working hours should be permanently established.

The format reinforces the firm's highly pragmatic stance on adaptable hours. Employees must favor the idea, it is true; but productivity levels under gliding time must match or exceed productivity attainments of a previous system. Data on tardiness, absenteeism, and turnover must be reported. And flexitime must not hinder a department's internal work functions or restrict departments in their coordination responsibilities.

Summary Comment

Eastern Air Lines approaches flexitime from a contingency or "it depends" point of view, believing that the system may be workable in some departments and not in others. It rejects an all or nothing philosophy whereby flexitime would be used in all departments regardless of their business function, or it would not be used at all. The company believes it is proper for nonoperational departments to consider the feasibility of adaptable hours. From all indications flexitime is a success at Eastern Air Lines.

Scott Paper Company

Scott Paper Company introduced flexible working hours (the company identifies its plan as "adaptable hours") on a trial basis at its Philadelphia headquarters office in November 1972. Approximately 130 out of a total of 1,200 employees were included in an initial pilot program that ran until March 1973. During the experiment the company looked at factors such as level of efficiency, absenteeism and tardiness, possible difficulty of supervisory control, employee satisfaction, service problems, building security, and proper length of the lunch period. Initial results were encouraging.

In March 1973 the company decided to expand its experiment with adaptable hours. For approximately the next three months all employees at Scott's corporate headquarters complex worked under the new time plan. This expanded trial study also proved to be successful, and in May 1973 the firm extended adaptable hours to cover all employees at the corporate headquarters.

Results

A managerial questionnaire provided the company with positive feedback on how the program had been received. Managers' overall responses were favorable.

A more current determination of results is also available. Scott's vice president of human resources wrote to me in 1976 and said, in part: "We have encountered almost no operating difficulties under the program, although we had anticipated many. Our employees' reaction has been overwhelmingly favorable, and problems are still minimal after over three years of experience."

The Specific Time Plan

When plotted out, the specific time plan at the headquarters location looks like this:

FST	CORE TIME (excluding 35-minute lunch break)	FQT

| 8:00 A.M. | 9:30 A.M. | | 4:15 P.M. | 5:45 P.M. |

As shown, flexible starting times range between 8:00 A.M. and

9:30 A.M., and flexible quitting times range between 4:15 P.M. and 5:45 P.M. Bandwidth, therefore, runs from 8:00 in the morning until 5:45 in the afternoon. Core time is from 9:30 A.M. until 4:15 P.M. At the extremes, a person who starts at 8:00 A.M. works until 4:15 P.M., and a person who starts at 9:30 A.M. works until 5:45 P.M. According to company policy, within the limit specified, days may begin on the quarter-hour, that is, 8:15, 8:30, 8:45, and so forth, with a 35-minute lunch period. The schedules thus produce a 7.7-hour day and a 38½-hour week.

Basic Operating Guidelines

The manager of each department must analyze the operating requirements of his or her department to determine what hours of work are required within the department and what level of coverage must be maintained within that time framework (that is, how the department should be crewed during those hours). Final approval of these work hours rests with the staff or division officer to whom the department reports.

Within the time framework established, the individuals working in the department are given maximum flexibility in scheduling their work hours consistent with efficient operation of the department. It follows that in some groups (for example, among telephone operators and receptionists) individual choices may be quite limited. The company's aim, however, has been to provide as broad a choice as possible.

Employees' work schedules are selected or assigned on a weekly basis. If an unforeseen problem or emergency requires a change within the week's schedule, approval of this change must be requested from the department head. However, even though workers have this option to change their schedules on a weekly basis, in actual practice little change occurs. The company informs me that most employees find a convenient schedule and stay on it except in unusual circumstances.

Each department head is charged with the responsibility and accountability for seeing that nonexempt and exempt employees working in his or her department do not abuse the freedom the flexible hours program permits.

All nonexempt employees record their own work time on a weekly departmental time sheet. If either daily or weekly overtime is worked in any week, the employee must initial a small overtime box

inserted on the time sheet. For all employees exempt from the overtime requirements of the wage-hour law, no time records are kept.

The company designates its plan as one of adaptable hours.
Using definitions given in Chapter 3 of this book, however, the Scott
plan is better described as a modified version of adaptable hours. I say
this for two reasons. Work schedules are selected or assigned to individual workers on a weekly basis. Thus no employee is able to select
daily, at his or her discretion, a work starting time. Second, interval
frames and time frames are a part of the Scott plan.

In short, the Scott plan is not one of adaptable hours in the strict
sense of our definition. Nor is it a rigid staggered hours plan. It is essentially a flexitour arrangement. Its structure places it in that twilight
zone between flexitime and staggered hours. Without question, however, the Scott plan is one of flexible hours, and the evidence strongly
indicates that the Scott Paper Company is very satisfied with its flexible hours program.

Occidental Life of California

Included in the company's literature is the statement: "We strive
for employee commitment rather than compliance." Possibly this
proclamation has something to do with the firm's ventures into flexitime. Occidental Life of California has instituted working-time
patterns offering combinations of adaptable hours and staggered
hours. For convenience—and because in actual practice it is sometimes difficult to separate the two forms—both plans are viewed here
as being incorporated within the concept of flexitime.

This insurance company currently has flexitime plans in effect at
the Los Angeles headquarters at Occidental Center, as well as at its
Head Office for Canada (H.O.C.) at Toronto.

Initial Trial Experiments

Before it began using flexitime the company was on fixed hours.
Following a detailed study of various working-time patterns in 1972
and early 1973, the company decided to undertake a three-month
flexitime trial experiment beginning in March 1973. Some 700 clerical, administrative, and technical employees were included. The company chose three test situations: Planning, because it represented a
technical area; Insurance Services, because it included many clerical

operations and interacted with other operating departments; and the Head Office for Canada, because it represented a cross section of operations but on a smaller scale.

During June 1973 the company made an assessment of the pilot program and discovered that a number of advantages had been realized. (1) There was a reduction in lost time due to tardiness and personal business. (2) More productive work took place before 8:00 A.M. and after 4:30 P.M. because of fewer work interruptions. (3) Many employees were able to adjust their work schedules to fit their life-styles. (4) Travel time was reduced, generally between 30 minutes to one hour per day. (5) There was a better use of resources in such areas as keypunch and computer testing. No major disadvantages were noted.

An Expansion of Flexible Work Hours

During June and early July of 1973 the company reached the decision to expand the arrangement throughout the home office; thus, during the latter part of July some 3,500 employees at Occidental Center in Los Angeles began working under a flexible work-hours program.

To a degree, the nature of the work was a determinant of flexible starting times. Most employees were able to choose starting times between 7:00 A.M. and 9:00 A.M. In the planning division, flexible starting times were 6:30 A.M. to 10:00 A.M. Systems and programming workers, because of computer-time availability, had the 6:30 to 10:00 option.

It was recommended that each area of responsibility work out its own schedule after giving careful consideration to work flow, co-ordination with other departments, the field force, the public, supervisory availability and capability, and potential conflict with night-crew employees. It was the company's recommendation that as many employees as possible be allowed to choose their own starting times.

During the first three months of the headquarters-wide program, division heads were instructed to monitor operations, especially in terms of (1) employee starting times, (2) productivity, (3) effects on internal and external communications, (4) effects on punctuality and absenteeism, (5) effects on commuting, and (6) overall viewpoints of employees and management.

Because of Occidental Life's new work-hours arrangements, the firm received regional as well as national television headlining that summer. ABC-TV crews filmed and interviewed employees, and the Occidental story ran on the ABC evening news with Harry Reasoner. The national network was impressed with the possibility that flexitime, if widely adopted, might be one way to unclog the traffic in big cities. The report ended with the punch line: "In the words of one commuter, it's not the work that's hard, it's just getting there."

Results

Internal communications (Is the employee at work? Am I able to phone him at his office? Is he available for consultation?) often are more difficult under flexitime. Better communications planning, however, helps overcome the problem, says the company. On the plus side, morale improved. In some areas there has been greater productivity, and there have been virtually no reports of a decline in productivity. Tardiness has almost disappeared.

Close to 65 percent of the employees report to work before 8:00 A.M. About 30 percent come to work at 8:00 o'clock. Married women say that getting off work in midafternoon gives them more time to do their chores before their husbands reach home and provides them more time to be with their children. And single women like having more leisure to get ready for evening recreation.

The flexible work-hours report appearing in July 1974 contained an overall summary of the viewpoints of both managers and nonmanagement-level employees. In general, the workforce viewed flexitime with approval:

Very positive	14%
Good	77%
Noncommittal	4%
Negative	1%
No comment	4%

That was the latest formal assessment made by the company. I received a letter in 1976 from a vice president who said: "There is no later analysis and we do not presently plan to make another survey since, in general, this program is continuing to provide the benefits to both employees and the company."

Early Friday Closings

In combination with the flexible hours program the company has an "Early Friday Closing Program" that runs from May through October.

On Fridays during those six months, employees can work a straight 5½ hours, with one 10-minute break. This means that an employee who comes to work at 7:00 A.M. is able to leave work at 12:30 P.M. A top management official says: "We have been able to sustain this program under the condition that we do not lose any productivity, and with the exception of one of our 27 divisions this has been the case."

Summary Comment

Occidental Life's flexible hours program is proving to be effective. A company vice president renders an interesting observation on why the flexitime program is successful: "When an employee has a free choice of when he comes to work, he doesn't look on us as the bad guys who are dictating to him."

California State Automobile Association

A pilot flexitime program was launched at the main office in San Francisco during September 1973. Approximately 100 employees from the underwriting services and public services departments were involved.

The company's 7½-hour workday was continued under gliding time, but in accordance with these innovations:

FST	CORE TIME (excluding lunchtime)	FQT
7:30 9:00		4:00 5:30
A.M. A.M.		P.M. P.M.

Pilot Program Results

Employees were surveyed during September — regarding their expectations on whether flexitime would work — and during October, following one month of actual work under the new system. Actual results were quite similar to those anticipated. Respondents believed that the program would work well in the future, and that commuting problems would be lessened considerably under flexitime. The sentiment was virtually unanimous that adaptable hours be continued.

Management was also surveyed one month following initiation of the pilot program. According to their measurements, employee morale increased and absenteeism and tardiness decreased.

A follow-up survey of all employees was carried out in March 1974 after a six-month trial period. It was found that employees did not arrive at work late (after 9 A.M.), nor did they take unfair advantage of the system's privileges. Most of them experienced definite savings in commuting time. From a company standpoint, the findings were supportive. As described by a top corporate official: "The results were excellent, with everyone cooperating with fellow employees to see that the work flow was uninterrupted and that service to members continued in a businesslike manner."

Flexitime Is Extended Throughout the Company

It was decided during March 1974 to expand gliding time companywide and offer it to some 3,000 employees located throughout 57 offices in northern California and Nevada. The plan went into effect in April 1974.

Information announcements went out to all employees one month prior to implementation. For example, from an executive vice president's office:

> As participating employees, you will continue to work your usual 7½-hour day. However, you will be permitted to choose the time each day when you begin and stop working. Your lunch periods will also be flexible and may be as short as a half hour. Your schedule may vary from day to day just as long as you work 7½ hours each day and conform to the time during the main part of the day designated as core time. Your manager will have all the details once the program is introduced next month in your department or district office.

Prior to the use of flexitime, companywide explanatory announcements also went out to all management personnel. District managers were encouraged to coordinate sliding time systems with their respective regional manager. At headquarters, managers were instructed to plan directly with their respective assistant vice president. Managers were asked to handle several important matters.

First and most important, develop a flexitime system for your department or district office. Establish which hours during the day members are served most frequently, telephones are busy, mail is processed, and so forth. Determine if the work flow can benefit from employees arriving earlier; staying later.

At the main office the core-time frame was set at a standard 9:00 to 4:00 for most employees. The company realized that core time was dependent to some extent on the work situation; thus, district office managers had responsibility and authority to vary core-time designations based on such factors as size of the office and work-flow requirements. As mentioned above, however, different district office variations had to be coordinated with the regional manager.

Under the new system, timekeeping requirements have not been changed. Nonexempt employees continue to fill out time cards on a daily basis, reporting the exact time work begins and stops. There are no mechanical time-recording devices. Employees realize that abuses in timekeeping could cancel out flexitime.

The California State Automobile Association also offers the option of debiting and crediting working hours. Recall that the normal workday is 7½ hours. A nonexempt employee is able to work an additional 30 minutes a day (8 hours total) because the work contract calls for no overtime pay until after 8 hours on the job.

Some Employee Quotes

"Freedom! I feel the CSAA trusts me."

"Knowledge that my time schedule can be changed if necessary is a good feeling."

"If I'm late, I can make up the time and not be a nervous wreck."

"I get to pick up my child early from the day-care center."

"I can shop before stores close in the evening."

"I avoid the crowded bus."

"Commuting is made incredibly easier. I miss most traffic both ways by working between 7:30 and 4:00. The 8:30 to 5:00 schedule would lengthen traveling time for me by at least one hour."

"I work best in the morning."

"Since I telephone the east coast with some frequency, the morning hours allow me more flexibility in calling because of the one-, two-, and three-hour time difference."

"Flexitime encourages promptness. You get in earlier, and you get out earlier."

"This is just wonderful. Please keep it on."

Dividend Day

CSAA has come up with an interesting innovation, one that would harmonize well with the flexitime concept. It is "dividend day." At the time of this writing the idea was under active consideration at the company.

How might it work? Each employee would be on a four-week cycle. During the first three weeks of each cycle an employee would work an 8-hour day. Thus, the employee would accrue an extra $2\frac{1}{2}$ hours per week and a total of $7\frac{1}{2}$ hours at the end of the third week. During the fourth week the employee would work a $7\frac{1}{2}$-hour day for four days and use the accrued $7\frac{1}{2}$ hours as a dividend day off.

Since the cycle consists of four weeks, it would be possible that departments could have a quarter of their staff begin the cycle on different weeks. Therefore, only a quarter of the staff would have time off on the same fourth week. Since any day of the fourth week could be a dividend day, all those eligible probably would never be gone at the same time. And of course the company could build in controls to avoid such a potential difficulty.

Another feature: Should an absence occur during the three-week cycle, the employee would work an 8-hour day during the fourth week for each day he or she was absent. If the absence were longer than four days, the week would not count and the cycle would be delayed one week.

Summary Comment

Flexitime appears to be working well at CSAA. In a recent letter to me a management official says: "Since 1974 little attention has been given to the flexitime program — at least internally. Simply put — it works for us. The selling point, I believe, is not to the employees but to management, who are afraid of anything so new."

Alexander Hamilton Institute

This relatively small New York City firm prepares and publishes newsletters, which are mailed on Friday afternoons to a business and

professional clientele. Flexitime was adopted mainly to relieve employees from pressures of rush-hour transportation and to maintain
or improve productivity.

Setting Up the System

The materials manager and personnel coordinator reports that
prior to the introduction of gliding time the workday started at 8:45
A.M. and ended at 4:30 P.M. The normal workweek was 35 hours.

After investigating various plans in relation to the firm's business responsibilities, management selected gliding time as the most viable alternative. The specific time plan that it put in operation took
this form:

FST	CORE TIME (with a 45-minute fixed lunch break)	FQT
8:00 A.M.	10:00 A.M.	3:00 P.M.	6:00 P.M.

As shown, the 8:00 A.M. to 10:00 A.M. period became the flexible
starting time; 10:00 A.M. through 3:00 P.M. was designated as core
time (lunchtime was fixed at noon to 12:45 P.M.); and the flexible quitting time fell anywhere between 3:00 P.M. and 6:00 P.M. Bandwidth,
therefore, extended from 8:00 A.M. to 6:00 P.M.

Implementation of the program necessitated a shifting of deadlines in every department in order to afford broader choices of starting and ending hours — while still enabling the firm to meet the Friday
afternoon mailing deadlines. The company president personally
briefed employees in groups of ten, pointing out the desired advantages of flexible working hours:

> With flexitime you are given the opportunity of making better
> use of your time. For example, on any one day you may work during
> the core-time hours only, and then make up the hours on any other day
> of the week. You may do this to suit your own convenience or to cope
> with fluctuations in the workload without having to work overtime.
> Your finishing time is no longer directly related to your starting time on
> that day. Your concern will be to complete 35 hours per week. You will
> be able to add or deduct hours on any day as long as you total 35 hours

per week. You will find that you will not be as tightly controlled as before and therefore will have more discretion over your work and your private life.

Results

Most of the company's experiences with flexitime have been positive. Employees adapted swiftly to new deadlines, some of which were advanced as much as half a day. The firm has been able to handle an increased number of subscribers to its publications with no increase in personnel and no appreciable increase in overtime. Joint planning and teamwork resulted in efficient handling of peaks and valleys.

One department head reported that employees demonstrated even more maturity in their work behavior, showing reliability in processing materials whether the department head was present or not. In addition, the company has noted an improvement in productivity, and employees have taken a more personal interest in their work.

A recent letter received from company president James M. Jenks contains a number of interesting observations:

> Overall, our experience with flexitime has been satisfactory and we intend to continue to use flexible working hours. If flexitime has a limitation, it arises from the desire of nearly everyone to leave the office early on Fridays. We feel, however, that it is necessary to keep the office open after the core time on Fridays. There has been some resentment among those people who have been asked to remain on duty after the core time on Friday against those people who, because of the nature of their duties, are not asked to remain on duty after the core time. However, these problems are not great; they are overcome through cooperation among the people who are asked to stay and who work out among themselves the minimal coverage of the duty that we require. Nonetheless, there is some small amount of resentment and friction caused by this factor.

> We believe that having flexible working hours is an attractive feature to people we interview for employment. Since we are a small organization and not in great competition for workers, and since there is no shortage of labor at the present time, I cannot say that flexitime has enabled us to hire people who would not have taken the job anyway. I doubt if two jobs ever come out exactly equal in a prospective employee's mind. If they did, however, I think that flexitime would be a factor that would favor the employer who offered it.

Summary Comment

At Alexander Hamilton Institute flexitime serves essentially a small white-collar workforce. On the basis of information received from top management officials, it is correct to say that flexitime is proving to be a highly satisfactory working-time pattern.

Hewlett-Packard Corporation

Hewlett-Packard is an international electronics firm with headquarters in Palo Alto, California. The firm manufactures a variety of quality products, including calculators and electronic office equipment. The corporation first experimented with flexible working hours in 1967 at its plant in Boeblingen, Germany. A few years later, in 1972, the system was initiated at Hewlett-Packard's Medical Electronics Division in Waltham, Massachusetts. Currently, approximately 90 percent of the company's employees, at 22 separate worldwide manufacturing facilities, are involved with flexible working hours.

According to William R. Hewlett, president and chief executive officer of the firm, one main reason for initiating a flexible workhours program at Hewlett-Packard was ". . . to allow our people greater flexibility in arranging their personal schedule. They can plan their workday to gain more time for family leisure, conduct personal business, avoid traffic jams, or satisfy other individual needs." Central corporate goals are to maintain a position of leadership in the industry in terms of employee relations, to innovate, and to show commitment to employees.

The Specific Time Plan

Employees are on an 8-hour workday. Under the company's gliding time system, workers are able to vary their schedule daily. In most instances, the specific time plan for day-shift employees is set up like this:

FST	CORE TIME (excluding 30-minute lunch break)	FQT

6:30   8:30   3:00   5:00
A.M.   A.M.   P.M.   P.M.

In this plan, day-shift workers may arrive at any time between 6:30 and 8:30. They have a 30-minute lunch period and may leave at any time between 3:00 P.M. and 5:00 P.M. — after completing an 8-hour day. Core time runs from 8:30 A.M. to 3:00 P.M.

At Hewlett-Packard, individual divisions or departments have the option of revising arrival and departure hours to best suit their needs (as is also the case at the California State Automobile Association).

Swing- and graveyard-shift employees also have the flexibility to begin and leave within 2-hour periods; however, no specific time frames are predetermined by headquarters. Department managers during the two shifts have responsibility for determining a work schedule that will accommodate any necessary shift overlap and still maintain the spirit of flexitime.

In the operation of the system, workers are not required to sign in and out each day. Hewlett-Packard does not use time clocks, but operates on an honor system instead. Some divisions do make use of a time record card as a source document for payroll purposes. This card, however, is completed by the individual employee on a weekly basis.

With employees coming and going at different times, it is essential that persons be careful not to disturb others at work. Those who wish to converse are asked to do so on their own time in an area away from the work site.

Controlling Potential Problems

With a program that allows so much flexibility, several problems are inevitable. Of particular concern to Hewlett-Packard are customer and co-worker communications, shift coordination, and the scheduling of overtime.

Since employees are arriving at different hours, communication with others can become more difficult. However, employees found that once they became aware of the "typical" schedule of other employees, no problem in fact existed. Instead, because workers were arriving and leaving at several different times, offices actually got more coverage over a longer period of time.

Another potential problem concerns departments whose products or services require a 24-hour operation. To accomplish departmental goals and still allow employees some flexibility of work hours, Hewlett-Packard has encouraged supervisors to involve affected work groups in determining the most acceptable means of achieving both company and employee objectives.

A concern of some supervisors is the adequate monitoring of the program. Faced with the possibility that employees will be on the job from 6:30 A.M. to 5:00 P.M., some supervisors feel they must put in longer hours. The company has attempted to reduce this concern by encouraging supervisors to delegate more responsibility to their lower-level employees.

Results

After the flexible hours system was used on a companywide basis for approximately one year, a joint survey of supervisory and non-supervisory personnel was taken. The "All Employees Survey" provided some valuable feedback to the firm. According to employees, production and efficiency increased, tardiness and absenteeism were reduced, morale was higher, and commuting problems were reduced. Another big winner, from the standpoint of employees, was their right to schedule work hours in conjunction with off-the-job interests and activities.

At about the same time as this survey was taken among all employees, another was taken among supervisors. Their responses show a trouble spot in the area of "Interfacing with Other Departments." All their other responses were supportive of flexitime.

Overall, the combined inputs of management and non-management people show that flexitime at Hewlett-Packard is a definite success. Here is the overall response:

Program is successful	95%
Program is somewhat successful	3%
Program is unsuccessful	2%

Reactions of Employees to the Program

The following quotes illustrate employee feelings about the flexible work-hours program at Hewlett-Packard Corporation:

"A less rigid atmosphere is more conducive to productivity."

"Since each employee may select hours that are more suitable to his or her own wishes, the time at work is in less conflict with other interests."

"The increased freedom to have more prime time at home has improved attitudes."

"The program gives a staff-type benefit to all employees."

"It creates a feeling of job worth instead of just putting in hours."

"The employees have the freedom of choice. This is a good step toward humanizing the job."

"Creativity isn't an 8:00 to 5:00 operation."

"The employee has the freedom to choose a work cycle that coincides with his efficiency cycle."

"An individual's working hours are not controlled by bells, but rather by personal integrity."

Summary Comment

At Hewlett-Packard Corporation flexitime has proved to be a definite asset. A 1976 letter sent to me by a Hewlett-Packard vice president reads: "We continue to be very satisfied with the way flexitime works and it is now a way of life in the company for most people. It would not be something we could take away without very severe morale problems and strong understandable reasons for doing so."

John Flaherty, Hewlett-Packard's personnel manager at Waltham, Massachusetts, attended the National Conference on Alternative Work Schedules in Chicago in 1977. He mentioned to me that the firm's flexitime program continues to be most successful.

John Hancock Mutual Life Insurance Company

This firm provides an especially interesting case study of working-time alternatives. The Boston-based organization currently has four different programs all operating simultaneously. Coexisting in harmony are flexitime, staggered hours, a 4-day-workweek plan, and a fixed 5-day-workweek program.

The firm began studying rearranged workweek alternatives in 1969, and its investigations led to pilot studies in four operating divisions. The 4-day-workweek trial began in 1972, and was twice extended so that additional data could be obtained. Approximately 16 divisions comprising 600 employees were involved.

The 4-day workweek evolved into a permanent arrangement in 1973. Currently there are approximately 2,500 employees on a 4-day schedule—2,000 in the home office and 500 in group field offices located throughout the country. Overall, the company has had favorable results with the system. But this working-time pattern is not our main subject matter.

The Flexible Time Plans in Most Departments

At John Hancock the work hours for employees on a fixed 5-day week were (and are, for those still on the plan) 8:20 A.M. to 4:30 P.M. For employees working under flexible hours the arrangement takes this other form:

FST	CORE TIME (excluding lunch period)	FQT
7:30 9:00 A.M. A.M.		3:40 5:10 P.M. P.M.

Flexible starting time falls between 7:30 and 9:00 in the morning, while flexible quitting time falls between 3:40 and 5:10 in the afternoon. Quitting time is determined by starting time. Employees who start at 7:30 A.M. are able to leave at 3:40 in the afternoon. Employees starting at 9:00 can leave at 5:10. Core time under this program is 9:00 to 3:40, with lunchtime excluded from the calculations.

Within the time plan it established, the company set up two options, primarily to accommodate the problems of production-line managers.

Option A. Under this option an employee can start work at any time between 7:30 and 9:00, and can leave work at any time between 3:40 and 5:10. Workers develop their own schedule, provided they work 7½ hours. Option A is essentially the working-time pattern on which this book is focused, namely, flexitime.

Option B. Under this option, by utilizing "interval frames" and "time frames," employees may elect starting times between 7:30 and 9:00 so long as these are mutually agreed upon by the employees and their managers. The chosen starting time can be changed only by the mutual consent of the two parties. This option is most frequently used in large production processes that must meet specific machine deadlines. Option B is essentially a staggered hours plan.

The Time Plan in Group Systems Development

In addition to the companywide flexible hours programs described above, there is also an experimental program in Group Systems Development that should be mentioned. The program involves some 50 people and is based on the following time plan.

FST	CORE TIME	MIDDAY FLEX	CORE TIME	FQT
7:00 A.M.	10:00 A.M.	11:30 A.M.	1:30 P.M. 3:00 P.M.	6:30 P.M.

As shown in the diagram, an employee is required to be present for only 15 specific hours each week, even though he or she must work a total of 37½ hours over the week. The other 22½ required hours can be put in at the employee's discretion during the bandwidth between 7:00 A.M. and 6:30 P.M.

Another feature of this plan should be noted, namely, the midday-flex period. Flexitime plans discussed previously in this chapter contained core times covering the entire period between the FST and FQT bands — exclusive of the lunch period. In Group Systems Development at the John Hancock Company, a midday-flex period spans the two hours between 11:30 A.M. and 1:30 P.M. Such an arrangement presents the employee with additional alternatives. Should an employee decide to begin work at 7:00 A.M., take a minimum 30-minute lunch break, and work through the rest of the midday-flex period, he or she would complete the required 7½ hours at 3:00 P.M. On the other hand, should the employee choose to take the entire 2-hour midday-flex period for lunch and off-the-job pursuits, he or she would finish work at 4:30 in the afternoon.

Numerous interesting possibilities also await the employee who decides to begin the workday at 9:00 A.M., as a study of the time plan above will show the reader who is willing to make the simple calculations.

Especially because of the high degree of flexibility afforded by this particular arrangement, the company uses automatic time accumulators to facilitate the tracking of hours worked by each employee.

The 4-Day Workweek and Flexitime

At the John Hancock Insurance Company, flexitime and staggered hours coexist harmoniously with both the 4-day work schedule and the fixed 5-day work plan.

The 4-day plan operates successfully at John Hancock and is strongly accepted in many other companies. Because in the appropriate setting it has proved to be both workable and satisfactory, and because only a small number of organizations are presently using flexible hours and 4-day-workweek plans simultaneously, it is important to examine the matter more closely.

John Hancock reports that the 4-day workweek is a more complicated kind of program. This is so because the 4-day workweek changes some of the existing personnel policies—for example, the number of sick days granted, the definition of a vacation week, the definition of a half-day of work.

Under the company's flexitime and staggered hours programs, no changes are required in policies affecting overtime, earned days, or sick days, since the main thing that happens under these programs is that the employee's starting time is altered.

Summary Comment

As explained, the John Hancock Life Insurance Company uses four working-time plans simultaneously, including flexitime. In a letter written to me in 1976, a company vice president said: "Thank you for your letter with respect to flexible working hours. I am pleased to learn that someone is taking time to document the experiences of companies using this concept." John Hancock is one of a number of companies satisfied with flexitime, and is quite willing to share its experiences with flexible work hours.

Industrial National Bank of Providence

This bank, with headquarters in Providence, Rhode Island, has deposits in excess of $1 billion and a staff of some 1,700 employees at 49 branches throughout the state. It is the fourth largest banking institution in New England. In the early part of the 1970s, INB had no significant problems with absenteeism, tardiness, rush-hour traffic jams, or high employee turnover. Rather, its management was receptive to a program directed at enhancing individual responsibility and participation. An INB Internal Study included the observation:

> Given the significant societal changes of the last 20 years and the profile of workers of the 1970s and 1980s, the vital need for implemen-

tation of new concepts for organization design, job content, and accountability appears self-evident. If workers in the future have broader job expectations, seek more responsibility, and seek personal growth in jobs — will our present utilization patterns be sufficient to meet their needs?

A Pilot Program

In 1973 tests were conducted over a 10-week period in the consumer loan department's four sections: collections, credit and management, new accounts, and payments. Seventy-three employees participated in the trial program. Regarding job responsibilities, each section determined for itself the flexible starting and quitting times, the core time, and the lunch period. Automatic time-recording equipment was used to track employees' work time.

The collections section has some unique problems with time. The section is charged with contacting delinquent accounts. The best time to reach these customers is after the traditional workday, around dinner time and later. Before it was placed under flexitime, the section worked a standard 8:30 A.M. to 5:00 P.M. schedule. After the change to flexitime, the time plan looked like this:

FST	CORE TIME (excluding lunch break)	FQT
8:00 9:00 A.M. A.M.	3:00 P.M.	8:00 P.M.

Here we see an unusually long bandwidth, from 8:00 A.M. to 8:00 P.M. We also note the very broad flexible-quitting-time span. An additional innovation was built into the time plan in the collections section. Although daily core-time hours were required — as well as a specific number of total work hours per week — employees were not required to put in the same number of hours each day. Thus, total hours worked could vary from day to day, and at the worker's discretion (The reader may recall a similar provision in the Group Systems Development Department at the John Hancock Corporation).

An assessment of the system was made in the consumer loans section after the 10-week trial period. Findings were positive, and gliding time was expanded to include the accounting department.

Flexitime Results at INB

In the collections section, flexitime proved to be advantageous both to employer and to employees. According to the section head, many employees like the idea of getting off one or two days a week at 3:00 o'clock. When employees do depart at 3:00, they make up the time on other days when their efforts can be spent on the job more productively. More evening-hour work is also possible under individual flexibility — which is one of the section's objectives. Furthermore, as measured against the bank's record best months of the previous year, the section's efficiency in meeting its quota either improved or held its own.

What happens when the supervisor leaves at 3:00 in the afternoon and an employee works until 8:00 in the evening? "No problem," reports the collections section head. "The man has a personal quota to meet. If he doesn't do his job, our monthly report will show it. Therefore, it doesn't bother me if he is working without supervision. In fact, he probably works harder without the distractions of a full office and the temptation to talk with a lot of people."

In-depth interviews with supervisors in the consumer loans section indicate that flexitime is a success there. In addition to further reductions in tardiness, benefits take the form of better internal communications, a greater sense of individual responsibility on the part of employees, greater participation, and a team approach to solving problems of work coverage throughout the workday.

It is reported that the vast majority of INB's workers use flexitime to their best personal advantage, while fulfilling their job responsibilities during different hours. An illustration comes from the new accounts section. The section is composed primarily of female clerical workers. Normally, the workload is steady and most employees choose to work the earliest hours possible. But they display responsibility when the work becomes sporadic. The supervisor reports several occasions when workers who were planning to leave at the end of the 3:00 P.M. core time stayed much later to process paperwork that suddenly arrived from another department. The section head commented: "My section has a good attitude. They really use teamwork in regard to their jobs. They certainly do not abuse the system as far as handling the work flow."

According to the operations manager of the consumer loans section, management had hoped that the concept of flexitime would allow employees to share management responsibility for productivity and morale. "The results have exceeded our expectations," he says.

From the employees' standpoint, questionnaire surveys reveal that having more leisure time in the afternoon is the number one benefit. One employee states: "During daylight saving time, I can be on Scarborough Beach—an hour's drive—by 5:00 o'clock and have three hours of sunlight any weekday I want to." Another employee says: "I've got a family and personal things to take care of. I used to be reluctant to start a project after supper when I got off at 5:00. Now I start something right after I get home, and finish after supper. I now accomplish many projects that I used to put off until the weekend."

Summary Comment
In the words of the INB president: "Our program has demonstrated that the flexible workweek concept which enables employees to start and finish the workday as they desire within guidelines can meet the demands of the work flow and foster in employees a greater sense of individual responsibility."

Flexitime appears to be working well at Industrial National Bank. Numerous objectives of both the bank's managers and its employees are being achieved, owing in some measure to the introduction of gliding time.

The Nestlé Company

This international food-products company has its worldwide headquarters in Switzerland. Its headquarters in the United States is located in White Plains, New York. This latter headquarters has had the advantage of learning about flexitime directly from the parent company in Europe, which had had a number of years of experience with gliding hours on the Continent.

A System Established, and Revised
In the United States the Nestlé Company instituted flexitime in the summer of 1972 on a three-month trial basis. Some 700 management and nonmanagement salaried personnel at White Plains were involved. At the conclusion of the trial period a survey was conducted to determine if the company should continue the program. Results

were favorable, and in September of that year the program was put
on a permanent basis.

The program was monitored during the next two years. In early
1974 the auditing department, which had been conducting a cycle
audit, reported that some abuse had occurred in the initial flexitime
schedule. It was suggested that the program be subjected to further
study. Thus, a task force composed of key White Plains managers was
set up in August 1974 for the purpose of reviewing the program and
recommending specific changes. As a result of the latter study, effective January 1975, the system was altered in that core-time periods
were expanded. On that same date the system, as revised, became operational.

A 35-hour workweek remains in effect. An employee does not
have to work a total of 7 hours each day in that workweek. The number of hours in a given day may vary somewhat, so long as a workweek
totals 35 hours. In addition, employees on business trips, vacation,
and paid sick leave are credited with 7 hours per day.

The current flexitime schedule is:

Monday to Thursday

FST	CORE TIME	MIDDAY FLEX	CORE TIME	FQT

| 8:30 A.M. | 9:00 A.M. | 12:00 P.M. | 1:30 P.M. | 4:30 P.M. | 6:00 P.M. |

Friday

FST	CORE TIME	MIDDAY FLEX	CORE TIME	FQT

| 8:30 A.M. | 9:00 A.M. | 12:00 P.M. | 1:30 P.M. | 3:30 P.M. | 6:00 P.M. |

As shown, the company uses two different time plans: one in effect from Monday through Thursday, the second operational on
Fridays only. Other specifications are a short flexible-starting-time
band on all five days, midday flexibility, morning and afternoon core

times, a Friday afternoon core time of less duration than that in effect from Monday through Thursday, and finally an FQT on Friday afternoon that begins at 3:30 instead of 4:30.

Summary Comment

The flexitime schedule currently in effect at the Nestlé Company is proving effective. Some 750 salaried employees are presently included in the program. A vice president's assessment submitted to me recently reads: "We believe the revised schedule has resulted in improved efficiency while still permitting useful flexibility."

Metropolitan Life

Metropolitan Life is one of the nation's largest insurance companies. Although the corporate headquarters is located in New York City, the organization maintains what it identifies as eight "home offices" throughout the country. The firm claims that numerous innovations have been instituted over the years to provide better service to policyholders and to create a work atmosphere more responsive to employee needs. As part of its continuing efforts in these directions, in 1973 the corporation began an active investigation into alternative work schedules.

Early Developments

During 1974 Metropolitan Life initiated a six-month experiment over a cross section of selected home-office operations. Both exempt and nonexempt employees were included in the program. From Mondays through Fridays participating employees continued on a 35¾-hour workweek, with each normal workday consisting of 7 hours and 9 minutes plus a 36-minute lunch break. In effect, quitting time was determined by adding 7 hours and 45 minutes to the employee's starting time.

The company identifies its system as "flexible starting times." It would be correct to say that, especially during the pilot stage, the program was essentially what has been described in this book as staggered hours. Some 31 different time frames were established, with intervals of five minutes between each frame. Table 3 lists only the first five and the last five time frames, which should be sufficient for clarification purposes.

Table 3

When employee begins work at:	Quitting time is:
7:30	3:15
7:35	3:20
7:40	3:25
7:45	3:30
7:50	3:35
9:40	5:25
9:45	5:30
9:50	5:35
9:55	5:40
10:00	5:45

The degree to which employees were able to utilize flexibility in varying their starting time depended on what the work situation allowed, as defined by management. Important criteria were maintenance or improvements in productivity, service to customers, and work flow.

After six months the experiment was evaluated in terms of its impact on productivity, the reactions of management and employees, and the manner in which employees utilized the schedule. The results were quite favorable. No adverse impact on productivity was noted, and the reaction of both management and nonmanagement employees was positive. Because the experiment showed that staggered hours could be applied successfully in a variety of areas, the company was confident that alternative work scheduling could be adopted on a more widespread basis. Described below are subsequent developments that took place at corporate headquarters in New York as well as at various home offices and computer centers.

Guidelines, and an Expansion of the Program

To ensure a smooth transition, the initial expansion was gradual. Task forces were appointed to help departments study whether alternative work scheduling was feasible, to determine schedules of implementation, and to assist management in preparing for the change in hours. Guidelines were developed as an integral part of the phase-in efforts.

Employee Job Coverage. Supervisors are to convey the message that employees have increased responsibility to fit work hours to the needs of the work situation. At the same time, managers and first-level supervisors have final responsibility. Possible job coverage imbalances might be remedied in a variety of ways: (1) Make clear to employees the approximate number of workers needed at certain times, and then let them decide among themselves who will work at what time. (2) Limit the range of starting times for the section or for particular workers. (3) Rotate early and late times to ensure fairness. (4) Request that certain key employees keep to specific times. (5) Require advance notice of significant changes from a regular pattern of starting time.

Monitoring Time Recording. All weekly salaried employees, exempt and nonexempt, must enter their starting time and their initials each day on the "Daily Attendance Register." Supervisors are to spot-check employees so as to confirm whether workers abuse the system or not.

Supervisory Coverage. Supervisory coverage during the early and late hours of the day is not feasible in most cases unless supervisors increase their own working hours. Such extended coverage is generally not found to be necessary. The company suggests that early and late hours can be handled in several ways: (1) Delegate minor levels of supervision to responsible lower-level employees (for example, team supervisor) at early or late hours in the day when only a small percentage of employees are expected. (2) Check on the following day's workload to decide whether an employee can start work early the next day without supervision. (3) Rotate early and late duty with another supervisor in the section. (4) Trade off with a supervisor from another section.

Secretaries and Flexible Hours. The degree to which a secretary may be permitted flexibility must be arranged between the secretary and the person for whom he or she is working. Some persons may require their secretaries to maintain the same hours as themselves, but consideration should be given to permitting flexibility to the secretary by adopting some of the following: (1) Use the dictaphone more frequently. (2) End the day with dictation that can be transcribed in the morning. (3) Share secretaries or make some other arrangement for telephone coverage. (4) Leave brief notes of instructions.

Communications Within and Between Departments. Departments should be made aware of those units that adopt an alternative work schedule. In addition, each department should let other departments know if employees will be available at early or late hours to handle interdepartmental work, or if, in fact, regular hours are to be maintained for such communications. As far as internal meetings are concerned, unless prior notice is given, meetings should be scheduled during core time.

Incorporating Flexible Hours with Staggered Hours

A most interesting evolutionary development has taken place at Metropolitan Life over the past few years. As mentioned, early applications of alternative schedules focused essentially on staggered hours. Even at the outset, however, the company was not rigidly determined to use staggered hours only. For example, when the company began applying that system in 1974, the following particulars were part of the total information package communicated to supervisors: "Limitations in flexibility may be needed only at the initial installation, if at all. After experience, the manager and supervisor may then allow a further degree of flexibility." Also stated: "An employee is late when not in the work area and prepared to begin work at the agreed-upon starting time. However, where the work situation allows reasonable flexibility, employees will not be recorded as late if they make up for time lost in the beginning of the day by working that amount of time at the end of the day."

In those instances where the individual is allowed flexibility in determining his or her starting time, for all practical purposes flexitour and flexitime will be seen as permeating a staggered hours system. In 1977, in phone conversations with research consultants at Metropolitan Life, I asked the question: "Is flexitime also part of your program?" Their answers were affirmative, meaning that the basic alternative work schedule in operation is one of staggered hours, but that in numerous departments additional flexibility is superimposed on the staggered hours framework. In short, for all practical purposes Metropolitan Life's overall plan today includes staggered hours, flexitour, and flexitime.

It is correct to say that the following results apply to the company's overall experiences with staggered hours as well as to the more recent developments whereby flexible hours systems are combined with staggered hours. (1) Most supervisors do not find their jobs more difficult. In fact, some find their jobs less so. (2) Lateness is no longer a major concern. (3) Employees tend to cut down on requests for personal time off. (4) In general, there is no negative impact on productivity. In most instances productivity levels are maintained, and in some instances they've even increased. Stated in a different way, the majority of managers feel that alternative work schedules have a positive impact on the effectiveness of the work group and the smoothness of the work flow. (5) There is no adverse effect in terms of amount of overtime. (6) Overall, the reaction of management to the company's new work systems is very favorable.

A Sampling of Employee Opinion
From materials sent to me by Metropolitan Life, here is a sampling of comments of nonmanagement-level employees.

"If flexible hours are discontinued, I may kill myself."

"I believe that an amount of self-determination in work conditions such as this will have the effect of encouraging employees to take on more responsibility for their own work and should result in increased productivity."

"If I get up earlier, instead of waiting around until it's time to go to work, I come in earlier."

"I can afford to allow very crowded trains to go by."

"Use of computer terminals is much more efficient and improves chances of completing work more rapidly because of both people and terminal availability over longer periods of time each day."

"Because arriving and departing from work is on an individual basis, I feel the company benefits, as there is no congregating in the morning nor mass stoppage of work at night while awaiting departure."

"With flexible hours, I don't have to worry about ruining my record with lateness."

"I am an early riser and the flexible hours are just fine with my home schedule: More time in the afternoon for myself; less crowds when traveling to and from work; perfect for early morning or late afternoon appointments."

"It has stopped me from calling in ill, if I cannot get up on time some mornings."

"I feel that the freedom of flexible hours has increased workers' morale."

"I like the flexible hours schedule because I don't feel like I'm a robot. I like being able to choose what time is better for me."

And from managers and first-level supervisors come these observations:

> "Fewer requests for personal time off."

> "Increase in morale since the pressure of arrival time has been removed."

> "Our unit performs development work on console terminals. This allows us greater utility without having to use overtime, since several of our people start early while others start late."

> "People are working at their most productive time; that is, people who were sleepy at normal starting times now come in later and are more alert."

> "A favorable effect. Workers enjoy being treated as responsible adults. No pressure to be in at a specified time."

> "When flexible hours went into effect, lateness disappeared."

> "Telephone calls from the field are spread over the morning hours."

> "Provides the opportunity to clear up more work before the telephone starts ringing."

> "Attitudes toward work and the company have improved."

> "It does take a lot of the strain out of subway and bus traveling. Also, doctor and dentist appointments, and so forth, can be made to agree with the hours—causing less requests to leave early."

> "Work flows better. Prior to this arrangement, idle time was experienced until work was received."

> "Flexible hours have made the supervisor's job less difficult. I rarely have to remind clerks to start work promptly."

> "Early in the morning I can get my work done with hardly any interruption because the office isn't that crowded. When the bulk of the employees come in I can devote more time to supervising my team."

> "Employees seem to feel they have more freedom and are trusted more by management. Consequently, they do a better day's work."

> "The employees like the idea of choosing work hours. Pressure is lessened somewhat."

> "They seem to work quicker and try to do more work before they leave."

> "They don't take a long break before they leave."

> "I have encountered no significant problem because of the flexible starting times."

Summary Comment

According to a research consultant's "conservative estimate," in excess of 15,000 exempt and nonexempt employees at Metropolitan Life were enjoying alternative work schedules in 1977.

Concerning the company's new working-time patterns, a vice president conveyed this message to me:

> The majority of Metropolitan's operations are now making use of flexible starting times. A recent companywide survey of management has yielded positive results quite similar to those of the 1974 evaluation of the flexible-starting-times experiment. Positive changes in employee work effectiveness and morale have been cited. While there are some localized administrative difficulties, the areas involved have found appropriate solutions in most cases. Furthermore, management indicates no substantial difference in the nature of the flexible arrangement. In short, we are very pleased with the way the flexible-starting-times program has worked at Metropolitan.

Lufthansa German Airlines: North and Central America Division

The headquarters of Lufthansa's North and Central America Division is located in East Meadow, New York. This international firm is of European origin, and it has gliding time systems in operation on different continents. In Chapter 4, information was presented on Lufthansa's operations in Europe. Now let us take a look at Lufthansa's approach to gliding time in the United States.

The Time Plan in America

Gliding hours are applicable for the 250 employees who comprise the general administrative and sales staff housed in Lufthansa's headquarters facility in East Meadow, New York. The system applies to all levels of employment including management. The program was installed in December 1970. Lufthansa had benefited from prior gliding time experiences at its headquarters offices in Cologne, West Germany, and consequently no formal trial experimentation took place in the United States. In America, the company believed it was not necessary to screen employee and management reactions before implementation.

Lufthansa's system in the United States is quite simple. Here is the time plan the company used in 1977.

FST	CORE TIME (excluding 45-minute lunch break)	FQT

8:00   10:00   4:00   6:00
A.M.   A.M.   P.M.   P.M.

Employees work 7¼ hours a day. They report for work between the
hours of 8:00 and 10:00 A.M. As depicted, the 10:00 A.M. to 4:00 P.M.
period represents the time when all employees are to be at work
(excluding the lunch break), and flexible quitting time spans the
hours of 4:00 to 6:00 P.M.

Employees are not required to give prior notice of reporting
time, nor are they required to arrive prior to 10:00 in the morning;
the only exception is a prearranged appointment before 10:00 A.M. of
which the employee has been advised.

Time clocks were introduced when gliding time was installed—
not for the purpose of checking on people, but to facilitate payroll
record keeping. The time clocks are for the use of persons at all levels.

Lufthansa informs me that the first month following installation
of gliding time represents the most difficult period of adjustment for
management. This is the period during which employees suddenly
seem unavailable at the time they are needed. However, the company's experience is that the problem resolves itself quickly. It requires mainly that a manager learn to plan and organize work during
the core hours.

Results

A top-level manager at the North and Central America Division
headquarters office wrote to me recently. The communication reads:

> The result—success! Greatly improved morale, absence re-
> duced, and tardiness obliterated. The criteria for measuring the effec-
> tiveness are not easily formulated. Employee morale and client reaction
> are more a matter of general awareness of apparent success, which is
> difficult to equate to statistics. Productivity has improved. This was
> evidenced in a coupled rationalization program through natural attri-
> tion, whereby an increased volume of work was handled by 4 percent
> fewer employees in the first year. We otherwise have not attempted to
> reduce the effects to statistics in productivity, since they can be mislead-
> ing.

Summary Comment

According to the latest information received from the company, gliding time is a very welcome and beneficial tool. At Lufthansa, gliding time is assisting management and employees in attaining their respective, yet mutual, goals.

Sun Oil Company

In May 1973 the Sun Oil Company embarked on an experimental four-month implementation of flexible hours at its administrative headquarters in Philadelphia. The participating group of exempt and nonexempt employees numbered 120 and was composed of engineers, technicians, and support people. These different groups utilized different periods of flexible starting times, quitting times, and core times. During the experimental program employees tracked time by using both the paper-log-sheet and the automatic time-recording methods. Attitude surveys were taken via questionnaire at the outset, midpoint, and end of the experiment to measure possible changes in employees' feelings toward work, supervision, and time-keeping methods.

Results

The major questionnaire findings were these: (1) The vast majority of respondents believed that the morale of fellow employees had "improved greatly" or "improved somewhat" under flexitime. (2) The majority of employees were of the opinion that flexitime had little effect on work-group efficiency. (3) To the question, "What effect has flexitime had on the efficiency of your group or department as relating to other groups/departments/outside sources?" a majority of respondents answered "No change." (4) A majority favored the automatic time-recording method of time tracking. (5) According to those surveyed, the "attitudes of supervisors" were about the same under adaptable hours as under the previous work system used.

Recommendations, and an Expansion of Flexible Hours

In September 1973 a flexible-hours status report was published. In addition to describing the engineering department's experiences, the staff study group issued a number of recommendations. First, it recommended that flexible hours be made available to all managers in the Philadelphia complex who wanted to use the system, with each individual manager deciding if and when he or she wished to adopt flexitime.

A second recommendation was that implementation be accomplished through the assistance of a small task force. A small group would be set up for the specific purpose of surveying each department's activity and its interfaces with other departments so as to identify appropriate core hours and to assist the manager in presenting the flexitime ideas to his or her employees. The small task force would consist of members of the human resources section, plus an outside consultant specializing in automatic time-recording equipment.

Third, the staff study group recommended that both exempt and nonexempt employees be presented with an opportunity to work under gliding hours. A fourth recommendation was that automatic time-recording devices be used for timekeeping purposes. However, the group also agreed that the decision on method of timekeeping be left to the individual manager.

A fifth recommendation related to how the specific time plans would be set. It was recommended that each department deciding to use flexitime should develop its own core hours. Core-hour preferences would be surveyed and appropriate hours would subsequently be identified so as to avoid the use of some 20 or 30 different sets of hours. It was hoped that two or three sets of core hours could be agreed upon for use within the headquarters complex.

During the autumn of 1973 top management reacted favorably to the list of recommendations. It was proclaimed that, effective January 1974, flexible hours would be available to all departments at the Philadelphia headquarters.

During the first six months of 1974 approximately 700 of the 1,200 employees at the Philadelphia complex adopted flexible hours. Over the next three years regional administrative locations in Valley Forge, Pittsburgh, Dayton, Detroit, and Tulsa installed the system. At present the total number of employees involved is approximately 1,400. They are a mixture of exempt and nonexempt salaried employees all primarily involved in administrative work.

Summary Comment
During 1976 I corresponded with a vice president of Sun Oil Company. I have permission to restate his evaluation:

At this time I feel the experience has been positive but not necessarily dramatic. At the time that flexible hours were installed in each department, the concept was viewed as a rather exciting new break from the traditional 8-hour day. Now that the newness has worn off, those areas having flexitime accept it as a standard part of the work pattern in their department. It is quite low key. Some employees use it often, and others have tended to stick with their standard 8-hour pattern most days and adhere rather closely to the standard starting and stopping times. I do not feel that this effect is unexpected, as we had hoped that each employee would make whatever use of this facility that he felt he needed and that he felt was appropriate to this own life-style and work patterns.

On the basis of information available, it would be erroneous to say that the vast majority of employees currently using flexitime at the Sun Oil Company are ecstatic at having the opportunity to work under this new time pattern. It is more realistic and appropriate to say that most employees perceive flexitime as providing a satisfactory work-hours arrangement. It is useful. It is better than the previous system used. It is a step in the direction of progress. But, "it is no big deal."

The Northwestern Mutual Life Insurance Company

The home office is in Milwaukee. This firm — the nation's seventh largest life insurance company — has 1.2 million policyholders, $32 billion of life insurance in force, and more than $8 billion in assets. Northwestern Mutual employs some 2,000 home-office people and is represented by a sales force of over 3,500 full-time agents operating in 49 states. Nonexempt employees at the home office are represented by the Office and Professional Employees International Union, which is affiliated with the AFL-CIO.

Developing the Variable Hours Program
The company gave major thought to the possibility of changing its working-time pattern in 1972 and 1973. It began a conscious effort to provide sound answers to such questions as: "Does it really make any sense to require that everyone come to work and leave work at the same time?" and "Does it serve either the interests of the firm or its work force?" In 1973 the answer to both questions was no.

The company set up a task force composed of one representative from each home-office department. The objective was: "To continue developing a responsive corporate environment by establishing work schedules that afford maximum selectivity and convenience to our home-office employees compatible with operational and service requirements."

After considering a number of approaches to the rearranged workweek, the task force selected "variable hours" (the term it preferred) as the best alternative. A recommendation was made to top management that a six-month trial program be initiated. Following management approval, plans were formulated; and beginning in October 1973 a six-month program was ushered in at the home office. About 1,800 employees, both exempt and nonexempt, were included. All departments were involved.

The specific time plan took this form:

FST	CORE TIME (excluding 30-minute lunch break)	FQT

7:00   9:00   3:00   5:00
A.M.   A.M.   P.M.   P.M.

The 7½-hour workday remained in effect. Flexible starting time ran from 7:00 to 9:00 A.M., flexible quitting time was from 3:00 to 5:00 P.M., and core time covered the period between 9:00 A.M. and 3:00 P.M.

Throughout the trial period, NML measured the effectiveness of the program, especially in terms of service, employee attitudes, supervisory attitudes, reactions of union officials, tardiness, absenteeism, and morale. The union provided no resistance. Union officials were kept informed during the planning and experimental stages.

During the trial program, certain issues surfaced and had to be resolved: inadequate phone coverage after 3:00 P.M.; apprehension over lack of supervision during certain work hours; some slowdown in delivery of interdepartmental services; and difficulty in scheduling meetings. As matters evolved, these issues did not prove to be overwhelming limitations. Overall, the trial program was judged to be successful, and plans were developed to allow more employees to work under variable hours.

Recent Results of Variable Hours at NML

Not counting the experimentation period, the first full year of variable hours use was 1975. Available information provides the following particulars:

Productivity Gains. Unit cost figures show that the company is doing better under variable hours, when comparisons are made with the previous work system. In 1975, two critical measures of cost — acquisition of new business and maintenance of business already on the books — were less per $100 of premium than in 1974. The company believes that some of this improvement was due to variable hours.

Absenteeism, Including Sick Leave. The number of days lost per employee, for all reasons, dropped from 5.8 in 1974 to 4.7 in 1975, the lowest average since 1969. The figure of 4.7 days works out to be an absenteeism ratio of 1.8 percent.

Employee Turnover. The company's turnover of nonexempt employees in 1975 was 14 percent — the lowest since World War II. In 1968 turnover was 34 percent, dropped to 17 percent by 1974, and then took another dip in 1975.

Tardiness. The company claims that it no longer experiences employee tardiness. When an employee arrives during the FST band 10 minutes later than anticipated, he or she works 10 minutes longer during the FQT band.

Excused Time. As the company phrases it, "We also stopped subsidizing those extra long lunch hours that involve shopping trips, dentist appointments, and the like. We now get 37½ hours per week on the job out of each full-time employee." Related to this point is the discovery that 50 percent of the firm's employees are at work before 7:30 A.M. and 80 percent are in before 8:00 A.M.

Advantages of Variable Hours

In addition to the positive results enumerated above, Northwestern Mutual identifies a number of advantages stemming from its operations and locations, advantages that take the form of benefits to employer, employee, and community citizens. Company managers have said in their communications with me:

"Our employees think it's marvelous. Jackie no longer sits at her desk reading a paperback from 7:00 to 8:00 A.M. because her husband drops her off on his way to work."

"It's helped make recruitment of new employees easier."

"It's kept NML in the forefront as a progressive employer in the State of Wisconsin."

"Our employees get a lift by talking about it to their friends and acquaintances."

"It's leveled out the 8:00 A.M. and 4:00 P.M. congestion around our building, particularly since a 42-story building has been constructed just across the street."

"It spreads out the traffic flow on city expressways and downtown streets."

"Incoming mail is opened, read, distributed, and acted upon earlier in the day."

"It provides an extra hour of telephone service to both east and west coasts."

"It further developed our trust in people to do what is right."

"Supervisors are delegating more management responsibility."

"People see tangible evidence that they are influencing their work situation."

"It's a boost to our Affirmative Action efforts—a boon to the working mother."

"It stretches our imaginations—has made us more receptive to part-time jobs, job sharing, and other innovative arrangements."

Summary Comment

During April 1976 a U.S. Senate Subcommittee held hearings in Washington on "Changing Patterns of Work in America." On April 7, 1976, Northwestern Life Insurance Company vice president M. E. Jacobson testified for 15 minutes before that subcommittee. His entire presentation concerned the subject of flexitime. The executive's presentation included these remarks: "Flexible hours . . . [are] the most visible step to improve working conditions our company has taken in the last ten years. . . . I urge this subcommittee to further examine flexible hours as a way of improving the quality of working life in America. Our experience is totally positive and one of the few changes introduced where nobody loses—everybody wins."

M. E. Jacobson mentioned to me in a 1976 letter: "We have had flexible hours at Northwestern Mutual Life since October 1, 1973. We are enthusiastic supporters of the concept. By 'we' I mean both the management staff and the clerical staff think that the variable hours system is a very positive influence in our climate."

In brief, the system is working well at NML. It is proving to be advantageous both to the company and to its employees. Some 2,000 employees, both exempt and nonexempt, work under variable hours. All departments at headquarters are involved. The company thinks it is probable that variable hours are being used in some of the 113 general agency offices associated with NML. However, because general agents are independent businessmen, Northwestern Mutual does not consider them employees of the company and does not maintain full particulars about their office practices.

When I spoke with M. E. Jacobson in Chicago in 1977, he said that the company's flexitime program continues to be a big success.

Pacific Gas & Electric Company

Pacific Gas & Electric Company, a public utility, maintains its headquarters in San Francisco. Design-drafting is the single largest department operating on a formal flexible work schedule. It is one of six departments reporting to the vice president of engineering, and it provides staff assistance to functional engineering departments in designing the company's facilities, including hydroelectric, nuclear, and fossil-fuel power plants; gas and electric transmission facilities; substations and offices; and service center and maintenance buildings. The department workforce numbers in excess of 500 people.

The basic workweek consists of 5 days, with 37½ hours of work time. Each workday is limited to a maximum of 8 hours (other than overtime), because of the prevailing labor laws and the company's agreement with the Engineers and Scientists of California, the union that represents the designers and draftsmen.

Flexitime was installed departmentwide in early 1974 on a six-week trial basis. Automatic time-recording equipment was rented for the experiment. Employee and supervisor attitudes were measured by opinion questionnaires completed prior to the start of operations and immediately on their conclusion.

Because of the favorable initial results, decisions were made to purchase the automatic time-recording equipment, expand the trial program to cover 12 months, and monitor the program over that time period.

Monitoring the Program and Measuring Results

The specific time plan in use during the initial six-week trial period, as well as during the entire 12 months, took this form:

FST	CORE TIME	MIDDAY FLEX	CORE TIME	FQT

7:00 A.M.	9:30 A.M.	11:30 A.M.	1:30 P.M.	3:30 P.M.	6:00 P.M.

As shown, the FST span was from 7:00 to 9:30 A.M., FQT covered the 3:30 to 6:00 P.M. range, and there was midday flexibility between 11:30 A.M. and 1:30 P.M. Core time was 9:30 to 11:30 in the morning and 1:30 to 3:30 in the afternoon.

I mentioned that throughout the trial year the program was departmentwide. A clarification should be added. There was "minimum coverage" in the department. Minimum coverage is defined as the fewest number of employees required to be on the job in each work group during the normal 8:00 A.M. to 5:00 P.M. business day. Each first-level supervisor was responsible for determining the minimum coverage for his or her work group. This minimum was based on the requirement of providing satisfactory departmental service.

Data derived from payroll records, opinion research, and personal observations were used in measuring results in nine key areas. The following paragraphs describe the impact of one year of flexible work hours in the design-drafting department.

Employee Attitudes and Perceptions. Employees were asked to assess morale, job satisfaction, personal productivity, and feelings of independence under flexitime, as contrasted with the system previously in use. For each of the four factors, responses showed a decided shift in the direction of "Has increased under flexitime." There was also a "much improved relationship with the supervisor" under flexitime. This latter finding is probably attributable to the fact that employees were no longer questioned about tardiness, long coffee breaks, personal phone calls, and the like, since these actions no longer detracted from the work time expected of the employee.

Another interesting finding appeared in the responses to the question, "If I were seeking new employment, how important would flexible hours be?" Among the 458 respondents, about 42 percent said flexitime would be a "very important consideration," 46 percent said it would be a "somewhat important consideration," whereas only 12 percent were of the opinion that it would be an "unimportant consideration." And when asked the question, "Should flexible hours continue?" 453 employees answered "Yes" (about 99 percent) and only 5 employees said "No."

Supervisors' Reactions and Observations. In the "Supervisor Opinion Survey" taken after one year of operation, 36 of the 37 supervisors said that flexible hours should continue. More significant, however, is that 77 percent of these supervisors rated the overall benefit to the company as "significant" or "great"; only 2 supervisors perceived "no benefit."

A high percentage of the supervisors identified "improved morale" and "feeling of independence for employees" as significant gains under flexible hours. Most of them noted "design squad productivity," "relationship with their employees," "their own level of job satisfaction," and "availability of time for personal business" as being better or improved.

Productivity. From management's position, a most important concern about flexible work hours relates to productivity. In the design-drafting department, employees do not commonly perform short-term, repetitive work tasks that lend themselves to easy productivity measurements.

Concerning productivity, 79 percent of the employees who responded to the questionnaire believed that their personal productivity increased under adaptable hours. Similarly, about 72 percent of the first-level supervisors said that the productivity of their work group increased. The company estimates that the productivity gain is in the range of 2 to 3 percent, or over $250,000 per year.

Sick Leave. Under fixed hours, employees frequently used sick-leave time to cover medical appointments. By contrast, under flexitime, employees at their option are able to adjust their work schedules to minimize this type of absence.

Company figures show that 1- to 4-hour sick-leave absences

averaged 3 hours per employee in 1974 as compared with more than 9 hours in 1973. Similarly, 5- to 7-hour absences were reduced in 1974. The company claims it captured approximately 58 percent of the partial-day absences. Based on an average of 574 employees during 1974, this meant an annual savings of about $20,000.

Time Off for Personal Business. Because of the proximity of the downtown San Francisco work location to retail stores, financial institutions, government offices, and medical and legal services, company employees have a strong incentive to handle personal affairs during the normal workday. The availability of flexible work hours freed the employees from concern about taking time off during work hours at the expense of the employer. The company claims it has gained much of this productive time.

The supervisors surveyed stated almost unanimously that a reduction in the use of company time for personal business had occurred, while close to 80 percent of the nonmanagement-level employees agreed with that view. In addition, about 92 percent of the responding employees reported that time available for their personal business had increased under flexible hours.

Effect on Department Operations. From the design-drafting department's perspective, flexitime has proved successful. The nature of the work, lack of public contact, close proximity of all employees, and effective supervision—all are factors that had a cumulative impact and prevented any really adverse operational problems from arising.

The Supervisor Opinion Survey reveals no significant problems in internal or external communications. (As pointed out elsewhere in this chapter, some firms do experience internal communications problems under flexitime.) Individual engineers experienced occasions when a designer or draftsman was unavailable, but they stated that having squad members present after the former quitting time was a valuable trade-off in that communications or information could be passed on through individuals in the work groups.

Use of Building Facilities. A major source of worker complaints prior to use of the flexible hours system was the long waiting time for elevators during peak load periods. Also, heavy congestion in the company cafeteria was a source of dissatisfaction.

Both the Supervisor and Employee Opinion Surveys show a

large reduction in elevator waiting time. While no specific question was asked about the cafeteria congestion, this ceased to be a common complaint. The company's judgment is that mitigation of these two annoyances can only help to improve employee morale and upgrade the work environment.

Commuting to Work. Since a high percentage of people who work in San Francisco live outside the city, a major employee benefit of flexible work hours is the option of commuting to and from work during nonpeak travel times. Changes of 30 to 45 minutes in departure time can often be translated into travel-time reductions of as much as 50 percent. Company surveys show that under flexitime, about 62 percent of the employees reported a significant increase in the convenience of commuting to work and 65 percent reported a decrease in commuting time.

Under the fixed hours concept there was little that could be done when disruptions in commuters' schedules were caused by adverse weather conditions, traffic tie-ups, or transit system strikes. Now, under flexible hours, the employee has to cope with the problem of completing the allotted hours of work. No longer is the company expected to absorb time lost because of commuters' transportation problems.

Alternatives to the Use of Automatic Time Accumulators. Manual timekeeping by each individual and an honor system with no time reporting are other methods that can be used with flexitime. The company's experience with manual posting of weekly time cards demonstrated that a large percentage of employees waited until Friday afternoon to make entries for the week. It was felt that this type of manual bookkeeping would not serve the company's purpose. It was also the consensus of management that the honor system would be impractical.

The company concluded that automatic time accumulators would be superior to both manual timekeeping and the honor system.

Summary Comment
The 15th Annual Convention of the American Institute for Design and Drafting was held in 1975 in Arlington, Texas. Speaking at the Convention was Kenneth L. C. Dorking, manager of the design-drafting department at Pacific Gas & Electric Company. This

company official spoke about the firm's experiences with gliding time. His talk was entitled "Flexible Work Hours: A One-Year Review." As part of his concluding remarks he said:

> The advantages and benefits . . . should be sufficient cause for organizations located in congested, metropolitan population centers to consider the use of flexible work hours. By providing our employees with a greater sense of independence and enabling them to better utilize their time, the department has been rewarded with a more responsive and satisfied workforce. The operating guidelines have been well accepted by the employees, yet provide the supervisor with the means to control the work group and to set minimum levels of coverage during the 8:00 A.M. to 5:00 P.M. normal business day.
>
> Properly administered in an appropriate work situation, flexible work hours can be a valuable asset for both the employee and the employer.
>
> One note of caution. Once your employees experience flexible work hours, it will be very difficult to return to fixed work hours. However, if you try it, I think you will like it.

All the information that I've received from the Pacific Gas & Electric Company leads to the conclusion that in the firm's single largest department flexitime has proved to be a definite asset to employees and management.

Sandoz: Colors & Chemicals Division

The firm is a U.S. subsidiary of Sandoz Ltd., a Swiss drug company. The headquarters of the parent firm is in Basel, Switzerland. Sandoz has established locations in Atlanta, Georgia; Charlotte, North Carolina; East Hanover, New Jersey; Hudson, Massachusetts; as well as Chicago and Los Angeles.

Let us focus on the New Jersey site, where the American home office is located, as well as the Sandoz Colors & Chemicals Division. It is here that an extensive gliding hours program has been put in operation. At the Colors & Chemicals Division, union support or nonsupport of flexitime is not a factor in that only a handful of the 1,300 employees are unionized.

A Pilot Program

"Gliding work time" (the company prefers use of this term) has been used with great success by the parent firm in Europe, and is a

major reason why the system was adopted by the American subsidiary. Sandoz introduced gliding work time on a six-month trial
basis for 175 Colors & Chemicals Division employees in July 1972.
When the company surveyed employees two months later, 92 percent
responded that the program should become permanent.

Before the system was introduced, management and supervisors
seemed to be less enthusiastic than nonmanagement employees. Some
saw in the system a reduction in control over subordinates and,
therefore, a threat. Once managers and supervisors had experience
with gliding time, however, their attitudes became more favorable. A
follow-up survey showed that 91 percent felt they did not lose any
control over subordinates, 82 percent found their role as supervisor
the same or improved, 79 percent thought that production scheduling was as easy or easier, and none believed that production had suffered. In fact, 38 percent felt that production had increased.

An overall assessment of the six-month trial was positive, and for
the 175 workers involved in the experimental program, the system
was installed on a permanent basis, effective January 1973. During
the rest of that year gliding work time was expanded to cover approximately 70 percent of the 1,300 employees at East Hanover.

Accrual of Hours

The normal workday is $7\frac{1}{2}$ hours and the normal workweek is
$37\frac{1}{2}$ hours. The Sandoz plan offers debit-hours and credit-hours options. An employee has the option of working more than the normal
$7\frac{1}{2}$ hours each day and accumulating a maximum credit of 10 hours.
Similarly, the employee has the option of working less than the normal $7\frac{1}{2}$ hours per day, up to a maximum debit of 10 hours. The employee who has banked hours is able to spend this accrued time in the
form of extra time off at future dates. The employee who "owes" the
company time works extra hours in the future so as to make up and
pay back the hours owed.

Nonexempt employees paid weekly cannot work more than 40
hours a week, unless they are specifically authorized to work overtime. They can, however, accumulate plus hours at a rate of $2\frac{1}{2}$ hours
per week in excess of $37\frac{1}{2}$ hours per week, to reach their maximum
of 10 hours. At this rate it takes four 40-hour weeks to reach the maximum, assuming the employees start the period with a zero balance.

In order to accommodate this accrual of hours, the division's
previous practice of compensating all hours in excess of 8 hours per
day at a rate of time and one half was redefined as follows: "Only

those hours in excess of 8 per day which are specifically authorized as overtime by the supervisor will be compensated at a rate of time and one half." Hours in excess of 40 per week fall outside the program for nonexempt personnel paid weekly and must be authorized as overtime.

How do absences affect this accrual of hours? At Sandoz, absences attributable to illness, jury duty, and the like, are recorded in the absence column of the time record. An absence does not affect the gliding time program and is always based on a 7½-hour day.

In the company's view, accrual of hours enhances a flexitime program and provides for additional options.

Summary Comment

At Sandoz's Colors & Chemicals Division the gliding work-time system appears to be functioning well. A manager in corporate personnel operations issued this statement to me in 1976: "Our employees have accepted this workday flexibility with great enthusiasm, and we are quite pleased with the results."

Westinghouse Electric Corporation, Nuclear Center

Westinghouse, a very large corporation comprising about 35 "business units," employs some 160,000 people over numerous geographical locations. A leading division of the corporation—the Nuclear Center in Monroeville, Pennsylvania—has committed itself to a full-blown organization development program. An employee survey was conducted at the start of the OD program in 1973 to learn what employees thought about the organization and about their work. Based on the survey results, numerous specific programs were initiated with the aim of further developing an organizational climate of openness, trust, and interdepartmental cooperation. Flexitime was but one of those innovations; it was meant to deal with the complaint of nonexempt employees that they were treated as second-class citizens.

The Water Reactor Divisions at the Monroeville facility employs some 2,800 people. A flexitime pilot study was launched in this unit in April 1976. Some 700 exempt and nonexempt employees participated in the six-month trial program. Automatic time totalizers were used for time-recording purposes and a number of measurements were made before, during, and after the six-month period. Measurements of quantity and quality of work showed no significant changes. Use of overtime was about the same. Absenteeism dropped significantly under flexitime. Some exempt employees (not a majority) voiced a strong resentment to the new time-recording method imposed on them, believing they had suffered a loss in professional status. (Prior to the installation of flexitime, exempt personnel were on the honor system.) Overall, at the end of the trial period flexitime was viewed in a positive light, and the decision was made to extend the system to additional personnel.

In April 1977 some 2,800 nonexempt personnel — up to the level of vice president — were on flexitime. At the Nuclear Center the flexitime program did not include the option of debiting and crediting work hours beyond a week for exempt personnel and beyond a day for nonexempt personnel. (Westinghouse was a government contractor, and provisions in the Walsh-Healey Act required overtime pay for work in excess of 8 hours per day.)

Within the flexitime program, company policy required a ½-hour minimum lunch break. Furthermore, minimum staffing was required between 8:00 A.M. and 4:45 P.M. so as to guarantee satisfactory job coverage. The flexitime work schedule, based on an 8-hour day and a 40-hour week, took this form:

FST	CORE TIME	MIDDAY FLEX	CORE TIME	FQT

7:00 A.M.	9:00 A.M.	11:30 A.M.	1:30 P.M.	3:30 P.M.	7:00 P.M.

FST fell within the 7:00 to 9:00 A.M. band, and FQT was possible over a wide 3:30 to 7:00 P.M. band. Midday flexibility, extending from 11:30 A.M. until 1:30 P.M., resulted in a morning core time of 9:00 to 11:30 A.M. and an afternoon core time of 1:30 to 3:30 P.M.

Summary Comment

In April 1977 I spoke with the Director of Organization Development at the Westinghouse Nuclear Center; this official was intimately involved in planning and implementing the flexitime system. His assessment was that flexitime had paid off in reduced absenteeism and in higher job satisfaction and morale levels. Installation of flexitime was seen as a contributing program for continued organization development at Westinghouse.

First National Bank of Boston

Until the past few years nonexempt employees were on fixed hours in this company. The typical workday was from 8:45 A.M. to 5:00 P.M., or 7¼ hours plus an hour for lunch. The schedule offered a 5-day workweek totaling 36¼ hours. The bank introduced flexitime in a pilot setting in November 1973. Results were successful, and over the next three years about 1,000 exempt and nonexempt personnel went over to the new schedule. At the end of 1976 this number of employees represented about 30 percent of the eligible staff in the Boston operation. In 1977 the bank was reviewing the work schedules of departments not on flexitime to determine the feasibility of including them.

The bank's flexitime bandwidth typically spans the 7:30 A.M. to 6:00 P.M. period. Where a department converts to flexitime, it is mainly the department manager and supervisors who determine bandwidth, core time, flexible starting and quitting bands, and minimum staffing requirements for job coverage. In its program, where feasible, the First National Bank of Boston extends flexitime to both exempt and nonexempt personnel. The option of debiting and crediting work hours is part of the total program. Employees must work some hours each workday, but they are not required to work the same number of hours. The main criterion is that they work a standard workweek of 36¼ hours.

The bank uses Hecon Corporation's Flextime Machine. According to the bank, employees prefer the time accumulators to a manual system. Also, under the manual system the bank frequently experienced "time erosion." In other words, in instances where an employee was supposed to be at work at 8:45, actually arrived at 8:50, then entered 8:45 on the time sheet to avoid being docked as tardy, 5 minutes of time erosion occurred. The bank claims that the use of time accumulators eliminated the practice of making daily time entries on hand-posted attendance sheets and then manually totaling the entries at the end of each week. For the bank, the discontinuance of this manual operation translates into an annual cost savings of about $10,000.

A vice president reported on the bank's experiences in a talk that he gave at a national conference held in San Francisco in September 1976. He stated that flexitime had resulted in improved levels of morale, cooperation, and teamwork. About 90 percent of the staff on the flexitime program wanted it continued. Flexitime promoted cross-training, as supervisors were forced to implement, and staff members were required to learn, other jobs in their work units in order to maintain a minimum staff for daily work coverage. The system practically eliminated tardiness. Employees discovered that the system facilitated commuting to and from work, the accomplishment of personal business responsibilities, and off-the-job interests. As for productivity, in most departments flexitime did not produce increases. Certain departments, however, did note some improvements in output. In short, productivity levels achieved under fixed hours were maintained under flexitime in most departments.

Summary Comment

Overall, where flexitime has been installed at First National Bank of Boston, results have been positive. At the San Francisco conference a vice president conveyed the following conclusions:

> We look upon flexitime as an ongoing time system for us, and we are very satisfied with the results. . . . Our management and staff are both very pleased with the significant role it has played in the daily and weekly time features of the employees' work habits and work efforts. We believe that in certain departments where productivity can be measured we have reached a higher plateau of production and that it has been maintained. We also know that morale within flexitime departments is markedly better — both management and staff agree on that.
>
> Flexitime has given our staff an opportunity to participate in the decision-making process of determining hours of work and they have made and abided by their decisions. These decisions have in turn enabled managers and supervisors to more effectively fulfill their managerial roles. In closing, flexitime at the First has worked first-rate, and we suggest you consider it for your bank.

During the spring of 1977 I received further correspondence from the bank. Flexitime's effects remained positive.

Control Data Corporation

I shall conclude this chapter by turning the spotlight on Control Data Corporation, an organization that has had considerable experience with various flexible hours systems. Control Data is a large computer technology firm with business extensions over much of the world. Need for interdependence, rather than the pursuit of independence, is a vital part of the company's philosophy. The corporation views its fundamental purpose in these terms:

> Control Data is a worldwide business dedicated to improving productivity and the quality of life for individuals and organizations through the application of its computing technology, financial resources, and professional services. There are so many things to be done to improve productivity and quality of life everywhere through the use of computers, and the challenge is so great, that progress will be made faster through cooperation and pooling resources as opposed to individual company enterprises. Consequently, Control Data is seeking cooperative arrangements with other organizations in all parts of the world.

The company's flexible hours pilot programs were initiated in April 1972 in the Microcircuits Research Building, and were expanded to the Aerospace Division in July of the same year. Both facilities are located in the corporate headquarters complex in Minneapolis, Minnesota. Thirty days of preparation were necessary prior to actual implementation to work out guidelines, resolve conflicts, establish policies and procedures, gather employees' preferences, and communicate the approved schedules to all employees.

In July 1973, Control Data adopted flexible work scheduling as a companywide practice affecting some 30,000 employees in the United States and overseas.

As stated by the company, one of its major purposes in establishing flexible hours is to maximize employees' choices in establishing their working hours within the confines of the business environment where they work. The goal is to ensure that business and personal needs are both satisfied in an efficient and compatible manner.

Discussed below are policies and practices that have been implemented for all full-time and part-time Control Data employees at locations within the United States.

Policies and Practices Regarding Flexitime

Wherever feasible, individual employees are permitted to vary specific starting and quitting times, so long as they work the standard number of hours per day. Both exempt and nonexempt employees are included in the plan. For exempt employees, the program does not alter the normal minimum number of work hours per day or week. Nonexempt employees work an 8-hour workday and a 40-hour workweek unless they are scheduled for overtime.

As defined by the company, flexitime refers to the times an employee reports to work and departs from work. Changes in the number of days worked in a week, the accumulation of hours, or the carryover of hours to another week are not part of this definition.

Each division or facility establishes work-hour guidelines based on organizational and employee needs. Establishment of guidelines is the responsibility of the division or region general manager. In multidivisional facilities, coordination between organizations must also be achieved. Once guidelines are established, changes in them are to be coordinated in the same manner.

The monitoring of an employee's starting and quitting times is accomplished in a variety of ways, including the use of time clocks, sign-in sheets, and personal logs.

Additional Alternative Work Schedules

The discussion above mainly concerns *individual flexibility,* where each employee within a unit is allowed to vary his or her daily starting and quitting times, with no change in the total hours worked in a day or week. But the flexible hours concept at Control Data Corporation includes additional forms of work schedules.

There is the *summer hours* plan. Under it, individual divisions, operations, or facilities are permitted to vary work hours during the summer — provided that employees continue to work 8 hours per day and discharge their work responsibilities.

Another plan is that of *group flexibility,* where all employees within a department or work group are able to change their work hours concurrently as a unit and thereby work the same hours daily for one week. For example, group flexibility determined by functional units might take this form:

Production	7:00 to 3:30	½-hour lunch break
Crib	7:00 to 3:30	½-hour lunch break
Quality control	7:00 to 3:30	½-hour lunch break
Engineering	9:00 to 6:00	1-hour lunch break
Management	8:00 to 5:00	1-hour lunch break
Staff	8:00 to 5:00	1-hour lunch break

A fourth plan in effect is *staggered hours* — which encompasses, where possible, *flexitour.* Within departments, individuals may choose one of a number of options established by their respective managers and may work those hours daily for at least one week. The staggered hours plan is most likely to be in operation in assembly-line work and in multiple shifts. At most Control Data facilities the first shift works during the period 4:00 A.M. to 12:00 noon, the second shift works from 12:00 noon to 8:00 P.M., and the third shift is on duty from 8:00 P.M. to 4:00 A.M.

Although it may at first appear that employees working in functions that have more than one shift may not have much flexibility, a closer look shows that this is not necessarily true. At Control Data, where there are three shifts in a given work unit, the third shift is usually a small percentage of the total number of workers in that department. It is altogether possible that, with management approval, employees on the first shift may start work at an agreed-upon earlier time without interfering with the handful of employees still left from the third shift. This in turn "makes room" for certain numbers of second-shift workers who may want to come in earlier.

Where there are only first and second shifts, it frequently occurs that a first-shift employee prefers to come in earlier than the usual starting time (particularly during daylight saving periods); on the other hand, the second-shift worker often prefers to come in later. In short, this "pulling apart" of the two shifts can often be accommodated without disturbance of the work flow and the start-up machinery.

Control Data's experiences show that operations with multishifts are able to utilize alternative work schedules. The determining factor is the kind of business being done, not the shift. Because of equipment utilization, multishift operations, and product flow, the types of schedules used in the *manufacturing areas* of the company tend to be concentrated on staggered starting times and group flexibility rather than on individual flexibility.

How Managers Judged Flexible Work Hours

In 1975, follow-up questionnaires were administered to approximately 85 managers and 200 nonmanagement employees in three Aerospace work operations: production, engineering, and program/products/marketing. The administration was part of a three-year follow-up of the programs implemented in the Microcircuits and Aerospace Divisions in 1972.

At this point it would be appropriate for us to study in some detail Control Data's assessment approach and at the same time take a close look at the questionnaires and the responses—because in my experience with numerous company programs, one of the more thorough follow-up studies was that undertaken by Control Data. Furthermore, a detailed look at the questionnaires will give the reader some idea of how to carry out the assessment of a flexible hours program—should the reader's company decide to install a system on a trial basis.

Our discussion centers on Aerospace for three reasons: In both Aerospace and Microcircuits, the same questionnaire was used; responses in the Microcircuits survey were similar to those obtained in the Aerospace survey; and the Aerospace follow-up is even more recent.

Although the questionnaires concern all four forms of alternative work schedules in operation at the company, most reponses relate mainly to *flexitime* (see Questions 1 and 2 below), as that has had the most widespread applicability at Control Data Corporation.

Each respondent to the questionnaire was instructed to compare the new schedule with the previous system used.

Management Flexible-Work-Hours Questionnaire

1. What mode(s) of flexible work hours are being utilized in your department, section, or unit?
   - (a) Summer work hours   16%
   - (b) Staggered start times   38%
   - (c) Group flexibility   16%
   - (d) Individual flexibility   85%
   - (e) Standard hours   16%

   (The sum of the percentages exceeds 100% because many managers reported using more than one mode of flexible hours.)

2. Indicate how many people are utilizing each mode of flexibility.
   - (a) Summer work hours   3%
   - (b) Staggered start times   26%
   - (c) Group flexibility   14%
   - (d) Individual flexibility   41%
   - (e) Standard hours   16%

3. In your opinion, has the travel time of your employees changed going to and from work?
   - (a) It has increased   0%
   - (b) It has remained the same   20%
   - (c) It has decreased   80%

4. In your opinion, has the sick leave used by your employees changed?
    (a) It has increased   2%
    (b) It has remained the same   80%
    (c) It has decreased   18%

5. In your opinion, has the tardiness of your employees changed?
    (a) It has increased   5%
    (b) It has remained the same   47%
    (c) It has decreased   48%

6. In your opinion, has your department, section, or unit productivity changed as a result of flexible hours?
    (a) It has increased   53%
    (b) It has remained the same   42%
    (c) It has decreased   5%

7. In your opinion, has the absenteeism of your employees changed?
    (a) It has increased   0%
    (b) It has remained the same   73%
    (c) It has decreased   27%

8. In your opinion, has the communication between your employees and yourself changed?
    (a) It has worsened   8%
    (b) It has remained the same   76%
    (c) It has improved   16%

9. In your opinion, has the leisure time of your employees changed?
    (a) It has increased   69%
    (b) It has remained the same   28%
    (c) It has decreased   3%

10. In your opinion, has your department's, section's, or unit's telephone coverage changed?
    (a) It has worsened   17%
    (b) It has remained the same   66%
    (c) It has improved   17%

11. In your opinion, has the average start time of your employees changed?
    (a) It has become later by ½ hour   3%
    (b) It has become later by 1 hour   7%
    (c) It has remained the same   37%
    (d) It has become earlier by ½ hour   30%
    (e) It has become earlier by 1 hour   20%
    (f) It has become earlier by more than 1 hour   3%

Concerning how the flexible hours systems were judged by the managers, several conclusions stand out. About 85 percent of the managers used individual flexibility (some 87 percent in Microcircuits); more of the employees supervised by the managers worked under individual flexibility than under any other system then in use; travel time to and from work decreased; tardiness decreased; productivity increased; leisure time increased; and most employees were coming to work at earlier hours.

Overall, in the opinion of Control Data's managers, flexible hours benefit both employer and employee.

How Nonmanagement-Level Employees Judged
Flexible Work Hours

During 1975 a follow-up questionnaire was administered to approximately 200 nonmanagement-level workers. Listed on the survey were 24 questions (seven of them related almost exclusively to the nature of the company's business and, for this reason, are not included in the discussion below). A respondent, in completing the questionnaire, was instructed to compare flexible work hours with the previous system used.

Nonmanagement Flexible-Work-Hours Questionnaire

1. Flexible hours are:
   - (a) No good — 3%
   - (b) Better than nothing — 2%
   - (c) All right — 24%
   - (d) Great — 71%

2. Flexible hours make me feel that Control Data:
   - (a) Does not trust me at all — 1%
   - (b) Trusts me sometimes — 7%
   - (c) Partially trusts me — 32%
   - (d) Trusts me all the time — 60%

3. The time necessary to get from home to work has:
   - (a) Increased considerably — 5%
   - (b) Moderately increased — 16%
   - (c) Not changed — 21%
   - (d) Moderately decreased — 38%
   - (e) Decreased considerably — 20%

4. The pressures and frustrations of trying to get to work on or before a scheduled start time have:
   - (a) Greatly increased — 3%
   - (b) Moderately increased — 7%

    (c) Shown no change   17%
    (d) Moderately decreased   36%
    (e) Decreased greatly   37%

5. The need to leave work before quitting time has:
    (a) Increased greatly   1%
    (b) Moderately increased   11%
    (c) Shown no change   30%
    (d) Moderately decreased   30%
    (e) Decreased greatly   28%

6. The use of sick leave has:
    (a) Increased greatly   1%
    (b) Moderately increased   8%
    (c) Shown no change   40%
    (d) Moderately decreased   40%
    (e) Decreased greatly   11%

7. Leisure time has been:
    (a) Greatly reduced   5%
    (b) Moderately reduced   13%
    (c) Neither reduced nor increased   24%
    (d) Moderately increased   45%
    (e) Greatly increased   13%

8. Morale has:
    (a) Greatly degenerated   4%
    (b) Moderately degenerated   8%
    (c) Shown no change   10%
    (d) Moderately improved   56%
    (e) Greatly improved   22%

9. Attitudes toward the company have:
    (a) Worsened   10%
    (b) Remained the same   20%
    (c) Slightly improved   49%
    (d) Significantly improved   21%

10. Productivity has:
    (a) Greatly decreased   3%
    (b) Moderately decreased   8%
    (c) Neither decreased nor increased 24%
    (d) Moderately increased   53%
    (e) Greatly increased   12%

11. Abuses:
    (a) Are extremely abundant   3%
    (b) Are moderately abundant   18%
    (c) Are about the same in number 15%

    (d) Infrequently occur   57%
    (e) Are nonexistent   7%

12. Problems caused are:
    (a) All too numerous and are destroying produc-
        tivity   4%
    (b) Moderately inconvenient   15%
    (c) About the same in number   7%
    (d) Few   56%
    (e) None   18%

13. The need to supervise employees has:
    (a) Greatly decreased   6%
    (b) Moderately decreased   35%
    (c) Not changed   28%
    (d) Moderately increased   28%
    (e) Greatly increased   3%

14. The cooperation between departments has:
    (a) Greatly decreased   4%
    (b) Moderately decreased   22%
    (c) Shown no change   40%
    (d) Moderately improved   30%
    (e) Greatly improved   4%

15. Flexible hours are good:
    (a) From June through August   4%
    (b) From May through October   4%
    (c) From November through April   1%
    (d) All year round   91%

16. Interdivisional relationships have:
    (a) Greatly deteriorated   2%
    (b) Moderately deteriorated   9%
    (c) Shown no change   53%
    (d) Moderately improved   31%
    (e) Greatly improved   5%

17. Relationships between shifts have:
    (a) Greatly deteriorated   4%
    (b) Moderately deteriorated   10%
    (c) Shown no change   45%
    (d) Moderately improved   39%
    (e) Greatly improved   2%

Concerning how nonmanagement-level employees judged the flexible hours systems, these conclusions stand out. Some 95 percent said that flexible hours were "all right" or "great"; the systems generated feelings that the company trusted its employees; there were travel-time reductions; feelings of being pressured to get to work before a scheduled starting time were reduced; there was less need to leave work before quitting time to take care of personal business; leisure time increased; morale readings were more positive; attitudes toward the company improved; employees believed that productivity had increased; workers did not abuse the systems by taking unwarranted privileges; employees did not think that many new problems had been generated; and lastly, employees said that flexible hours are good throughout the year.

Overall, in the opinion of Control Data's nonmanagement-level workforce, flexible hours systems benefit both employer and employee.

Objective Measurements

In addition to reviewing the flexible hours programs through manager and nonmanager surveys, the company also examined various objective measurements.

Concerning *productivity* and *efficiency*, measurements were mixed. As far as the company has been able to determine, although productivity and efficiency did not deteriorate as feared by some, there was no measurable positive effect either. The company concludes that because of the presence of numerous variables, the effect of flexible hours on operation efficiency is unknown. Recall that on manager and nonmanager questionnaires, both groups were of the opinion that productivity and efficiency improved under flexible hours.

Regarding *turnover*, company data show a rising trend in turnover from 1971 through 1973, with a noticeable decline in 1974 and 1975. As stated by the company, whether or not the variation in turnover rates is attributable to working hours cannot be determined. The turnover figures used are total figures, including both voluntary and involuntary turnover. Because separation rates can be significantly affected by layoffs and other organizational factors, the effects of flexible hours on turnover cannot be determined from the available data.

In regard to the use of *sick leave*, objective data suggest no clearcut pattern. For example, company figures show a slight decline in sick-leave usage during the summer months of 1974. However, for the nonsummer months of 1974 such usage was higher than in previous years. In short, the effects of flexible hours on sick-leave usage cannot be determined without knowledge of the effects of other organizational variables.

Thus, the overall conclusion reached after studying flexible hours programs in Aerospace and Microcircuits operations is that the programs are favorably received by both management and non-management employees, but exert little positive or negative influence on objective measurements of productivity and efficiency, turnover, and the use of sick leave. As stated by the company, "The flexible hours concept will generate a favorable employee attitude impact when properly administered and utilized. This one individual positive result will most likely be more significant than all other criteria combined."

Summary Comment

When one looks into a kaleidoscope, pieces of colored glass appear complex, undergo constant change, and are viewed in different forms. So, too, job satisfaction and morale, motivation to work, productivity, and efficiency interrelate and are viewed in complex ways. Needless to say, these factors are of considerable importance to organizations. For instance, various alternative work schedules have been in operation at Control Data since 1972, and there is strong use of flexitime. Objective measurements, however, show no productivity and efficiency changes in a positive direction as a result of these installations of flexible hours. Evidence suggests a similar conclusion in regard to motivation to work. Yet there is no evidence that work motivation, productivity, and efficiency suffered under flexible hours.

So we are left with this: No apparent change in motivation to work, in productivity, and in efficiency has been shown by objective measurements. On the other hand, as measured through manager and nonmanager attitude surveys, significant change is noted in a positive direction for morale and job satisfaction. When viewed in terms of humanistic management, flexible work hours appear to be beneficial to Control Data mainly in the form of higher morale and job satisfaction levels. And where satisfactory productivity levels are maintained without added costs, attaining the goal of higher morale and job satisfaction is surely an important part of the ball game.

7

Alternative work schedules in the United States-outside the private sector

This chapter concentrates on organizations outside the private sector that have alternative work schedules in operation. A program at a nonprofit association draws our initial attention. Discussion then turns to alternative work patterns in municipal and federal government agencies. As in the preceding chapter, the major focus here is on individual flexibility or flexitime.

American Optometric Association (AOA)

The American Optometric Association is a nonprofit organization, similar in structure to that of the American Medical Association, American Dental Association, and American Hospital Association. The AOA represents some 20,000 practicing optometrists and students of optometry. It was founded as the American Association of Opticians in 1898; the name was changed to the American Optometric Association in 1919. The AOA is a federation of associations representing each of the fifty states and the District of Columbia. In addition there are zone and local optometric societies. The AOA maintains its national headquarters in St. Louis. It also maintains an office for federal government relations in Washington, D.C.

166

Mechanics of the Gliding Time System

The workforce at the AOA's St. Louis headquarters comprises about 70 full-time office workers organized into six "divisions." Each division is headed by a director, who is assigned his or her own staff. The managerial staff consists of about 15 members. Thus, in discussing "gliding time" (the Association prefers use of this term), we are talking about a system that affects a workforce of close to 100 people at the St. Louis headquarters.

Under the AOA's old schedule all employees reported for work at 8 A.M., had a 15-minute midmorning coffee break, took an hour for lunch, had another coffee break in the afternoon, and left work at 5 P.M. In other words, a fixed schedule was in operation.

The Association began using gliding time at its St. Louis headquarters in 1973 and has made few changes in the program since that time. Exempt as well as nonexempt employees have the opportunity to participate. The AOA's Washington office consists of only 25 employees and gliding time has not been adopted there. The Washington office communicates primarily with federal government agencies, and AOA employees have to be at work when government organizations are functioning — which means normal business hours. Furthermore, this office does not have the membership contact requirements that the St. Louis office has.

The AOA's headquarters is open 12 hours — 7:00 A.M. to 7:00 P.M. — Monday through Friday, and 4 hours on Saturday — 8:00 A.M. to 12:00 noon. Here is how the specific time plan looks:

FST	CORE TIME (excluding lunch break)	FQT
7:00 A.M.	10:00 A.M.	2:00 P.M.	7:00 P.M.

As shown, the plan has a very wide bandwidth extending from 7:00 in the morning until 7:00 in the evening: FST covers the 7:00 to 10:00 span, and FQT is possible any time within the 2:00 to 7:00 segment. Core time runs through the 10:00 to 2:00 period. Prior to the installation of gliding time the lunch break was 1 hour, and many employees continue to take 60 minutes for lunch. However, under gliding time, both the duration of the lunch break as well as its starting and ending times are flexible. Meal schedules are discretionary and are up to one hour in length, with prior authorization. The plan is in effect from Monday through Friday.

Because of the nature of their work, three or four employees are restricted from participating in the gliding time program and must continue to work a fixed schedule. These include the mail supervisor, the receptionist/switchboard operator, and the maintenance personnel. Nevertheless, some autonomy is provided in that these workers have the option of switching schedules with fellow employees who perform the same task.

Although the plan is termed gliding time by the AOA, in certain respects it's a composite of gliding time and flexitour. That is, employees in the program submit their intended work schedules to their supervisors seven days in advance of the applicable week. Although varied starting and quitting times are permitted, workers are strongly encouraged to adhere to the advance schedule submitted. A similar policy is in effect regarding lunch breaks. Employees may break for lunch at their own discretion, as long as the break is part of the advance plan schedule.

Employees punch the time clock at the beginning and close of their workday and lunch break. Management believes that people basically resent the punch-clock approach to timekeeping, and the Association is in the process of getting information on a new record-keeping computer system.

In accordance with the Association's definition, the workweek extends from Friday through the following Thursday. The workweek is based on 40 hours per week, with overtime pay in effect after 40 hours. The AOA has worked into its system an ingenious benefit, here described. The 12-hour bandwidth in effect Monday through Friday plus the 4-hour period on Saturday morning results in the following work situation: The employee must work a 40-hour week; however, *he or she may elect any 40 of the 64 hours.* This provision opens up all kinds of possibilities. Here is but one: An employee may choose to work (under the one-week advance plan submitted each Wednesday) 11 hours on a Tuesday and only 5 hours the next day. The reader can easily imagine and draw up all kinds of other working-time options.

Results

With implementation of its gliding time work schedule, the AOA is able to offer telephone service to its membership for 60 to 64 hours each week. Under the old work system, the 20,000 members spread from coast to coast found that some hours during the regular 8:00 to 5:00 day were without headquarters coverage. Because the headquarters office was located in the Central Time Zone, people on the east coast would have to call St. Louis an hour after they got to work. And California members had to call before 3:00 in the afternoon.

It was this very consideration that led the AOA away from installing the 4-day-workweek schedule and toward installing gliding time. On a 4-day schedule the Association would have been faced with the inconvenience of not having people at work during one of the normal workdays. But with gliding time the St. Louis office is open and has people available during normal workweek business hours coast to coast. If an optometrist phones from New York on his or her arrival at work, the St. Louis offices are open. The same thing for California — the St. Louis offices are open at 5:00 P.M. California time. In essence, here is a plan that promotes productivity. The AOA is in the business of providing information. With a 7:00 to 7:00 schedule, the AOA headquarters can better serve its nationwide clientele of its own members, other health associations, government agencies, and business suppliers. The office is now open throughout the usual business hours in all U.S. time zones.

Of course, there are additional ways to talk about productivity. Consider reductions in overtime. According to the Association, gliding time schedules result in an increase in the intensity with which people work. Jobs tend to be completed in minimum times; either the employee stays to finish the job in hand or comes in early the next day to get it finished. If a person has to put in a 12-hour day to get a job done, it counts toward his or her 40 hours. Extra reward takes the form of time off during the rest of the week. States the AOA: "Since installing the program we notice a substantial savings to the Association due to a considerable elimination of overtime. Gliding time eliminates practically all overtime." Under gliding time the St. Louis headquarters has had to hire only one additional switchboard operator, and the Association says the reduced overtime has more than paid for the additional operator.

When employees work with greater intensity, match their use of the flexible time bands to the workload, and complete their jobs in minimum times, these plus points add up to increases in productivity and savings. Correspondence received from the AOA corroborates this improved productivity: "Although the program is a complete success, we continue to study the actual effects of gliding time. We still continue to evaluate and analyze the workload to determine what work is actually given in 40 hours and if it has been performed. Thus far we are ahead of the work productivity level that was set up on our regular 40-hour-week program."

The Association has derived other benefits: "The attitude of our people is much better," morale has improved, and there is a reduction of the number of days lost through illness, especially those illnesses that are only an excuse for other personal problems. Furthermore, improvements are noted in working climate and in communications between employees, their colleagues, and their bosses. Consider this point about communications. Under gliding time, supervisors must work more closely with their subordinates in workload planning. Say, for example, an employee likes to come in at 7:00 in the morning whereas the supervisor does not arrive until 9:00. It is the supervisor's responsibility to see that the employee's workload is set up the day before so that the employee will be able to operate two or three hours without supervision. Two additional benefits are also noted by the Association: a reduction in turnover, and better recruitment responses when the flexible hours system is mentioned in advertisements.

A Sampling of Employee Opinion

"I feel better because I sleep when I need to and come in when I want. I just get a lot more done than I usually did before."

"I had a slight medical problem a few weeks ago, and I had to leave work early. I was able to make up my time and hang onto my sick leave. This way you can save your sick leave until you really need it."

"I am the supervisor of the secretarial pool, and have no difficulty in organizing the secretaries' schedules and in accomplishing tasks. I always have everyone here during core time, usually our busiest time. We get everything out on time and haven't had any complaints. And I have two women who like to take off early on Fridays. So, instead of both these women leaving at 2:00, one leaves at 2:00 and the other waits until 4:00. They switch off each week."

"In my area of supervision I observe that most employees prefer to shorten their lunch hour in order to leave earlier. One woman takes 45 minutes for lunch, but in general, the longest is half an hour. They found that an hour was just too long. They would eat and sit around, just waiting for one o'clock. Now they can take short lunches and do not waste the time."

"With gliding time I can arrange my schedule to fit my personal life, and if I'm doing something socially in the evening I can come in later the next morning and work later that day."

"When I work late, the phones slow down and the people here don't bother me. I can really get a lot done."

"I'm an insurance handler, and gliding time is marvelous for me. My husband works at an automobile assembly plant and gets to work at 6:30 in the morning. Now I go to work at 7 and we both get home by 3:00 or 3:30 P.M. and have the afternoon to ourselves. Why should I sit around the house and wait for 8 o'clock?"

Summary Comment

Apparently, gliding time (with a strong dose of flexitour added) is being used with great success at the American Optometric Association headquarters in St. Louis. An AOA director said in a letter that he wrote to me recently: "Since the inception of gliding time in our Association in 1973 there have been few changes in the program and we find it to be extremely effective."

City Government Employees of Inglewood, California

Flexible hours systems have been making some inroads into city and federal government agencies. At Inglewood, California, 33 municipal government workers participated in a flexitime trial program begun in 1973. The workers had been on a standard 8:00-to-5:00 schedule. With flexitime, working-time possibilities were extended in multiple directions:

FST	CORE TIME (excluding lunch break)	FQT
7:30 9:00 A.M. A.M.	3:00 P.M.	6:00 P.M.

Flexible starting time extended from 7:30 to 9:00 A.M., core time was established from 9:00 in the morning until 3:00 in the afternoon, and flexible quitting time was set at 3:00 to 6:00 P.M. We see, therefore, a wide bandwidth from 7:30 A.M. until 6:00 P.M., a large segment of core time running some 6 hours, and a rather generous 3-hour quitting-time range.

Use of flexitime among this small number of employees resulted in a more productive and satisfied workforce; consequently, about 300 employees, or 40 percent of the workers other than policemen and firemen, were offered flexible schedules. According to the city manager, sick leave for medical and dental appointments has dropped sharply. In addition, service to the public has improved. The expanded hours (7:30 A.M. to 6:00 P.M.) allow Inglewood's citizens to transact business with the city by telephone over a greater number of hours during a day. Similarly, citizens are afforded added opportunities to stop at municipal government offices on their way to or from work.

The extension of service hours has been accomplished without adding personnel. Also, overtime has been reduced drastically as employees match their use of the flexible bands to the workload and complete more tasks in minimum times.

The city manager says that flexitime is not a panacea for solving all employee morale problems, nor can it be universally applied. On the other hand, the city administrator believes that, when applied appropriately, flexitime can result in better public service in many government units, provide employees with opportunities to adjust hours to fit their needs, present municipal employers with a system for building a happier, more productive workforce—and at the same time reduce traffic congestion in cities.

City Government Employees of Honolulu, Hawaii

The alternative work schedules philosophy is being applied with considerable vigor in the municipal and county agencies of one of the nation's newest states, namely, Hawaii. The Hawaiian Department of Civil Service engages in a continuous study of innovative work-hours ideas, offers advice to various departments as to feasibility, and assists in the implementation phase.

The guidelines for working-time patterns in Hawaii are applicable to all agencies within the City and County of Honolulu. There, the philosophy is defined in this way: "Flexible working hours is a plan where individual work schedules are established within specified limits to suit the desires of employees." As shown in the following paragraphs, the Hawaii plan is a combination of staggered hours and flexitour.

In applying alternative work scheduling over various departments, the purpose is threefold: (1) to provide all eligible employees
the opportunity to participate in setting their own work hours within
specified time limits, (2) to improve productivity and ultimately
provide better service to the public, and (3) to provide a measure of
relief during peak-hour traffic.

Responsibilities of Department Heads

All department heads are responsible for implementing the
staggered hours–flexitour program within their jurisdiction. Wherever possible, managers are encouraged either to alter crew-type situations or to shift work duties so as to include the largest number of
employees.

As the concept of alternative work scheduling is interpreted in
Hawaii, four situations often preclude participation in the program:
(1) when employees are on a prescheduled shift-work basis, (2) when
employees must report at a preset time and place for transportation
to work sites, (3) when employees work in a crew situation where all
members of the crew must necessarily start and end work at the same
time, and (4) when the work circumstances of other employees do not
permit deviation from preset working hours.

A major consideration is that department heads make available
opportunities for employees to choose starting and ending work times
on the basis of individual needs, so long as those preferences can
coexist with the duties of the departments. It is communicated to
department heads that operational requirements, staffing, or other
work situations may change from time to time and require adjust-
ments to the starting and ending times of some employees.

The Specific Time Plan

Hawaii law requires that government offices be open to serve the
public between the hours of 7:45 A.M. and 4:30 P.M. Monday through
Friday except on legal holidays, and these requirements are incorporated within the specific time plan established. Starting times in the
staggered hours–flexitour program are between the hours of 6:00
and 9:00 A.M. and ending times are between the hours of 2:45 and
5:45 P.M., provided that the 8-hour work requirement is met by employees.

To ensure that requirements of the state law and adequate services to the public are met, it is necessary that a department head plan

to have at least one employee present in every office no later than 7:45 in the morning, and to provide adequate staffing throughout the day until 4:30 in the afternoon. Other employees may start between 6:00 A.M. and 9:00 A.M., as approved by their respective department heads.

Guideline Procedures

Let us look at the guideline procedures established. These pertain to all municipal and county agencies considering use of the new system.

1. Each department head shall set out the parameters of flexible hours for his or her particular department and initiate internal controls and procedures for its operation.

2. Within the limits set in this policy, the wishes of individual employees or groups of employees shall be considered when scheduling working times within a department.

3. The flexible hours staff study group will advise departments on implementing procedures, as required. The following procedures are recommended:

   (a) Each department establishes specific time frames. This will be made available to employees in work units or operations. For example, the starting times for the 6:00 A.M. to 9:00 A.M. time span may be designated at one-hour intervals (or half-hour intervals) along with the normal 7:45 A.M. starting time. The designation of starting times and the number of employees that will be allowed at each of the designated starting times should be controlled by the department.

   (b) Notify employees of the designated starting times available to them (or of the open time frame: for example, any time between 7:00 A.M. and 9:00 A.M. or between 6:30 A.M. and 8:00 A.M. or any other such time span, but within the limits of 6:00 A.M. and 9:00 A.M.).

   (c) Permit employees to make their choice of starting times known. It may be necessary to ask that more than one choice be made in the order of preference.

   (d) Accommodate employees wherever it is operationally possible by granting them the starting time of their choice or work out alternate choices. In the event the employee cannot be accommodated, the employee will revert to the 7:45 A.M. starting time.

(e) When two or more employees desire the same starting times and all cannot be accommodated, departments should be guided by the following considerations in the order listed.

(1) Do the employees belong to car pools?

(2) Can the affected employees work out an arrangement among themselves that is satisfactory to the department?

(3) As a final determination, apply jurisdiction seniority within the work location or operation of the affected employees. The department may also elect to rotate starting times among such employees over a logical and reasonable period of time.

In accordance with definitions given in Chapter 3, when individual employees are able to choose different starting and quitting times on a daily basis, flexitime may be said to be in operation. By contrast, when it is principally management that designates interval frames and time frames to which employees are assigned, one is talking mainly about staggered hours. In the Hawaii plan, employees are afforded some opportunity to select work frames—one aspect of flexitour. However, no "open season" arrangement is established whereby employees can select different tours. In brief, the program in Hawaii offers a combination of staggered hours and flexitour, but leans in the direction of staggered hours.

Summary Comment

According to materials at my disposal, the staggered hours–flexitour schedule is popular and successful in Honolulu. A top-level manager said in a letter to me: "The guidelines sent to you apply to all agencies within the City and County of Honolulu, not only to the Department of Transportation Services. Consequently, all of the agencies (departments) have implemented the program."

Social Security Administration

The Social Security Administration, with headquarters in Baltimore, Maryland, provides an example of a very large federal agency using flexible hours. The SSA was the first federal agency to try the idea. As explained earlier in this book, some alternative work schedules are structured mainly along the lines of group flexibility, flexitour, and staggered hours. In the Social Security Administration, however, the big emphasis is on flexitime.

As defined and used in the SSA, flexitime is a system of working hours that allows an employee to decide his or her 8-hour workday on a day-to-day basis. The individual who wants to can change the 8-hour period worked each day. Some managers as well as some professional and technical employees participate in the program; however, at the SSA, gliding time is mainly for nonexempt workers.

Where Flexitime Studies Were Conducted

Studies were conducted in at least eight large bureaus and offices. The first five identified below are described by the SSA as "operating bureaus"; the latter three are "staff bureaus."

> *Bureau of Disability Insurance (BDI).* An experimental program was started here in December 1974. More than 450 employees, mainly clerical and semitechnical, were involved.

> *Bureau of Data Processing (BDP).* Flexitime was introduced here in April 1974 to about 350 office workers at two locations in the Baltimore area.

> *Bureau of Retirement and Survivors Insurance (BRSI).* In May 1975 about 375 BRSI office workers in New York City began working under flexitime.

> *Bureau of Field Operations (BFO).* Gliding time began in August 1975 at nine of this bureau's district offices in the Atlanta, Georgia, region. Participating were 225 employees.

> *Office of Management and Administration (OMA).* Trials here began in June 1975, and included a total of 737 office workers.

> *Bureau of Health Insurance (BHI).* An adaptable hours program began here in June 1975 and covered 175 employees primarily in professional and staff functions.

> *Bureau of Retirement and Survivors Insurance (BRSI).* Flexitime was installed on a trial basis at the Baltimore headquarters of this bureau beginning in March 1975. Experiencing gliding time were 144 employees, including managers, project leaders, and administrative and clerical personnel.

Office of Administrative Appraisal and Planning (OAAP). The implementation date here was April 1975. All OAAP employees—analysts and support staff—participated.

Status of Flexitime at the Bureau of Data Processing

As noted above, the Bureau of Data Processing introduced flexitime in April 1974 to about 350 office workers at two locations in the Baltimore area. The trial run was successful, and the program continues with few changes. Here is how the time plan works at BDP:

FST	CORE TIME (excluding 30-minute lunch break)	FQT	OVERTIME ONLY
6:30 9:30 A.M. A.M.	3:00 P.M.	6:00 P.M.	7:15 P.M.

Each employee is free to come to work each day at any time between 6:30 and 9:30 A.M. The employee then completes his or her shift 8½ hours later (including 30 minutes for lunch). For record-keeping purposes, automatic time totalizers are used.

In general, supervisors are not included in the BDP flexitime program. Since employees in any units may be working at any time from 6:30 A.M. to 6:00 P.M., in the bureau's view it is essential that there be at least one supervisor on duty the whole time. Supervisors can, however, work staggered hours shifts, determined by themselves.

Working any more than 8 hours a day is overtime, for which an employee must have his or her supervisor's approval. Maximum overtime allowed per day is 3 hours.

How overtime operates at the Bureau of Data Processing is worth a closer look. The Flextime Machine records total time up to 7:15 P.M. At that time the "overtime day" ends. Therefore, an employee who secures approval to work the maximum 3 hours overtime must arrive so as to finish the 8½-hour stint (including lunchtime) by 4:15 P.M. For the employee who comes in as early as 6:30 A.M., overtime begins at 3:00 P.M.—provided, again, that the employee's supervisor has given approval of the overtime. One further point. On every occasion where employees work overtime, they must work at least one hour, but past that first hour they can record overtime in blocks of 15 minutes.

Status of Flexitime at the Social Security Administration

It is fortunate that a report was made available by the SSA in 1976. The following discussion pertains to an evaluation covering all eight bureaus. The reader is reminded that, owing to the inherent difficulties of attempting to exert rigorous experimental control in operational settings, measured changes in employee attitudes and organizational behavior that appear to vary with the introduction of flexitime may also reflect, in part, the concomitant introduction of other variables—such as increases in workload demands or modifications in staffing.

Keeping in mind that the SSA attempted to measure gliding hours in operational settings—meaning that the agency's primary concern was to continue to perform its business functions and get out the work—let us take a look at results.

Attitudes and Morale. In operating bureaus, about 80 percent of the employees and 60 percent of the supervisors judge flexitime to be an improvement over the preflexitime system. Responses from staff bureaus are also supportive of the new arrangement. In operating bureaus, some 90 percent of the employees state that "having a say" in deciding their work hours is important to them. Opinions of staff bureaus also register this sentiment.

In terms of job satisfaction, both employees and their supervisors report that employee job satisfaction increased under adaptable hours. For example, while about 32 percent of the employees rated their job satisfaction as "high" or "very high" before flexitime, 58 percent did so under flexitime.

Regarding morale, about 75 percent of managers in operating bureaus note an increase in employee morale. In staff bureaus, managers are almost unanimous in their opinion that the new work system has a positive impact. In a related finding, about 85 percent of the employees report that flexitime enables them not only to spend more time with their families but also to participate more actively in additional outside activities.

Leave Usage and Attendance. In both operating and staff bureaus, flexitime resulted in a slight reduction in use of sick time. Many organizations are well aware that employees' ability to care for their children is related to use of leave time. At the SSA, 75 percent of those who admitted to problems in fulfilling such obligations indicated that variable hours did in fact alleviate their situation.

As one might suspect, tardiness was reduced substantially at the SSA following installation of flexitime. Previously about 20 percent of the employees had difficulty in getting to work on time — as was reported in a questionnaire survey. With gliding time the figure was reduced to 7 percent. The proportion of supervisors who consider employee tardiness to be a major problem decreased dramatically, from 90 percent to only 16 percent. In one large operating bureau, supervisors report that the problem of tardiness no longer exists. Nearly all attribute this development to the adaptable hours program. In staff bureaus, the majority of supervisors report that employee tardiness in their component has fallen to an "irreducible minimum." In short, flexitime is associated with the virtual elimination of employee tardiness.

Productivity and Organizational Effectiveness. The SSA findings pertaining to productivity and effectiveness have a ring of similarity to other discussions in this book relating flexitime and productivity. That is, objective measurements of quality and quantity frequently show no significant productivity spurts following the installation of gliding hours. On the other hand, subjective data in the form of worker perceptions frequently suggest that flexitime is accompanied by an increase in productivity. Materials received from the SSA tend to support such conflicting conclusions.

Let us look first at *objective measurements.* In the Bureau of Disability Insurance, one group of 100 benefit authorizers working under gliding time was compared with an equivalent group of 100 benefit authorizers working under standard hours. Over a 17-month evaluation period there was no discernible difference between the two groups in the quality or accuracy of their work — both groups improved.

In terms of quantity as measured by average daily production, however, the productivity of the nonflexitime group declined while that of the flexitime group remained unchanged. It was concluded that " . . . at least a part of the flexitime group's ability to maintain the case output level can be attributed to the effects of flexitime." And an interpretation by the Bureau of Data Processing concludes: "Flexitime in BDP, at worst, causes no decrease in productivity and probably is responsible for some, albeit unquantifiable, increase." In another productivity study, it was found that the average number of cards keypunched per hour in the Office of Data Development increased substantially following the introduction of adaptable hours.

Another way to talk about productivity and organizational effectiveness is in terms of supervisory relationships. The proportion of employees who had positive feelings about their supervisors went from 65 percent before flexitime to 76 percent after flexitime. This was accompanied by a reduction in employee applications for reassignments.

Concerning productivity as measured by *subjective feelings and opinions,* the majority of the SSA studies dealing with employee perceptions generally yielded findings of a positive nature. A survey of employee attitudes subsequent to the introduction of variable hours shows that about 33 percent of the respondents felt that the new system improved the quality of their work, while another 25 percent thought it helped to improve their "accuracy." The supervisory evaluations, however, were somewhat less favorable than those of their subordinates. In the Office of Data Development, less than one percent of the employees saw a negative relationship between flexitime and the amount or accuracy of their work product.

In short, a substantial proportion of SSA employees working under variable hours perceive an increase in the amount and accuracy of their work product and specifically attribute this improvement to flexible working hours. Objective measurements of output are clearly more temperate in nature. On the other hand, there is little evidence that gliding time adversely affects job performance.

Transportaiion. A clear majority of the respondents are of the opinion that flexitime enhances employees' ability to get to and from work. This finding is observed across all bureaus studied. At the SSA locations in metropolitan areas, about 75 percent say it is easier to travel between work and home.

Interestingly, in the Baltimore area there has been some increase in the proportion of employees driving to work alone since gliding hours began. Specifically, about 13 percent abandoned car pools or public transportation. However, in New York City flexitime has no apparent effect on public transportation usage. Would this suggest that SSA workers find that New York City has a rather efficient transit system?

Implementation and Utilization. Close to 90 percent of all participating employees choose to be on duty by 8:00 A.M. At most bureaus
the reasons given mainly reflect personal choice and preference.
However, at one location where about 90 percent are at work by 8:00
A.M., some employees claim that parking spaces are generally not
available to those electing to arrive at work during the latter part of
the FST band.

In regard to time recording, the SSA relies heavily on the use of
automatic time totalizers. In most cases employees have no strong
feelings about having work time recorded in this manner. In one
bureau, many supervisors perceived that their subordinates were
largely negative in their feelings toward the use of time totalizers. In
actuality, however, less than 5 percent of the employees were opposed
to it. At New York City locations, 61 percent supported the use of automatic time totalizers while less than 13 percent objected.

At most bureau locations, employees and supervisors see few or
no problems stemming from the frequent differences in the hours
worked by both groups. At the Bureau of Data Processing, more than
90 percent say they do not experience problems in working different
hours from those their supervisors work. On the other hand, informal feedback from BDP supervision suggests that there are some
problems in providing supervisory coverage throughout the workday.

Two studies suggest that employees' ability to work overtime
and to utilize SSA employee services (such as the "Upmo" program —
Upward Mobility education classes) — is largely unaffected by the
gliding time program.

In brief, the SSA studies concerning implementation and utilization of flexitime show that most employees come to work at earlier
hours than under the previous fixed-hours program, the majority of
them are not opposed to the use of automatic time totalizers, few of
them object to a development whereby employees and their respective supervisors often work different hours, and good opportunities
still exist for employees to put in overtime.

Summary Comment
Recent evaluation reports show that flexitime is working well at
the SSA. Worker impressions of the system are very positive. Objective measurements indicate that the new system makes little or no
negative impact on productivity. In some instances flexitime does cor-
relate in a positive way with productivity increases. In most instances,

though, objective measurements show that productivity is largely unaffected — in a positive or negative direction — following installation of flexitime.

Federal Government: an Administrative Service Center

A second federal government agency that uses flexitime also provided me with helpful particulars. No objections were made to my wish to restate the department's gliding time experiences, so long as anonymity was guaranteed.

Background: Why Flexitime Was Adopted

An "Administrative Service Center" in a large federal department first became interested in flexitime in 1972, after officials read a selection of articles about the success of gliding time in West Germany. Tardiness problems were severe, centering on lack of punctuality in starting the workday on time and abuse of coffee and lunch breaks. A second troublesome issue was that of low morale. It was believed that flexitime would significantly reduce the intensity of these problems.

The Center had long recognized that the majority of complaints and discrimination grievances filed by employees had one thing in common: the initial confrontations between worker and supervisor frequently occurred because of the employee's failure to start the workday on time and to return from coffee and lunch breaks on schedule. Disagreements about lateness snowballed, resulting in subsequent grievances based on some unrelated incident. Once an employee had continuing difficulty in being prompt and had been singled out for reprimand by the supervisor for such transgressions, it was often predictable that trouble between them in some other form would follow.

Management found itself devoting an inordinate amount of time to tardiness issues. Discipline throughout the Center was not always applied. When it was applied, it was not always uniform or equitable. Employees taking breaks together for coffee or lunch were sometimes treated differently on returning late. One employee's supervisor would mete out a reprimand for the transgression while the other employee's supervisor would overlook it. This, of course, would cause subsequent problems to management when the chastised worker would compare notes with the other worker and demand to know why his or her own offense had been judged more harshly.

Early Experiences with Flexitime

The Administrative Service Center was at last given the go-ahead to experiment with flexitime. At the Center a labor force numbering close to 300 is engaged in a variety of work functions, including finance, payroll, personnel, procurement, and data processing. The experiment was launched after employee and supervisory committee discussions, union consultation, a secret ballot among employees in the work unit, and research into the legality of its implementation.

Some 40 employees were involved in the flexitime pilot program that began in November 1972. Job classifications covered those of clerk, secretary, technician, program analyst, and manager. Job duties included measurements of daily work production, developmental and analytical research, procedure writing, and supervision. In addition, segments of the test group were responsible for handling telephone calls both from the public and from other federal agencies.

During the pilot stage the bandwidth ran from 6:00 A.M. until 6:00 P.M., with core time at a minimum. Some problems developed. First, supervisors found it difficult to schedule meetings. There was no assurance that the entire staff would be in attendance. Second, supervisors expressed the viewpoint that they were unable to measure work production during those hours when they themselves were not on duty.

Within a year after the initial experiment had begun, decisions were made to expand flexitime throughout the Center and to include some 250 employees over a range of job classifications. This meant that changes had to be made in the specific time plan. Formulated was a flexible starting-time band from 7:00 to 9:00 A.M. and a flexible quitting-time band from 3:00 to 5:00 P.M. Core time was expanded to cover the period from 9:00 in the morning until 3:00 in the afternoon.

Results

After more than four years of flexitime use, the Administrative Service Center said that immediate benefits included reductions in tardiness and short-term absenteeism, and increases in morale and productivity. These advantages were clearly measurable in the beginning. Reductions in lateness and absenteeism were the most significant and permanent improvements. The Center further observed:

> As the glow of flexitime wore off and it came to be regarded by most employees as their inalienable right rather than a benevolent gesture of management, morale and production returned to almost the same levels that existed prior to flexitime. (It should be noted here that most of the uncontrollable factors which had caused morale to ebb before flexitime was introduced still persist today.) Conditions that affected morale and work productivity have remained nearly the same during the entire period flexitime has been in effect.

At this point I should like to inject a personal comment. I doubt that many managers—including those at the Administrative Service Center—would reject the argument that, in those cases where significant improvements in worker satisfaction and organizational efficiency are not perpetuated over the long run following the installation of flexitime, it is erroneous to conclude that the fault is rooted in the flexitime system itself. A more realistic assessment is that flexitime is perceived by most employees as a definite improvement over previous systems used. Satisfaction and morale tend to be higher following the installation of flexitime. It should be noted, however, that neither flexitime nor any other single procedure will, by itself, forever sustain higher satisfaction and morale levels.

It is a psychological fact that, for most employees, a satisfied need ceases in time to operate as a principal motivator of behavior. Although newly achieved satisfactions are indeed welcomed, these inevitably grow stale and the individual commences once again, with renewed vigor, to seek still higher levels of need fulfillment. In brief, where employees embrace flexitime and at future dates seek additional benefits from employers, don't blame flexitime.

Summary Comment

In general, flexitime use in the Administrative Service Center is assessed positively. For both the Center and its employees, gliding time is preferred over a standard hours system. On the other hand, the Center clearly recognizes that flexitime is not a panacea.

A few months ago I received a letter from a top official who was acting director of the Administrative Service Center at the time when flexitime was introduced there. His letter reads in part: "You may be interested to know that my personal position on flexitime is one of strong support. While I do feel there are instances in both the private and government sectors where flexitime would not work satisfactorily, there are many, many where it would. If for no other reason than to relieve the tension upon the employee of having to beat a clock each day when going to work, flexitime is worthwhile."

U.S. Geological Survey: Department of the Interior

During May 1975 the U.S. Geological Survey began a one-year experiment in flexible working hours among some 3,000 employees assigned to the Washington, D.C., area. This represented one of the largest single groups of employees in this area to utilize flexible hours. The agency aimed to grant full participation privileges to as many workers as possible. Any restrictions on employees' use of "flexitime" (the term preferred by the agency) was to be consistent with operational requirements, documented, and reported to the Administrative Division. Overall, about 15 percent of all employees were in some way restricted from using complete flexitime because of the nature of their work. Participants included scientists and engineers, technicians, managers and other professionals, and clerical workers. In other words, participants included employees at different levels holding different types of positions. Of more than 300 supervisors, all but 22 percent were able to participate fully in the program.

Most workers were on fixed hours prior to the installation of flexitime, and the normal workday extended from 7:45 A.M. until 4:15 P.M. With gliding hours, offices were open an additional two hours. The new time schedule took this form:

FST	CORE TIME (excluding lunch break)	FQT
7:00 A.M. 9:00 A.M.		3:30 P.M. 5:30 P.M.

Flexible bands were established from 7:00 to 9:00 in the morning and from 3:30 to 5:30 in the afternoon. Except for time off for a lunch break, core time spanned the 9:00 A.M. to 3:30 P.M. segment. Although an agencywide core time was adopted, each supervisor was given the authority to lengthen that core time if necessary for operational requirements. Only one office subsequently extended the core time.

In 1976 the U.S. Geological Survey made a formal assessment of the flexitime program. Major evaluation methods consisted of (1) a 62-item questionnaire completed by all employees, including supervisors at various levels; (2) a 33-item questionnaire for managers; and (3) a study of objective measures of productivity. Let us now look at the evaluation results.

Subjective Measures of Productivity Under Flexitime

The questionnaire responses relate mainly to perceptual judgments. As previously noted, subjective evaluations often concur with objective assessments, but at other times there is considerable discrepancy. Nevertheless, whether in concurrence or disagreement with objective measurements, questionnaire responses provide valuable input.

Quantity of Output. The inquiry on the all-employees questionnaire reads: "Do you feel the amount of work you accomplish has changed as a result of flexitime?" Thirty-seven percent thought the quantity had increased, 61 percent perceived no change, and 2 percent said there was a decrease. Supervisors were asked: "In your opinion has productivity within your office or work area changed since flexitime was implemented?" Twenty-seven percent believed there was an increase, 68 percent found no change, and 5 percent thought decreases had occurred.

Quality of Output. When asked about changes in the quality of work, 36 percent of respondents to the all-employees questionnaire said a quality increase had resulted, 63 percent believed there was no change, while 1 percent thought that quality had decreased under flexitime. Responses from supervisors were quite similar. A quality increase was reported by 32 percent, 64 percent said there was no change, and 4 percent believed that quality of work had decreased.

Absenteeism. Among supervisors whose employees participated fully in the system, 51 percent stated that absenteeism improved, 48 percent said it was the same, and 1 percent believed that absenteeism was worse. Among all employees, 49 percent said they used less sick leave because of flexitime. Most others reported no change in number of leave days taken because of sickness.

Tardiness. Seventy-one percent of all first-line supervisors expressed a belief that tardiness or lateness had decreased as a result of flexitime, 26 percent found no change, whereas 3 percent said it had worsened.

Amount of Overtime. In those offices where employees were paid for overtime, 23 percent of all first-line supervisors reported a substantial decrease in overtime, 39 percent said there was a small decrease, 23 percent saw no change, and 15 percent observed a small increase.

Quiet Time. Among responding supervisors, 73 percent felt they and their subordinates had benefited from more quiet-time opportunities. Most other supervisors found no change in opportunities for quiet time.

Quicker Work Starts in the Morning. Employees tend to start work in the morning sooner, according to 65 percent of all first-line supervisors. Most of the other supervisors found no change. Almost none of them were of the opinion that employees got off to a slower work start because of flexitime.

Objective Measurements of Productivity Under Flexitime

In 1976 the federal government published *Flexitime: Evaluation of a One-Year Experiment at the U.S. Geological Survey.* In reference to objective measurements of flexitime it states: "Productivity measurement is, of course, difficult, and for many Survey functions, impossible to approach effectively. However, major efforts were made, including discussions with several supervisors, to determine and analyze changes in productivity before and after flexitime was installed for those functions where measurement is possible."

Absenteeism. Actual work statistics for employees in the Washington area indicated a reduction of 7 percent in sick-leave usage and a reduction of about 1 1/2 percent in annual-leave usage following the installation of flexitime.

Turnover. In the year following installation of flexitime at the U.S. Geological Survey voluntary separation (the "quit rate") dropped to its lowest point, when measured over a five-year period. From a previous low of about 6 percent in 1971 and a high of 8 percent in 1973, turnover dropped to about 4.6 percent during the 1975–1976 year. In short, under flexitime the quit rate decreased about 25 percent over a five-year period. However, it is to be expected that these statistics also reflect factors other than the Survey's use of flexitime.

Quantity. Productivity was also measured in terms of number of maps produced, number of vouchers processed, and number of technical reports processed. At the Eastern Mapping Center, significant production increases were noted in each of the six operational sequences used in the production of maps. At the Special Mapping Center, map production showed an increase of better than 14 percent. In the Branch of Financial Management, the number of vouchers processed increased more than 13 percent. And in technical reports processed in the Water Resources Division, the increase was 6 percent. Again, however, in reference to all three areas—absenteeism, turnover, and quantity—it is to be expected that the statistics also reflect factors other than the Survey's use of flexitime.

Other Results

Job Satisfaction. "Before flexitime began, how would you rate your overall job satisfaction?" "How do you rate your job satisfaction since flexitime?" These two questions appeared on the all-employees questionnaire. In answering the first question, 11 percent of the respondents assessed their job satisfaction as "very low" or "low," whereas only 4 percent of those responding to the second question made similar assessments. Fifty-three percent responded that their job satisfaction was "very high" or "high" before the installation of flexitime, whereas 72 percent placed themselves in these two categories for the period following the installation of flexitime.

Employee Morale. Among all supervisors, 79 percent felt that morale had improved following installation of flexitime. Most of the others reported no change. A greater morale improvement was noted in those offices where all employees enjoyed more complete flexitime.

Working Conditions. Employees reported that flexitime resulted in an improvement in their general working conditions.

Abuses. In general, employees and supervisors agreed that abuses under flexitime were not greater in number than those occurring under fixed hours. In fact, both groups thought that greater abuse of working hours had occurred under the former work-hours plan, namely, fixed hours. Regarding the all-employees questionnaire, 10 percent thought that abuses had increased under flexitime, 28 percent thought that abuses had decreased, 62 percent reported no change. Among supervisors the responses read 15 percent "increase," 27 percent "decrease," and 58 percent "no change."

Arrival Time. Under the former work system all employees began work at 7:45 A.M. With flexitime 58 percent arrived at work prior to 7:45 A.M.

Travel Time. Among all employees on flexitime, 44 percent experienced no reduction in round-trip travel time to and from work. On the other hand, 56 percent said that travel time was indeed reduced. Travel-time reduction ranged from 5 minutes to more than 30 minutes.

Time with Family. A possible benefit frequently cited is the decrease in time that workers spend away from home because of the possible reduction in commuting time. When employees were asked how important they felt it was to have the flexibility to schedule personal activities before or after work, the majority indicated that this benefit was very important to them. A total of 69 percent of all Geological Survey employees reported that they were able to spend a greater amount of time with their families because of the installation of flexitime.

Time for Recreational Activities. This topical area also relates to lifestyle. According to respondents to the all-employees questionnaire, more than 50 percent of all employees were in a better position to participate in off-the-job recreational activities as a direct result of flexitime.

An Overall Assessment
The booklet *Flexitime: Evaluation of a One-Year Experiment at the U.S. Geological Survey* contains this compact summary of the impact of flexitime:

SUMMARY OF THE IMPACT OF FLEXITIME

Factor	Expected Change	Actual Change
Productivity	Increase or decrease	Some increase
Sick-leave usage	Decrease	Decrease
Annual-leave usage	Decrease	Decrease
Overtime usage	Increase or decrease	Decrease
Equipment utilization	Increase	Increase
Employee turnover	Decrease	Decrease
Transportation methods	Decrease in car pools	No change
	Decrease in bus usage	No change
Building operations costs	Increase	Minor increase
Employee morale	Increase	Increase
Quality of work	Improvement	Improvement
Job satisfaction	Increase	Increase
Working conditions	Improvement	Improvement
Management skills	Improvement	Improvement
Office communications	Impairment	Slight impairment
Communications with other time zones	Impairment or improvement	Improvement
Tardiness	Decrease	Decrease
Abuses of working hours	Increase	Decrease
Quiet time	Increase	Increase
Overall survey evaluation	Improvement or impairment	Improvement

Management's Evaluation. In assessing the one-year experiment, managers were asked to consider flexitime in terms of the following selection choices: "very successful," "successful," "only partially successful," "unsuccessful," "no opinion," Among responding managers at all levels, 86 percent judged flexitime as very successful or successful. Only 14 percent believed that the system was only partially successful. None said that flexitime was unsuccessful.

All-Employees Evaluation. As noted, about 85 percent of all Geological Survey employees had flexitime privileges—they were able to vary their arrival times each day. The opinions of this large contingent are summarized thus:

I like flexitime very much	78%
I like flexitime	18%
I have no opinion	2%
I dislike flexitime	1%
I dislike flexitime very much	1%

Summary Comment

In my possession are materials sent to me by the U.S. Geological Survey during 1976. The agency concludes: "Results of this evaluation indicate that the use of flexitime has been beneficial both to the Survey and to Survey employees, and that no major problems have occurred that would dictate a need to return to fixed working-hour arrangements."

8

Flexitime's drawbacks

Having examined various alternative work schedules and scrutinized their application in specific organizations both inside and outside the private sector, we focus now exclusively on flexitime. Based on information solicited from organizations named in this book and on other personal research investigations, this chapter concentrates on flexitime's limitations. The limitations listed are taken from those actually experienced as well as those that can be viewed only as potential. Consequently, although the title of the chapter is "Flexitime's Drawbacks," it should be understood that the drawbacks identified may or may not occur in an organization that establishes a gliding time program.

What follows is the specific identification of both actual and potential flexitime drawbacks. After each stated drawback is a brief clarification, including an illustration.

Some Jobs May Go Uncovered
Unless starting, quitting, and midday-flexibility bands are given adequate employee coverage, customer service may deteriorate.

Illustration. A large home-building and remodeling center located on the outskirts of an eastern city has a flexitime plan. The company is open five days each week from 7:00 A.M. until 5:30 P.M. Employees work an 8-hour day and 40 hours per week. FST is between 7:00 and 9:00 in the morning, and FQT spans the 3:30 to 5:30 P.M. period. Core time extends from 9:00 in the morning until 3:30 in the afternoon, interrupted only by a ½-hour fixed lunch break. Within the flexible time schedule, workers in each sales department coordinate as a team in arranging their own individual working hours. The store manager is required to see that sales areas are adequately staffed at all times.

According to the manager, problems with the schedule do arise, as there are occasions when salespersons fail to synchronize work arrival and departure times. Whenever this type of failure occurs, a time segment exists during which a department area is not adequately staffed.

The System Is Difficult to Apply on Assembly Lines and with Multiple Shifts

Assembly-line operations, especially in combination with multiple shifts, may preclude application of flexitime. Under such work conditions, staggered hours may be the most viable alternative for a firm that desires to incorporate an alternative work schedule.

Illustration. An assembly-line foreman in an automobile manufacturing plant says to his subordinates: "Flexitime? Maybe it would be nice, but it wouldn't work here. All you guys know that you've got to be here in the morning when we start the line, and we've all got to leave nine hours later and with everything in order for the next shift. Here we have to come to work, and leave work, at the same time."

Some Job Functions Prevent Employees from Participating in the System

The duties and responsibilities of certain jobs make it impossible for persons holding those jobs to be included in flexitime arrangements. For example, at Scott Paper Company in Philadelphia, some groups of workers (for example, telephone operators and receptionists) may be quite limited in their individual choices. At the American Optometric Association's headquarters in St. Louis, the receptionist/switchboard operator and maintenance personnel fall into this category. At the U.S. Geological Survey, 15 percent of the employees are excluded from participation because of the nature of their jobs. Eastern Air Lines and the Pacific Gas & Electric Company also exclude certain jobs from flexitime coverage.

Illustration. At a midwest manufacturing firm that produces electrical components for automobile ignition systems, a personnel director says: "We're a big, complex outfit. If I don't know anything else, I do know that when you initiate a new type of benefit you've got to include people in all departments. In our firm flexitime would work in some departments, but not in others. And even within a particular department where the plan might be workable, some workers might have to be excluded from participating. Since we couldn't use it plantwide, we won't consider it. All we need is to open another can of worms. We've got enough interdepartmental friction as it is."

Additional Problems in Organizing Training Classes

Where most employees at a firm work a fixed workday schedule, almost all of them are at the company location during operating hours. Setting up training classes is less difficult, as employees are already at the job site and able to participate. Such may not be the case under flexitime. It is probable that not all workers will be present or available for training sessions within flexible starting and quitting segments.

Illustration. At a small firm in Michigan that makes an assortment of brass fittings, the production superintendent says: "We don't pay the highest wages here, and we experience rather high turnover. Quite often we set up training sessions from 4:00 P.M. until 5:00 P.M. We can't have those very people who need their skills upgraded leaving at 3:30 or 4:00 in the afternoon. As I understand it, they'd have a right to leave work early under most of those flexitime programs. We couldn't let that happen here."

An Increase in Buffer Stocks May be Necessary

An increase in inventory of buffer stocks, and additional distribution locations for parts and in-process supplies, may represent additional costs.

Illustration. A watch manufacturer installed flexitime. In more than one department, in-process inventory supplies had to be distributed over a larger number of locations in order that supplies would be immediately available to employees coming to work early or quitting late. The added inventory plus the greater amount of space taken up by the additional buffer-stock locations constituted increased costs, according to the company.

More Costs Because of Physical-Plant Energy Requirements

Employees performing work functions over a greater span of hours may produce additional costs associated with the energy requirements of the physical plant.

Illustration. Let us take the case of the headquarters of a large insurance firm employing a great many clerical workers. Assume that the flexible-quitting-time band extends until 8:30 P.M. In various offices where large numbers of employees extend their workday until close to 8:30, additional office lights will remain turned on during evening hours (at least during the winter months). In other words, more electricity is consumed in this work situation than in a situation where the 8:00 A.M. to 5:00 P.M. fixed schedule is in operation. Added energy requirements mean higher costs to the firm. In addition, extra energy usage runs counter to national conservation programs.

Less Management Flexibility in Calling Meetings

Where many employees are not available outside the core time, management has less flexibility in determining when to hold meetings. At the U.S. Geological Survey it was found that 13 percent of all managers above the first-line supervisor frequently or occasionally set up meetings outside the core time. Some employees were not able to attend those meetings.

Illustration. Earlier this week office manager Harry Smith received a communication from the company's comptroller urging all managers to familiarize themselves with new expenditure reimbursement policies and procedures. Harry had intended to hold a meeting Friday afternoon during core time for the purpose of explaining the new program to the office workforce. But he forgot to call the meeting. It is now late in the afternoon on a Friday preceding an extra-long weekend. Harry assesses the situation and concludes that he cannot call the meeting during the flexible-quitting-time band because not that many employees are at work. They've already left for the day.

Lunchtime Talking May Interfere with Work

Especially where a flexitime program includes a midday-flex period, added options available to employees may, in certain instances, interfere with and distract other persons at work.

Illustration. One business firm, located in the downtown area of a large city, supplies linens and towels to various companies. Many of the firm's office workers eat lunch while seated at their desks. Under the fixed hours system, people talking and laughing over lunch caused no drop in efficiency because no one was on the clock. Everyone was on lunch break. Now, however, under flexitime and a midday-flex band, some people sit at their desks and talk over lunch, while other employees are at their desks nearby trying to work.

Cafeteria Hours May Have to Be Extended

Where a firm provides cafeteria facilities to its employees, the cafeteria may have to remain open for additional hours. The extra hours mean additional company expenditures, especially in the form of labor costs. Whether the problem is solved by adding full-time workers, adding part-time workers, or using overtime, all three methods necessitate higher costs.

Illustration. At a large eastern insurance firm a fixed workday previously began at 8:30 A.M. Now, with adaptable hours, flexible starting time ranges from 7:30 to 9:30 in the morning. As a result, the company cafeteria opens 1½ hours earlier in the day.

Car-Pool Arrangements May Be Disrupted

Following installation of flexitime, the employee preferring the car-pool method for getting to and from work may experience more difficulties in making transportation arrangements. For example, after the Social Security Administration installed flexitime in its Baltimore offices, a number of employees no longer used car pools.

Illustration. Mary, who works at a west coast electronics firm, says: "Before flexitime, working out car-pool arrangements was a cinch. Everyone had to arrive at work at the same time, and there were all kinds of car pools. Now, under flexitime, there are not as many car pools when I want to go to work."

Latecomers May Find a Parking Lot Filled with Cars

As documented by the experiences of the many companies discussed in this book, after flexitime is incorporated most employees arrive at work at an earlier hour. Granted, most people who switch to an earlier arrival hour do so because of personal preference. Yet there are instances where earlier arrival may be dictated by other reasons. For example, being able to find an open parking space may be a main reason for arriving early. At one Social Security Administration location in the Baltimore area, just that development—and explanation—did occur.

Illustration. At a public utility located in an industrial park outside a medium-size city, an employee says: "Out here we've got the company parking lot, and that's about it as far as parking goes. The company has a variable hours plan. Whenever I come to work near the end of the flexible-starting-time band, I have a hell of a time finding a parking spot. That's probably a main reason why I've been coming to work earlier than usual."

Managers and Professionals May Perceive a Loss of Status

As the reader recalls, at some firms where flexitime was brought in, managers and professionals were included among all employees who had to "punch in and out"—or use the Flextime Machine, if that time-recording instrument was purchased. Many managers and professionals accept the new practice, realizing that it is important for time-recording purposes. Yet some may perceive such a requirement as a loss of status.

Illustration. A large eastern bank uses gliding time. Even the assistant manager is "on the clock," which previously was not the case. He says: "Although I don't voice this in the bank, I don't mind telling you that flexitime lowers my professional status. At least that's my opinion."

An Additional Time System May Mean More Confusion

Some firms have multiple working-time patterns in operation simultaneously, all arrangements interfacing with one another. For example, at Eastern Air Lines, the John Hancock Life Insurance Company, and the Control Data Corporation, four systems operate in conjunction with one another.

Illustration. The comptroller at one firm (not one of those listed above) says: "Even with all our latest computer hardware, I must confess that at times it's a bit bewildering—having different working-time patterns in operation at the same time."

Purchasing Sophisticated Time-Recording Equipment Costs Money

With a fixed workday schedule, a relatively small firm may use a simple manual system to record work time and find that system to be quite satisfactory. When installing a gliding time system, however, a firm may decide to change over to more sophisticated time-recording equipment. Where an organization converts to flexitime and does update its time-recording hardware, the new equipment requires additional expenditures.

Illustration. At a midwest company that manufactures an assortment of heavy-duty brushes used in sweeping and cleaning streets and sidewalks, the comptroller says: "Actually, I think flexitime would work here, but we would incur added expenditures in purchasing more sophisticated time-recording equipment. Employees probably would like the plan, but I don't think it would result in any hike in productivity."

Internal Communications Within a Department May Be Weakened

In contrast to a working-time pattern that compels all employees to be at work during a fixed time frame, a pattern that allows employees to choose different work hours at their individual discretion may make it more difficult for employees within a department to communicate with one another.

Illustration. At a supply company that has incorporated variable hours, the office manager says: "At 4:00 P.M. yesterday I planned to talk to Jane, a clerical worker, about the quality of the latest work she turned in. But I discovered that she had gone home at 3:30, at the end of the core-time period."

Internal Communications Between Different Departments May Be Weakened

This point concerns the issue of interface. Can people working in two different departments contact one another? As the reader recalls, under flexitime, Hewlett-Packard Corporation had trouble with interdepartmental communications. As the company phrased it, some problems arose in "interfacing with other departments."

Illustration. One morning the head of design engineering at a boat manufacturing firm wished to phone Jim Jackson, assistant manager in the purchasing department, to inquire whether equipment received did indeed match order specs. The engineering official was not able to talk to the manager in purchasing. The secretary said, "I don't know for sure when Mr. Jackson will be here this morning. Sometimes he comes in early, and at other times he arrives near the end of the flexible starting band."

External Communications with Outside Organizations May Be Weakened

Under flexitime, communications between two different organizations may be weakened.

Illustration. An official at a business supply firm wanted to talk with the assistant manager of purchasing at a manufacturing company. The supply firm had sent the company a large shipment of goods. On receipt of the order the manager in purchasing was alerted by "In-Bound Shipment" that the shipment received was in error. Quality of merchandise received did not match quality specifications ordered. The manager in purchasing left word that the supplier should phone him. During the late afternoon on a particular Monday the supplier phoned, but was instructed to call back on the following day, as the assistant manager—working under a flexitime schedule—had already gone home.

More Sophisticated Planning, Organizing, and Control Are Necessary

Under gliding time it is especially necessary that a manager carry out the planning, organizing, and control functions effectively. Poor planning and organizing will compound control problems.

Illustration. At a commercial laundry where flexitime is in operation, Phyllis arrived at the office on Tuesday morning at 6:30—the earliest flexible starting time. Between 6:30 and 8:00 she was busy at work putting customer bills into envelopes and sealing the envelopes. On that same morning the supervisor, Mr. Laws, arrived at work at 8:00. As Mr. Laws walked into the building he said to himself: "Let's see. Yesterday I forgot to give Phyllis the latest customer billings. The first thing I must tell her is to bring those customer accounts up to date before she makes up the bills and mails them out."

Resentment Among Those Not Able to Leave Work Early

On initiating a flexitime program, companies observe that most employees prefer to start the workday toward the front end of the FST band. They are then able to end the workday early, at or near the beginning of the flexible-quitting-time band. But many organizations find it necessary to provide work coverage over an entire workday. Consequently, some individuals preferring to depart early are not allowed to do so.

For example, Alexander Hamilton Institute in New York City detects some resentment among those who are asked to remain on duty beyond the afternoon core time. Also, the reader recalls that survey questionnaires to employees frequently include a question along the line of: "Do you feel resentment toward those employees who leave work early?" This clearly indicates that organizations are concerned over a possible backlash effect.

Illustration. At a packaging firm on flexitime, an office worker says: "All too often my boss wants me to work after core time. It bugs me when I see others go home at 3:00 in the afternoon."

The System May Be Cumbersome for a Large Organization

Especially in large organizations where coordination is vital over an intricate network of departments, gliding time may be cumbersome and result in confusion and extra costs in the planning, organizing, and control functions.

Illustration. A manager at a giant petroleum corporation said: "We have thousands of employees. Under a flexitime plan it would be next to impossible to keep track of the comings and goings of our workers. Monitoring the system would be a gigantic headache. Such a plan would be too costly to implement in our company."

Overtime-Pay Requirements May Run Counter to Debit and Credit Options

Firms installing flexitime programs that include the option of debiting and crediting work hours may experience additional difficulties on federal contract work.

Illustration. A manufacturer of office furniture has a flexitime program offering crediting and debiting options. The firm's employees view the program with great enthusiasm and satisfaction. In the past the company was not a federal government contractor. More recently, in investigating the possibilities of obtaining government contracts, the company learned that such contracts require that employers pay their employees overtime-pay rates for work in excess of 8 hours a day. Management then realized that this requirement would clash with the debiting and crediting provisions in the company's flexitime work schedule.

Having seen 21 different drawbacks, the reader may be tempted to conclude: "Now that I've read this chapter, my present thinking is that flexitime isn't such a great idea." Such an assessment, however, would be a bit premature. The reader should keep in mind a statement made at the beginning of this chapter, namely, that the drawbacks identified should be considered as potential only. They may or may not occur in an organization that establishes a flexitime program.

Let us now examine the positive side of the ledger.

Flexitime's advantages

Flexitime offers an extensive variety of benefits to various segments of society. The main purpose of this chapter is to identify those multiple benefits. In this as in the preceding chapter, the rationale is that the effects are real but not inevitable.

In actual situations, benefits interrelate with one another and are not exclusive to a particular category. For reasons of organization and clarification, however, the advantages of flexitime are discussed under five major headings.

Benefits to the Community

Gliding time benefits communities in various ways, some of which may be peculiar to a particular locale. In general, however, five specific advantages stand out.

Reduction in Rush-Hour Traffic Congestion

As masses of automobiles enter and leave metropolitan areas during rush hours, congestion is sure to result. Traffic congestion is experienced directly by drivers and passengers in automobiles, trucks, and buses; but pedestrians are also directly affected, sometimes to the extent that attempting to cross a main boulevard on foot is about as safe as attempting to walk across the Indianapolis Speedway during an Indy 500 race.

Illustration. A city government official in Chicago says: "Should large numbers of organizations in a metropolitan area incorporate flexitime, less congestion would be experienced by drivers and passengers in vehicles. Furthermore, pedestrians would experience greater safety."

Tax Savings Through Less Road Building

The greater the crush of cars on the periphery of a city and on its inner streets during peak rush-hour traffic, the more intense the lobbying for new expressways and for wider roads. Needless to add, road building and additional maintenance costs hit the citizenry in the pocketbook.

Illustration. A transportation officer in one midwestern city reports: "Should large numbers of organizations in a metropolitan area incorporate flexitime, traffic otherwise occurring during peak rush-hour time periods would be spread over a greater number of hours. Such a development would place less pressure on existing road arteries, and one result could well be less clamor for bigger and better roads."

Energy Savings Through Better Gasoline Mileage

Recently the Environmental Protection Agency assessed the impact of altered work schedules on energy consumption by commuters in urban areas. The EPA report shows that flexible schedules could result in reduced energy consumption by commuters because of increased travel speed from improved traffic flow.

Illustration. An employee at a Los Angeles insurance firm says: "Our company has flexitime. I do believe that I get a little better gas mileage when commuting to and from work. I don't have to start and stop the car as often because I don't hit as many traffic jams. With the flexitime program, I don't have to drive to and from work during rush hours."

Reduction in Noise Pollution

Industrial audiologists are increasing the extent to which they monitor noise levels in manufacturing facilities. There are also demands from private citizens for reductions in maximum noise thresholds allowed for products ranging from snowmobiles to power-driven lawnmowers. In addition, more communities are demonstrating concern over noise levels. Whether or not the French-British supersonic transport Concorde should be allowed to land at east coast airports is a recent case in point. In brief, the issue of noise is a subject of deep and widespread concern.

Illustration. An environment specialist phrases it this way: "When tens of thousands of people leave their homes and apartments at the same time and begin driving to work, excessive noise pollution results. With expansion of the use of flexitime, the movements of a city's workforce is distributed over wider time spans. Fewer automobiles on metropolitan streets at a given time means a reduction in noise levels."

Less Public Transit Equipment Saves Taxpayers Money
Massive applications of flexitime would assist communities and taxpayers through a leveling out in the need for expensive peak-hour public transit equipment.

Illustration. A California administrator voices the comment: "In metropolitan areas, additional subway cars and/or buses are required to handle the flood of people on their way to and from work during peak commuting hours. Through expansion of gliding time programs and the accompanying varied starting and quitting work times, less strain would be placed on a transit system during what now are critical time periods. In brief, cities would not require as many pieces of equipment to move people. Reductions in the need for this equipment represent savings to taxpayers."

Off-the-Job Advantages to Employees

Gliding time is in harmony with the trend toward greater freedom of choice and discretion in the use of time and the pursuit of interests off the job.

Off-the-Job Benefits
A great variety of off-the-job benefits await the employee eligible to enjoy flexitime, as frequently noted in preceding chapters. More free time in the morning or afternoon, more leisure time to engage in personal off-the-job interests and activities, time to take care of personal business, more time for the family—these are all major advantages to be derived through flexitime.

Because so many illustrations on the same theme have already appeared throughout the book, only one is included here.

Illustration. Under a fixed hours plan Diane worked a standard 8:00-to-5:00 day. Because she had little free time during the workweek, she took care of her errands on Saturday. After the company brought in flexitime, Diane was able to discharge most errand obligations on late afternoons *during* the workweek; consequently, Saturday became a day with more freedom for spontaneous activities.

Advantages to Employees Directly Related to the Job

There are at least 15 interrelated benefits attributable in part to flexitime that tie in directly to an individual's job.

A More Logical Alignment of Off-the-Job Interests with Job Responsibilities

A framework is established that provides for a more logical alignment of an employee's off-the-job interests with his or her job responsibilities.

Illustrations. Consider Pete and Dan, who tend to be natural early risers and who enjoy tennis, golf, gardening, and all kinds of other outdoor activities. Under gliding time, by exercising their early-starting-time option, they're able to depart from work at an earlier afternoon hour; consequently, they have more free time in which to indulge in their favorite outdoor activities after work. By contrast, consider the special interests of Susan, an unmarried career woman. Susan enjoys occasional dating during the week; thus, on the morning after a date she can arrive at work at a later hour, namely, at the end of the flexible-starting-time band.

A Reduction in Employees' Commuting Problems

In different ways, flexitime reduces the number of problems confronting employees trying to get to and from work.

Illustrations. Eric, working under flexitime for a government agency in New York City, is actually able to get a seat on the subway by adjusting his starting and quitting times. Elaine, an employee for the same agency, says that during the winter months, because of gliding time, she's able to take the subway after finishing work, get off at her station, and walk home before dark. There is less likelihood that she'll be mugged when walking home during daytime hours.

Less Congestion in the Work Environment Itself

Besides enabling workers to avoid a lot of congestion on the way to and from work, flexitime offers a continuation of this same luxury in the work environment itself.

Illustration. Doris is employed by a large insurance firm that has its headquarters in a 42-story office building in New York City. She works in an office on the 29th floor. She reports: "Flexitime is great. Before we had flexitime there was a lot of waiting in line at elevator doors in the morning. Then there was the same waiting in line for an elevator at the end of the day when everyone left the building at about the same time. The same thing was true in using the company cafeteria. There was always quite a line. On those days when I chose to eat lunch at the sandwich shop or cafeteria down the street, you guessed it — more lines. That's all a thing of the past. With flexitime, elevators aren't crowded any more. And we've got midday flex from 11:30 to 2:30. People using the company cafeteria don't have to wait in lines now. With lunchtime spaced out over three hours, there's not the noontime crunch. No big lines, and no difficulties finding a vacant table. Another great feature is that on days when I go to the sandwich shop or cafeteria down the block, I don't have to go at noon. I go about 11:30 in the morning or after 1:00 in the afternoon, when it's a lot less hectic."

A Less Fatigued Worker

Flexitime can have the effect of reducing fatigue. In general, a more rested worker is a more efficient worker.

Illustration. Consider the case of the Larsons, a Florida couple who take their two children to Disney World on a Sunday. The family leaves home at 8:00 A.M. Awaiting them is a two-hour drive in their car. After a full day at Disney World the family arrives back home at 8:00 P.M. feeling happy but exhausted. As Mr. Larson falls into bed at 11:00 he says to himself: "Thank God the company where I work has gliding time. Instead of getting to work at 8:00 as usual, tomorrow morning I'll check in at 9:00 when core time begins."

Less Frustration and Anxiety in Trying to Get to Work on Time

An employee suffering from frustration and anxiety is frequently not an effective performer. Although often attributable to causes that have little to do with the employee's job, frustration and anxiety can also be produced by the ordeal of trying to get to work, especially when the ordeal is "normal." A fixed hours system allows only one reporting deadline. The person makes that deadline or does not. Flexitime provides multiple options.

Illustrations. The Scott Paper Company administered a questionnaire to its employees. One question concerned feelings of frustration in getting to work. Most workers replied by saying that they experienced less frustration under flexible hours, mainly because they were permitted to arrive later in the morning. At the Social Security Administration headquarters, workers say they experience less tension and anxiety on a particular workday when they oversleep. Here also there is no rigid and narrow definition of work starting time. Workers still get to work on time even though arrival on that day is at a later hour. A third company, Qantas Airways, found less employee tension and anxiety because there was less fear of being docked pay for lateness.

Less Need to Own Two Cars

Women constitute nearly 40 percent of the nation's workforce In situations where a man and his wife work for different organizations, frequently two cars are needed in the household.

Illustration. In Los Angeles, both Mike and his wife Marilyn work, but for different employers. Mike's company operates under a gliding time plan; Marilyn's does not. Mike adjusts his starting and quitting times to fit Marilyn's fixed hours schedule. On his way to and from work, Mike is able to drive Marilyn to and from her job.

Reduction in Job Dissatisfaction Levels

The job dissatisfaction issue relates directly to questions of humanistic management. Gliding time specifically aims to reduce a worker's feelings of job dissatisfaction.

Illustration. Larry perceives his job as "deadly boring," but flexitime at least allows him to choose the hours when he "prefers" (not "desires") to work on his "boring job."

A Spread of Democracy in the Workforce

Flexitime promotes democracy in a workforce as nonmanagerial employees join the ranks of managers having rights to flexible working hours.

Illustrations. Managers and professional employees usually enjoy considerably more discretion in determining their work hours than most other workers do. In walking out of the office a manager says to his secretary: "I'll be back in 15 minutes." During that time the manager may be engaged in solving an interoffice job problem. On the other hand, he might have decided to reward himself with a 15-minute break. Likewise, take the case of a college professor who establishes office hours during which students are able to discuss some aspect of course content with him. To a large extent, the professor establishes office hours suitable to his own preferences. In short, gliding time gives nonmanagers and nonprofessionals the rights to flexible working hours.

No Need to Wait Around Before Starting Work in the Morning

The U.S. Geological Survey questioned its supervisors in the Washington headquarters area regarding their work experiences under flexitime. Included on the questionnaire was the question: "Do you feel that your employees tend to have 'quicker starts' in the morning as a result of flexitime—that is, do employees tend to start working sooner in an effort not to distract those who have arrived earlier?" The vast majority answered "Yes."

Illustration. Debby is employed by a public utility firm and until a year ago worked under fixed hours. Official starting time was 8:30 A.M. On some days Debby arrived at the office between 8:00 and 8:15, whereupon she read the newspaper or filed her nails until she could begin work at the official starting time. The company converted to flexitime last year. Now when Debby arrives at work early she can get a quick start and begin her workday immediately, if she prefers.

No Need to Wait Around During Lunch Break

Especially where a specific gliding time program includes a midday-flex band, an employee is able each day to select not only the time at which to begin lunch but also the duration of the lunch period. Thus, a worker exercises lunch-break options to correspond to his or her on-the-job and off-the-job responsibilities on a particular day.

Illustration. Gloria works for an insurance company that uses gliding time. On Monday of last week she felt like taking an hour for lunch. On Tuesday she wanted instead to take 30 minutes for lunch and get back to work as soon as possible, so as to be able to go home earlier that afternoon.

An Earned Right to Leave Work Early

Firestone–Canada asked gliding time employees: "If others are working and you are all caught up, how do you feel about leaving before they do?" Less than 10 percent of the respondents answered "Guilty."

Illustration. Stanley is an office worker at a machine shop that is on flexitime. He claims: "Before we went on flexitime, other workers often gave me the fish-eye look when I'd ask the boss if I could leave early. With flexitime, I don't have to ask anyone if I can leave early. Now, whenever I leave — at the start of the flexible-quitting-time band — I've earned the right to do so."

The Employee Is Treated as an Adult

Related to freedom and autonomy — but not synonymous with them — is the wish to be treated as an adult. Adultlike behavior includes a need to discipline oneself and assume responsibilities. It is true that the behavior of many individuals — even "adults" — seems childlike in its lack of self-discipline, ability, motivation, and readiness to demonstrate maturity. Offering flexitime to childlike adults may well boomerang and bring dire results to an organization.

On the other hand, countless numbers of people do want addi-

tional opportunities to demonstrate that they are capable of disciplining themselves, thus proving to themselves and others that they are
responsible human beings. Certainly for most employees in this category, flexitime is a system offering opportunities and rewards.

Illustration. Roberta works in the insurance claims department
of a large insurance firm. In her words: "I like flexitime for
many reasons. It may sound dumb to say this, but with flexitime
I definitely feel that the company is treating me in an adult manner. The flexitime system itself conveys to me the following message: You are an adult. You are responsible. You are capable of
disciplining yourself. You choose your starting and quitting
times. As a mature employee you will do your job well, but during the times of the day that you yourself choose."

Recognition of Individual Differences Among Employees
Flexitime supports the proposition that there are individual differences among people. The system accommodates different life-
styles and helps people "do their own thing."

Illustration. A manager in a city government department using
flexitime explains individual differences among people in this
amusing way: "Flexitime, among other things, recognizes that
there are people who are born into the world 15 minutes to an
hour late and will always be 15 minutes to an hour late for everything. Therefore, they just can't get started early in the morning. There are also the eager beavers who are always up and
moving at the crack of dawn, but who run out of gas about 3:00
in the afternoon. The early risers and the late risers average
out."

A Morale Boost
High morale is characterized by *esprit de corps* — group spirit and
pride shared by those in the group, a sense of mutual dedication and
resourcefulness aimed at goals of task accomplishment and group satisfaction. Naturally, it is the hope of every organization that a group's
energy will be positively directed so as to support the goals and programs of the organization.

Illustration. Winifred works at a firm that installed flexitime
about three years ago. As she puts it: "There's no question about

it. The overall morale of my group has definitely improved, and to a great extent the change is because of the company's flexitime program."

An Increase in Job Satisfaction

As repeatedly demonstrated in this book, the introduction of gliding time is almost always accompanied by an increase in an employee's feelings of job satisfaction. In surveys conducted at the Social Security Administration's offices at Baltimore, at the Alexander Hamilton Institute in New York City, at the Industrial National Bank in Providence, and at about every organization examined so far, the conclusion is the same.

Illustration. Kathy works on circuit boards at an electronics firm. She reports: "I like flexitime. Not only that, I like my job better now too. What does this mean? Well, now that we're on flexitime I'd think twice about quitting. I feel that my total job situation has more pluses now. It's more rewarding. It's a job that I'd hesitate to give up. I guess this all adds up to the fact that my degree of job satisfaction is higher under flexitime."

Advantages to Organizations Based on Objective Measurements of Productivity

It is one thing to measure productivity and to record changes in upward and downward directions. Even this objective is sometimes difficult to accomplish, as in unstructured and ambiguous problem situations. It is quite another thing to isolate and identify precise causes of productivity change. Where an organization's productivity increases or decreases following installation of flexitime, it is often unwarranted to assert that flexitime caused that change.

A few companies have been able to establish an experimental group working under flexitime and to compare its performance with that of a control group not working under flexitime. In most organizations, however, flexitime has been introduced into work groups and subsequent production changes were recorded while the organizations continued to carry out their regular business functions.

In spite of obstacles, organizations aim to measure flexitime's effects on productivity. Subjective measurements of results should be included. That is, how do managers and nonmanagers *feel* about flexitime? What are their *opinions* and *attitudes*? Do they *perceive* that flexitime is causing changes in productivity? At the same time, organizations must go beyond subjective perceptions and study flexitime in terms of objective measurements—"hard data."

Most organizations believe that at least six factors serve as objective measurements of productivity: employee turnover, absenteeism, tardiness, amount of overtime, quantity of work produced, and quality of that work. Conclusions stated here on flexitime's effects on productivity use these six factors as an analysis framework. Again, the reader is reminded that most conclusions are not based on scientifically controlled experimentation.

Employee Turnover Does Not Increase
Turnover is costly to an organization, especially where an employee's departure follows this pattern: The employee is skilled, becomes dissatisfied with the firm, and subsequently quits. Companies frequently welcome the departure of undisciplined and marginal performers, but when true contributors show strong tendencies to leave the company it's a far different story

How does flexitime influence the turnover statistics of a firm? Most likely, there is no significant change in rates of turnover following installation of flexitime.

Illustration. A manager at a public utility said: "We've got flexitime. Although the system doesn't decrease turnover, as far as we can determine it certainly doesn't cause any increase in turnover rates either." The statement is applicable to most companies in most industries.

A Reduction in Absenteeism Rates
It is highly improbable that flexitime will cause absenteeism to rise. Following installation of the system, absenteeism will perhaps remain at levels similar to those occurring under a previous work system. But it is most likely that absenteeism rates will drop—because, under flexitime, employees can take care of personal matters without using sick-leave time or other company time.

Illustration. What happens at most firms is similar to this manager's picture: "Our absenteeism went down after we put in flexitime. We discovered that employees actually take more of their *own* time, and not the company's, on such things as visiting the doctor or dentist, going to the bank, getting the car repaired, and getting a haircut."

Significant Reductions in Tardiness

One of the most pronounced effects of flexitime is observed in the area of employee lateness. Use of the system has virtually eliminated problems of tardiness and lack of punctuality. Objective measurements strongly support this conclusion.

Previously, at a western utility, an employee would frequently arrive late because of a bad traffic tie-up. Now, under adaptable hours, whenever such a development occurs, the company does not absorb the time loss. The employee extends his or her workday to make up for the loss.

Illustration. A production superintendent says: "We've experienced dramatic reductions in tardiness. In effect, the person penalized by lateness is the worker himself. On any given day, if a worker's actual starting time is 15 minutes later than he desired, his quitting time is delayed 15 minutes."

Amount of Overtime Is Not Increased, and Sometimes Is Reduced

As described in previous chapters, Gulf Oil—Canada, the American Optometric Association, and the municipal government of Inglewood, California, all experienced a reduction in the amount of overtime after they began using flexitime. On the other hand, available information shows that not all flexitime users have had the same experience. The following assessment would seem valid at this time: After the initiation of flexitime, amount of overtime shows no change, or there is a slight reduction in its use. It is unlikely that flexitime causes an increase in the use of overtime.

Illustration. This manager's evaluation is similar to the findings of most flexitime users: "Generally speaking, at our company gliding time has not made a significant difference in terms of amount of employee overtime. In some departments, however, overtime has been reduced somewhat because of flexitime. One thing we are quite certain about is that flexitime does not cause more overtime use."

Output Is Not Lower under Flexitime

Performance can be evaluated in terms of the amount or level of units produced over a given time segment. In general, flexitime does not appear to have a negative effect on the quantity of units produced or processed. Although not the general rule, some organizations observe an increase in quantity of output where employees work under gliding hours.

Illustration. Organizations using adaptable hours generally report results similar to those reported by a manager in an electronics firm: "In our organization, performance, measured in terms of the quantity or number of units produced, is not affected by flexitime. At least this tends to be the case in most departments. In other words, quantity of work produced is about the same under flexitime as under the previous system. It should be pointed out, however, that in some departments it has been noted that quantity has risen when employees worked under an adaptable hours schedule."

Quality of Work Remains the Same, or Is Higher

When contrasted to the results achieved under a different working-time pattern, the quality of one's performance under gliding time may remain the same, or be improved. Only infrequently does the quality of a worker's performance show deterioration under flexitime.

Illustration. Prior to Hewlett-Packard's conversion to flexitime, most errors made by computer personnel occurred during the first 30 minutes on the job. It appeared that people would end a previous workday when it was *time* to stop. In most instances they would stop in the middle of a task or operation instead of working until its completion. That is, they were more time-oriented than task-oriented. In contrast, under flexitime, computer personnel became more task-oriented near the end of a day. They were more likely to stop work on completing a task rather than stop work because of a particular time of day. Starting a workday with a new task resulted in fewer errors and better-quality work.

A point of view is now in order. In using turnover as the example, one may ask: "If flexitime shows no change, why is the program an advantage?" What is essential here is to view flexitime's benefits and detriments from a systems perspective. In other words, where results take the form of significant benefits in numerous other areas (for example, job satisfaction and morale) while at the same time turnover rates *do not rise,* use of flexitime is advantageous.

Other Benefits to Organizations

In addition to objective measurements indicating that productivity either remains at the same level or shows improvement under flexitime, the new working-time pattern offers additional advantages to organizations.

An Expanded Workday Allows for More Contact with Clients
Many organizations using flexitime establish and maintain a wider bandwidth than do organizations using fixed hours. Many of these organizations are able to utilize the extra hours in ways that provide more service to clients without thereby adding to the direct labor costs. This is done, of course, in two ways: (1) building FST and FQT bands into the system, and (2) requiring adequate work coverage over all hours in which facilities remain open. With facilities open over more hours, organizations in both the private and public sectors are afforded additional opportunities to deal with their respective clients.

> **Illustration.** At one municipal government agency, the manager in charge of automobile licenses and vehicle registration said: "No question about it, we do a better job now of dealing with the public. Our offices are open more hours each day. Now people can phone us, and come to our offices, during hours when we'd have been closed under the previous work system."

Leaving Late Messages During the FQT Band
As described in previous chapters, some organizations detect a trouble spot with flexitime in matters of internal communication. Although the legitimacy of this issue should not be downgraded, at the same time it should be pointed out that flexitime has built into it a compensatory mechanism that helps eradicate both actual and poten-

tial internal communication problems. Flexible quitting time, especially when the band is wide, allows both managers and nonmanagers opportunities to leave late messages for fellow workers. As the reader recalls, an engineer at Pacific Gas & Electric Company thought the FQT band helped compensate for workday occasions when it was difficult to communicate with other employees.

Illustration. Late one afternoon near the end of the FQT band, the assistant manager of a bank's new-accounts department wrestled with the problem of what strategy would best convince a potential new client to bring his business to the bank. The assistant manager identified the problem in writing and placed the memo on John White's desk, hoping the matter would be acted upon first thing in the morning. John White usually arrived at the bank each day prior to the assistant manager; on arriving at the bank the next morning, White worked out his list of suggestions and had the information available when the assistant manager walked into the bank.

A Better Opportunity to Hire Skilled Workers During Tight Labor Markets

A firm offering a flexitime work schedule has an advantage over firms of similar size and prestige not using the plan. Flexitime is a definite aid to a company's recruiting and hiring program. Firestone Corporation–Canada is one of a number of companies holding this view.

Illustration. A personnel manager at a medium-size company reports: "Although our firm doesn't have flexitime now, we're considering adopting it. A major company in the area has installed flexitime. Frankly speaking, we're afraid we may lose a number of skilled employees unless we install flexitime."

A Better Opportunity to Hire Female Employees

Flexitime is an excellent vehicle for recruiting and hiring female employees.

Illustrations. A Social Security Administration official says of flexitime: "It is attractive to the unmarried career woman for whom dating and other social activities are vital. In different yet equally beneficial ways, it serves the needs of the working mother who wants to see her children off to school in the morning before she departs for work. Or perhaps she prefers to work early in the morning and arrive home at about the same time as her children return from school."

The System Promotes Cross-Training

It is advantageous for companies to have employees who are able to perform well on more than one job. Especially in non-unionized organizations, a qualified and cross-trained worker is able to fill in for a fellow worker during the latter's absence. Productivity is not likely to suffer when temporary job situations are handled by capable people. Many employees desire opportunities for cross-training. It tends to increase the employee's overall sense of job satisfaction. Finally, cross-trained employees are in an advantageous position in regard to promotion eligibility.

Flexitime requires adequate job coverage. Positions must be staffed at all times. It is therefore necessary in some cases that people learn more than one job—to be able to cover for one another. Cross-training is promoted in such a work climate. For example, at the U.S. Geological Survey, about 10 percent of the agency's employees in the District of Columbia area experienced more cross-training under flexitime.

Illustration. At one firm using flexitime, an office worker said: "We're a small company with fewer than 50 people. Under fixed hours I had to do my job, but I didn't have to be concerned with what other people did. Now we're under flexitime. It works. But I had to learn more jobs, because frequently we have to fill in for one another."

Improved Communication over Different Time Zones

Organizations, like human beings, strive to improve their communication effectiveness. Situations in which flexitime may create internal communication problems have been mentioned in earlier chapters. On the other hand, flexitime can greatly increase an organization's ability to communicate by phone with other companies across the country—as well as with divisions of its own company at widely scattered locations. For instance, because of flexitime, organizations like the Northwestern Mutual Life Insurance Company and the American Optometric Association are able to maintain phone contact between their respective offices in different geographical areas and in different time zones throughout the full workday. This was not possible under previous fixed hours work scheduling.

Illustration. An international firm has its headquarters offices in New York City and its western division headquarters in San Diego, California. When all company locations were on fixed hours, personnel in New York were unable to contact personnel in San Diego until late morning because of the three-hour difference between eastern and western time zones. Now that the western division is on flexitime, its offices are open—though not fully staffed—two hours earlier. Consequently, on every workday, communication lines between east and west coast offices are open and can be utilized for two additional hours.

Quiet Time for Work Requiring Special Concentration

In certain work situations, an individual or a small group needs quiet time during which to work out particularly difficult problems requiring special concentration. Flexitime offers that individual or that small group this quiet-time advantage.

Illustration. Martin, a scientist with an aerospace firm, works in research and development. In his section the FST band begins at 5:00 in the morning—highly unusual for most firms, but not an unusual time to begin tackling certain scientific problems. Martin frequently begins his workday at 5:00 A.M. True, on those days his workday is over early in the afternoon. But the main reason why he often arrives at that early hour is to take advantage of the quiet time for work, when not many others are there.

The System Promotes Participation and a Team Approach to Problem Solving

Sophisticated organizations encourage participation in problem solving and a team approach to decision making. Flexitime works in both these directions. It acts as a magnet drawing managers and non-managers together. For example, at its headquarters in St. Louis, the American Optometric Association noted a closer relationship between supervisors and employees in the planning, organizing, and controlling phases of the work. Questionnaire surveys in the same organization brought out attitudes confirming this development. Teamwork and participation in problem solving are features of a smooth-functioning flexitime program.

Illustration. A medium-size company in the midwest uses flexitime. A clerical employee offered this thought: "Before, it seemed that the supervisor's intention was to tell us what to do one minute before we were supposed to do it. We were not called upon to say much about planning and organizing our work. Now things are different; we're on gliding time. With people coming and going at different hours, more advance planning and organizing of work are necessary. The boss works *with* us now, and not just in exercising control. We all work together. He seems to want our ideas and suggestions."

Increased Loyalty to the Organization

Where people working under flexitime like the system — and the vast majority do — they tend to think about their employer in more favorable terms. Attitudes that are positive often translate into overt behavior that is supportive of an employer.

Illustration. An employee at a midwestern manufacturing firm tells this story: "About three years ago a lot of guys in the shop began talking rather seriously about forming an independent union, but it never got beyond the talking stage. I don't know if all that talk about a union scared the company, but two years ago management brought up the flexitime idea. It sounded good. Anyway, we've been on flexitime for almost two years, and just about everybody likes the program. Incidentally, last year a big national union tried to organize the shop, and they didn't get to first base. Although I can't say for sure, I do believe that the workforce is a little more loyal to the company now. The flexitime program in operation may be one reason."

Development of a Healthier Organizational Climate

Where gliding time fosters teamwork, participation in decision making, greater job satisfaction, and higher morale levels, the strong possibility exists that employees will be more trustful of company intentions and less resistant to change.

Illustration. States a worker at a firm in Dallas, Texas: "We've got an adaptable hours plan. To make it really work everyone works together as a team. We're not distant from one another. We share ideas, and we're not afraid to try out new ways of doing things. The adaptable hours plan is an example. Especially since we've been on that new work schedule, the overall atmosphere or climate at work is even more positive."

Thirty-seven flexitime advantages have been examined in this chapter. It is important to be reminded that a number of the advantages may never materialize. While all of them are real, none of them is inevitable.

10

How to set up
a flexitime
program
in your organization

Do flexitime's advantages outweigh its disadvantages? Where organizations adopt flexitime, does the change represent a step in the right direction? Such questions cannot properly be answered with an absolute "Yes" or "No." More valid as an initial response would be "It depends" or "It is contingent."

Since no two organizations are exactly alike in all ways, it is imperative that each organization critically analyze its own particular situation to determine whether flexitime is feasible. What is the *organization's function?* What type of organization is it, and what does it do essentially? Also, what is the *nature of its business requirements?* Who are its owners, creditors, suppliers, and customers, and what are their expectations? Would adoption of gliding time present legal obstacles? What are the *organization's objectives in regard to flexitime?* What particular problems does the organization hope to solve by installing the system?

Concerning its *societal responsibilities*, if the firm were to adopt flexitime, would there be a significant impact on the community?

Part of the content of the opening pages of this chapter is based on my revision of information contained in *Flexitime — A Guide*, by Barbara L. Fiss (Washington, D.C.: U.S. Government Printing Office, 1975), pp. 7–17.

221

Which types of *employee wants* are basically satisfied, which types are activated but largely unsatisfied, and what is the order and intensity of feeling about unsatisfied wants? And what of the *organizational climate?* Throughout the various hierarchical levels and in the many different vertical and horizontal interrelationships, are attitudes mainly open, positive, and receptive to change; or closed, negative, and resistant to change? In appraising flexitime, all these major question areas deserve consideration.

Many readers are perhaps now saying: "I agree, but such an approach is too general. What I'm looking for are specifics, not glittering generalities. If I'm interested in considering flexitime for my organization, how do I go about it? Give me specifics." This chapter is aimed at fulfilling just such a request. What is presented is a sequential outline of suggested steps to follow, from a determination of flexitime's feasibility to an evaluation of an extensive flexitime program in operation.

Determining the Feasibility of Flexitime

An Outline of Suggested Steps

1. *Establish a Feasibility Study Group.* This initial group should be small, numbering not more than five persons. The group's work will involve considerable time, and it is recommended that the group be composed mainly of employees whose permanent positions in the organization are of a staff nature. Also, select individuals who occupy positions that provide them with an overview of the operation of the organization (for example, personnel, planning, employee relations).

2. *Define Your Objectives.* What unique characteristics and special problems exist in your workforce? Are *human relations* problems critical — issues such as group morale, employee satisfaction, trust, loyalty, organizational climate, and the like? Or are the main problems *workload* or *task* in nature?

3. *Define and Describe Your Workforce.* Prepare a detailed staffing document if none is available. Include:
   (a) Total number of employees
   (b) Number of supervisors and other workers
   (c) Number and kinds of jobs

This document will provide you with the basic information needed to determine the amount of flexibility that may be possible. Furthermore, it will provide you with information useful at a subsequent stage — when analyzing flexitime results.

4. *Tentatively Identify Work Groups to Be Excluded.* As explained in preceding chapters, the nature of some jobs and the need to provide adequate job coverage frequently disqualify certain jobs from flexitime scheduling. Such jobs may require the use of staggered hours, flexitour, group flexibility, or fixed hours. Shift personnel, telephone operators, cleaning and maintenance crews, security guards, cafeteria workers, and health-unit members are examples of employees who are oftentimes excluded from flexitime participation. On the other hand, since not all organizations are identical in all respects, particular jobs should not automatically be disqualified from inclusion in the system. Especially at this step, a judgment as to inclusion or exclusion should be tentative and not absolute.

5. *Examine Workload and Interface Factors.* At least three basic activities should be performed at this step.
   (a) Identify peak workload periods. Do workloads in the different sections of the organization vary, with a light or heavy load occurring at different times of the day, week, or month?
   (b) Quantify these factors where it is possible to do so.
   (c) Identify interdependency among departments, offices, groups, and individuals.

6. *Involve the Union.* Where employees are represented by a union, the bargaining unit will have a definite interest in management's flexitime plans. The organization should recognize that the involvement of union representatives will contribute to and assist in subsequent worker understanding and acceptance of flexitime. At least this is true where union officials accept and support the plan. In brief, the organization should consider taking the following actions:
   (a) Inform the local union of management's intent at an early stage in the flexitime feasibility study. Go through the joint union-management cooperation committee, if

one exists, or invite the union to send a representative to a briefing session.

(b) Seek out the views of union spokespersons.

(c) Keep the union informed of progress and new developments.

(d) Appraise the union's reaction to the flexitime concept. If a union is going to take a stance of opposition, or offer counterposition suggestions, it is best to get such views out in the open sooner rather than later.

As it works through the six steps leading toward a decision on flexitime's feasibility, the study group is obtaining specific information on a number of important questions. Does the flexitime concept have application to the organization's problems? Does it appear to offer some solutions? Given the organization's basic function and the nature of its business requirements, which jobs and workloads could be included in the flexitime program and which would have to be excluded? Do the excluded positions constitute a large part of the workforce, or are they a fairly self-contained unit? What kinds of problems could result from their exclusion? What is the union's reaction to the flexitime idea?

Once the appropriate steps have been taken, the study group should interpret the data and be in a position to submit a report to the appropriate organization head as to whether or not the use of flexitime would be advantageous. If the report is unfavorable, then further flexitime study is not needed. If, on the other hand, the report is favorable, attention should then focus on the next major step, namely, carrying out a flexitime pilot study.

Carrying Out a Flexitime Pilot Study

In the process of setting up a trial run, two alternative procedures present themselves. One: Install flexitime for a limited number of months in all departments and units where feasibility is indicated, and measure results at the end of that period. Two: Install flexitime for a limited number of months in one or more representative work units and, after the elapsed time period, measure results.

Especially for medium-size and large organizations the latter procedure is definitely preferred and recommended. Installing flexitime in a selected number of work units provides an additional way to confirm or question the study group's original conclusion, namely, that flexitime would prove effective if installed. Furthermore, it is far less costly than incorporating the system throughout the organization only to find that it is unworkable. In brief, the limited approach provides an additional checking device, is less complicated, and is the least costly way to test the system.

An Outline of Suggested Steps

1. *Identify the Work Unit or Units to Be Included.* Included in this initial step is the need to make decisions on how flexitime is to be assessed. One way to go about this is to determine the work units to be included under flexitime (referred to as the "experimental group") and, on the basis of various performance and employee acceptance factors, to compare these units with "identical" work units not included under flexitime. The latter units (the "control group") would continue working under the schedule in use at the time.

   But a second way is available to organizations that find it inexpedient to set up an experimental work unit during ongoing business operations. They can apply flexitime to departments and jobs in their everyday functioning and compare these results with those obtained prior to the innovation.

   I've chosen to focus on this latter approach for three main reasons. (1) The "Before–After" method is practical. (2) If the method is used correctly, the results are valid and meaningful. (3) It may be the *only* reasonable way for small firms to assess flexitime. For example, an organization with a total workforce of 50 employees is not in a position to establish experimental and control groups.

2. *Enlist the Support of Participating Department Managers.* Explain the nature of the experimental program with the aim of gaining the cooperation and support of participating managers. Department managers should in turn assist in communicating program particulars to managers at lower levels. Also, at this point the study group and participating

department managers should mutually determine the specific time period within which the pilot test of flexitime will
take place.

3. *Identify the Job Positions to Be Excluded from the Program.*
   Primarily on the basis of job coverage needs, managers
   should be instructed to identify positions in their respective
   units that must be excluded from participation in flexitime.

4. *Enlist Union Cooperation.* If a union exists, discuss program
   particulars with union officials and aim to win their cooperation and support.

5. *Determine Core Time.* The team of study-group members and
   department managers should establish the specific core-
   time band.

6. *Determine Flexible Time Bands.* The management-staff team
   should establish the FST and FQT bands.

7. *Consider Legal and Regulatory Requirements.* The organization
   must make certain that the core band as well as the FST and
   FQT bands are not in conflict with legal and regulatory
   requirements.

8. *Select Criteria for Evaluating Results.* This issue involves finding the best method to measure success or failure of the
   flexitime system in the pilot setting. The key lies in the
   careful selection of those elements that provide the most
   valid basis for measurement.

   (a) Identify appropriate criteria—those factors that take the
       form of targets or goals (often discussed in terms of
       standards), and that must be attained to a reasonable
       degree if operations are to be defined as successful.

       Chapter 9 deals with flexitime's advantages and in
       various ways is a discussion of criteria. As shown there, it
       is important that an organization establish *objective cri-
       teria* in the form of "hard measurements" of operations.
       Levels of employee turnover, absenteeism, tardiness or
       lack of punctuality, overtime, quality of product or serv-
       ice, and quantity are six criteria frequently included as
       important objective measurements of performance and
       productivity. The organization aims for low-level read-

ings in the first four of the criteria and high-level readings in the latter two. Each organization is of course
unique and should therefore aim to identify additional
productivity criteria peculiar to its own business function.

In addition, there are *subjective criteria*. These involve the feelings, attitudes, perceptions, and behavioral
tendencies of employees. Group morale, level of job satisfaction, and work motivation are important subjective
barometers.

(b) Design tests to measure flexitime results. Selecting the
criteria for these tests is a two-step process: it necessitates identifying both objective and subjective standards.
In addition, however, test instruments must be formulated for measuring the degree to which the standards
are achieved.

The tests are not actually used until a later step is
undertaken, that of evaluating results. However, as part
of the overall task of selecting criteria, it is expedient to
go ahead with constructing the test instruments; they
will then be available for later use.

Later in this chapter, and where appropriate, I
shall present specific and rather complete test instruments.

9. *Plan for Building Maintenance, Custodial Services, and Security
Personnel.* Identify the positions in these job classifications
that are affected by the pilot study. Work out necessary
rescheduling of crews.

10. *Plan for Record Keeping.* Decisions must be made as to
whether work time is to be recorded. If it is, the organization must then decide which form of time recording is most
compatible with its business requirements. Manual, mechanical, and electronic devices constitute the alternatives. Especially if the automatic time totalizer method is selected for
use in the pilot study, the organization should establish a
rental or lease arrangement with an appropriate manufacturer. Also, whatever the time-recording method selected,
discuss the issue with union representatives and aim to enlist
their cooperation.

11. *Orient Unit Supervisors.* Approximately six weeks prior to the trial run, the organization should begin holding orientation meetings with the supervisors of the units included in the pilot program. The aim is to explain the program to them in depth, to alleviate any of their concerns, and to gain their enthusiastic cooperation and support.

12. *Communicate Program Particulars to Employees Involved.* Approximately three weeks prior to initiation of the flexitime pilot program, details should be spelled out to employees. Essential ingredients should be communicated both orally and in writing, and designated officials should make themselves available for question-and-answer sessions. Openness, two-way communication, and a climate of trust should prevail. The overall message should be: "Flexitime may prove beneficial both to employees and to the organization; therefore, let's give it a trial run." The vast majority of employees in the pilot units will probably be eager to participate in and work under the new schedule.

   Supervisors of the units involved should be encouraged to participate in the overall task of disseminating information to employees. The direct feedback they get from their subordinates will benefit them greatly in fitting the program to the real situation.

13. *Work Under the Program—and Monitor It—During Its Trial Run.* Barring unforeseen delays, employees should begin work under flexitime on the target date previously determined. During the trial run, officials should monitor the program, aiming to remove any bugs that may develop.

14. *Evaluate Flexitime Results in the Pilot Setting.* It is at this stage that the test evaluation procedures discussed in Step 8 are applied. Also, the procedures examined later in this chapter in the section entitled "Evaluating Results of an Expanded Flexitime Program" are useful in evaluating flexitime in its pilot phase.

Let us assume that flexitime has proved successful in the pilot setting—employees and supervisors like the system and prefer it to the work schedule previously in use, and objective measurements show productivity levels at least as high as those attained under the previous work schedule. A decision should now be made not only to continue use of flexitime in the units included in the pilot trial, but to extend it wherever feasible throughout the organization.

Planning and Developing an Expanded Flexitime Program

Especially at this point, attention should focus on determining which departments and job positions should be included in the expanded flexitime program. The process comprises several steps.

Enlarge the Committee
1. *Involve Line Managers.* Line officials representing a diagonal cross section of the organization should be added to the study committee. Details of the flexitime pilot program should be communicated to those managers. This accomplished, their ideas and suggestions should be solicited.

2. *Consider Including Union Representatives.* Many organizations will attest to the fact that unions want to be kept informed about what is going on. It is essential to maintain open communications with the union at each major step along the road toward a full-fledged flexitime program. Union cooperation will increase understanding and acceptance of the program — it is vital.

Determine Committee Assignments, and Develop a Game Plan
Three major activities must be performed, and in a synchronized manner. First, the planning process requires that the study group investigate a number of "topics of concern" and gather all the additional information that is needed about them. Certain topics (identified below) may be assigned to individual committee members while others will be topics for consideration by the entire committee. Second, an approximate target date should be established for implementing flexitime in appropriate departments throughout the organization. Third, the committee should prepare a schedule of meetings to ensure that as many members as possible will be available to discuss the topics of concern.

Seven main topics of concern must be investigated as part of the overall game plan.

1. *Determine Core Time.* Establishing too large a core-time band
   will negate the concept and reduce the number of positive
   results that flexitime can bring. On the other hand, too small
   a core time could result in lack of adequate job coverage,
   disruption, and inefficiency. It is therefore necessary to establish a balance that fits the particular requirements of your
   organization. For example, in which sections of the organization is contact with the public on a regular, volume basis? Are
   workloads on certain days heavier than on others? How regular or irregular is the work scheduling or the setting of
   production deadlines? Is one and the same core time appropriate over the entire organization or should various in-
   terrelating departments be grouped and several core times
   identified?

   Typically, core time comprises four to six hours of each
   workday. As confirmed by various organizations discussed in
   this book, no one magic core-time band will fit all organizations. Core time must be custom-built for your organization.
   As the reader recalls, core time may take the form of one
   wide block of time interrupted only by a lunch break. Another possibility is to introduce the midday-flex band. This
   will split core time into two separate periods, and the results
   will be one core-time band in the morning and another in the
   afternoon. When there's doubt as to the number of core-time
   hours that is most appropriate, it is suggested that you go on
   the long side. If a change is in order in the future, employees
   will find it much easier to accept if it goes from six to five
   hours, say, rather than vice versa.

2. *Determine Flexible Time Bands.* The size of the FST and FQT
   bands will in part be a function of the number of hours contained in the core time. Where flexible time bands are large, a
   considerable amount of flexibility is introduced into the system.

3. *Consider Legal and Regulatory Requirements.* Some of the legal
   and regulatory considerations discussed in Chapter 5 are also
   applicable at this stage. Your organization naturally wishes to
   avoid legal entanglements. Is your organization in the private
   or the public sector? What do federal and state laws say
   regarding your proposed flexitime program? In what ways

are the various laws applicable to your organization? If a certified bargaining unit exists, what specifics are spelled out in the contract regarding matters such as the duration of a normal workday, when it should begin and end, overtime pay, and maximum number of consecutive hours that may be worked without a break.

At this point in the planning process the organization should have gathered quite a bit of information about legal requirements, as this issue received some attention when plans were developed for a flexitime pilot test.

4. *Identify Departments and Jobs to Be Excluded.* It was recommended that the study group planning the widespread application of flexitime be enlarged to include line managers. This enlarged group should focus on the total organization and make decisions as to which departments and jobs might have to be excluded from the flexitime program. The following suggestions should prove helpful.

   (a) Request that supervisors identify positions that should be excluded from participation in flexitime.
   (b) Ask supervisors to state reasons why the positions should be excluded.
   (c) Study alternatives such as reorganizing work flow, regrouping duties, and reassigning personnel.
   (d) When it is "finally determined" which positions *must* be restricted, identify those jobs and prepare a list of sound reasons that explain why those jobs have to be excluded from flexitime participation.

5. *Select Criteria for Evaluating Results.* This subject has already been discussed and will not be repeated here. The reader should refer to Step 8 in the section entitled "Carrying Out a Flexitime Pilot Study." It is quite possible to employ those same criteria and tests in planning for widespread applications of flexitime.

6. *Plan for Building Maintenance, Custodial Services, and Security Personnel.* An extension of the organization's workday may require rescheduling the work hours of certain personnel. For example, if maintenance and custodial crews generally discharge their work functions prior to or after normal work

hours, an extension of the organization's workday will require rescheduling the work hours of these crews. If these activities are carried out during work hours, discussion may still be necessary to ensure minimum disruption. In addition, schedule modifications may also be in order for security personnel.

7. *Plan for Record Keeping.* Where plans call for extending flexitime and where the automatic time totalizer has been selected as the time-recording instrument to be used, an organization should work out a rental or lease arrangement with an appropriate manufacturer. This type of equipment may be purchased at a later date, if flexitime does indeed prove successful throughout many departments.

In many organizations, a simple manual system may be used. For example, if a sign-in/sign-out system is employed, everyone enjoying the benefits of flexitime should use it, including management. A procedure whereby all employees sign a register in the order of their arrival at work has advantages over the use of a sheet on which workers simply write in their names next to a preprinted time. This latter approach can easily lead to abuses.

After all the necessary actions described in this section have been accomplished, implementation of the system must be considered.

Implementation

Coordination and communication are the keys to success. Where these two functions are carried out effectively, implementation of an expanded flexitime program should be a relatively simple process.

Coordination

1. *Identify Those Persons and Groups That Will Be Involved with Implementation.* Examine the various committee assignments to identify those individuals and groups that will be involved with the implementation of flexitime or will require information about it.

2. *Chart Lead-Time Particulars.* In previous meetings, lead times

were discussed. This information should be compiled, and then depicted in chart form.

3. *Assign People to Carry Out Specific Aspects of the Coordination Process.* Based on interest in the flexitime concept, job position held, and understanding of the implementation requirements, individuals should be assigned to carry out specific coordination activities.

Communication

Lack of good communication can be catastrophic. Here are some suggestions for ensuring good communication among all levels of employees.

1. *Prepare Instructions for Supervisors.* Written instructions should be prepared for supervisors. The document should spell out supervisors' responsibilities. Distribute the written instructions to appropriate management-level personnel about six weeks before the expanded program is to begin.

2. *Hold Meetings with Supervisors.* The organization should schedule meetings primarily for the benefit of first-level supervision. Encourage a free question-and-answer exchange, and aim for open discussion and a two-way flow of ideas.

3. *Provide Supervisors with an Additional Information Source.* Give supervisors the name and number of an official who will answer questions for them in the future — after the program has begun.

4. *Consult with Union Representatives.* Solicit the union's views as to the most effective methods of communicating essential details to employees. Discuss the use of the union newsletter, if such a medium exists in your organization.

5. *Prepare Information Sheets for Distribution to Employees.* Information sheets should be prepared containing clear statements on what flexitime is and how it works. Distribute the information sheets at least three weeks in advance of the date on which the program is to be launched. At the same time, provide workers excluded from flexitime with a written explanation of why their jobs had to be excluded.

6. *Use Additional Communication Channels, Where Available.* If your

organization regularly publishes an employee newsletter or magazine, use it to promote the flexitime program. Such publications provide excellent channels through which to explain essential details. Construct hypothetical questions along this line: "How will the flexitime program affect me in terms of . . . ?" Or, "Under flexitime, what will happen in terms of . . . ?" Provide clear answers to the questions you introduce.

7. *Convey Top Management's Enthusiasm.* Enthusiasm is contagious, especially where employees and supervisors perceive it among top managers. Aim to obtain top management's oral and written support for the flexitime program.

Launch the Program

After the essential coordination and communication activities enumerated above have been successfully completed, the expanded program can officially be launched — in conjunction with the commencement target dates previously determined.

Evaluating Results of an Expanded Flexitime Program

After a flexitime program has been fully implemented, it is of urgent concern that the organization be able to measure results and compare them with the goals and standards determined in the planning stage. In other words, how has flexitime affected work motivation, productivity, group morale, and job satisfaction?

In order to take measurement readings, the organization must have measurement instruments at its disposal. One suggestion is to compute productivity-level attainments and conduct a survey of employee opinion on the subject. But such procedures are properly criticized as "too general." I have therefore devised procedures to assist organizations in making a more specific evaluation of their flexitime program. Although subject to slight modifications to fit the particular needs of individual organizations, to a great extent the procedures presented here are applicable to all flexitime users.

Administer Questionnaire to Employees

The questionnaire for all participants other than managers might be administered at three different times during the first year of flexitime operations: after three months, after six months, and after one full year. (1) At the top of the first page, write a brief introductory section applicable to your specific organization. It should explain the nature of the questionnaire, why it is being administered, and the answering procedure. (2) Inform respondents that they are to remain anonymous. This should encourage honest and sincere answers. However, add two open-end lines: one calling for identification of department or work unit, the second inquiring whether the respondent is an exempt or nonexempt employee. These brief identifications will pinpoint particular departments or work units where trouble spots might occur and where corrective action might be in order.

The following 40-question format is designed to elicit attitudinal responses pertaining to productivity, and reveal on-the-job and off-the-job satisfactions and dissatisfactions in particular areas. In completing the questionnaire, *employees are to compare flexitime with the previous work-hours system used.* For each question, ask the respondent to select one answer only, and to place an *x* on the line adjacent to the answer chosen.

THE FLEXITIME WORK-HOURS QUESTIONNAIRE
FOR EMPLOYEES

1. Car-pool arrangements under flexitime:
   _____ (a) More difficult to arrange
   _____ (b) No effect—about the same as before
   _____ (c) More easily arranged
   _____ (d) I did not, and do not now, use car pools

2. Travel time to work:
   _____ (a) Less time is required
   _____ (b) About the same as before
   _____ (c) More time is required

3. Travel time from work:
   _____ (a) Less time is required
   _____ (b) About the same as before
   _____ (c) More time is required

4. Finding a vacant parking spot on arrival at work:
   _____ (a) Easier
   _____ (b) About the same as before
   _____ (c) More difficult
   _____ (d) I do not drive my car to work

5. Arrival time at work:
   _____ (a) I usually arrive at work earlier under flexitime
   _____ (b) No change
   _____ (c) I usually arrive at work later under flexitime

6. Amount of time during the workweek for taking care of personal business:
   _____ (a) Significantly more
   _____ (b) A bit more
   _____ (c) No change
   _____ (d) A bit less
   _____ (e) Significantly less

7. Amount of time during the workweek for off-the-job recreational pursuits:
   _____ (a) Significantly more
   _____ (b) A bit more
   _____ (c) No change
   _____ (d) A bit less
   _____ (e) Significantly less

8. Amount of time to spend with family:
   _____ (a) Significantly more
   _____ (b) A bit more
   _____ (c) No change
   _____ (d) A bit less
   _____ (e) Significantly less

9. Child-care arrangements:
   _____ (a) Easier under flexitime
   _____ (b) No change
   _____ (c) More difficult under flexitime
   _____ (d) I have no children at home

10. Amount of leisure time:
    _____ (a) Significantly more
    _____ (b) A bit more
    _____ (c) No change
    _____ (d) A bit less
    _____ (e) Significantly less

11. Job coverage (work stations adequately crewed):
    _____ (a) Better job coverage under flexitime
    _____ (b) No difference in job coverage under flexitime
    _____ (c) Job coverage has deteriorated under flexitime

12. Internal communications within my department:
    _____ (a) Easier
    _____ (b) No apparent change

_____ (c) More difficult

13. Communications with other departments:
    _____ (a) Easier
    _____ (b) No apparent change
    _____ (c) More difficult

14. Feelings I get when talking with fellow workers not on flexitime:
    _____ (a) They show resentment and wish they were on flexitime
    _____ (b) They mainly express indifference – they couldn't care less
    _____ (c) They prefer their present work system to flexitime

15. Feelings I get when talking with people in other organizations not on flexitime:
    _____ (a) They show resentment and wish they were on flexitime
    _____ (b) They mainly express indifference – they couldn't care less
    _____ (c) They prefer their present work system to flexitime

16. Feelings of guilt on days when others still working see me leave work early:
    _____ (a) More guilt under flexitime
    _____ (b) No change
    _____ (c) Less guilt under flexitime

17. Alignment of off-the-job interests and job responsibilities:
    _____ (a) Smoother under flexitime
    _____ (b) No apparent difference
    _____ (c) Less smooth under flexitime

18. Fatigue during work hours:
    _____ (a) Less under flexitime
    _____ (b) No apparent change
    _____ (c) More under flexitime

19. Quick starts on arrival at work in the morning:
    _____ (a) I wait around more and get a slower work start under flexitime
    _____ (b) No apparent change
    _____ (c) I wait around less and get a quicker work start under flexitime.

20. Personal freedom and independence:
    _____ (a) More under flexitime
    _____ (b) No perceived change
    _____ (c) Less under flexitime

21. Quantity or amount of work I turn out:
    _____ (a) More because of flexitime
    _____ (b) No perceived change
    _____ (c) Less because of flexitime

22. Quality of work I produce:
_____ (a) Has deteriorated because of flexitime
_____ (b) No perceived change
_____ (c) Has improved because of flexitime

23. Efficiency and productivity of my work unit as a whole:
_____ (a) Have increased under flexitime
_____ (b) No apparent change
_____ (c) Have decreased under flexitime

24. Opportunities for my own quiet time (periods during which even more concentration is possible):
_____ (a) More under flexitime
_____ (b) No apparent change
_____ (c) Fewer under flexitime

25. Amount of cross-training (learning experiences that enable me to perform a greater number of jobs):
_____ (a) More under flexitime
_____ (b) No apparent change
_____ (c) Less under flexitime

26. Participation in problem solving, and teamwork in decision making:
_____ (a) More under flexitime
_____ (b) No apparent change
_____ (c) Less under flexitime

27. My loyalty to employer:
_____ (a) Greater under flexitime
_____ (b) No change
_____ (c) Less under flexitime

28. Organizational climate:
_____ (a) Is more positive, open, and warm under flexitime
_____ (b) No change
_____ (c) Is more negative, closed, and cold under flexitime

29. Treatment as an adult:
_____ (a) I'm treated in a more adult manner by employer under flexitime
_____ (b) No apparent change
_____ (c) I'm treated in a less adult manner by employer under flexitime

30. Lateness (arrival at work after core time begins):
_____ (a) I'm late more often under flexitime
_____ (b) No change
_____ (c) I'm late less often under flexitime

31. Absence from work because of sickness and other reasons:
_____ (a) I'm absent less often under flexitime
_____ (b) No change
_____ (c) I'm absent more often under flexitime

32. Abuses of the system (taking unwarranted advantage of flexitime):
_____ (a) Are extremely abundant
_____ (b) Are moderately abundant
_____ (c) Are about the same in number
_____ (d) Occur infrequently
_____ (e) Are nonexistent

33. Supervisory availability:
_____ (a) Supervisors are more available under flexitime
_____ (b) No change
_____ (c) Supervisors are less available under flexitime

34. Flexitime makes me feel that the organization:
_____ (a) Does not trust me at all
_____ (b) Trusts me sometimes
_____ (c) Partially trusts me
_____ (d) Trusts me all the time

35. Morale (group spirit, group resourcefulness, and commitment to employer goals) under flexitime has:
_____ (a) Greatly degenerated
_____ (b) Moderately degenerated
_____ (c) Shown no change
_____ (d) Moderately improved
_____ (e) Greatly improved

36. My job satisfaction as a result of flexitime is:
_____ (a) Significantly lower
_____ (b) Somewhat lower
_____ (c) The same as before
_____ (d) Somewhat higher
_____ (e) Significantly higher

37. My overall feeling about working under flexitime is:
_____ (a) I like it
_____ (b) I'm not sure
_____ (c) I don't like it

38. Our flexitime program leaves me feeling:
_____ (a) Very satisfied
_____ (b) In general, satisfied
_____ (c) Uncertain
_____ (d) In general, dissatisfied
_____ (e) Very dissatisfied

39. When I consider working for another organization that uses fixed
working hours, flexitime seems:

    _____ (a) Very important

    _____ (b) Fairly important

    _____ (c) Of minor importance

    _____ (d) Of no importance

40. Flexitime is beneficial to:

    _____ (a) The employee

    _____ (b) The organization

    _____ (c) Neither the employee nor the organization

    _____ (d) Both the employee and the organization

Administer Questionnaire to Managers

Managers should also be surveyed on their judgments about
flexitime. The questionnaire might be administered at three different
times during the first year of flexitime operations: after three months,
after six months, and after one full year. A number of suggestions
made in reference to the preceding questionnaire are also applicable
here. Supervisors should be informed that they are to remain anonymous. However, the department or work unit should be identified.
Also, the respondent's management *level* should be stated — with
"foreman" (or equivalent title) defined as the first level of supervision.

The following 40-question format is designed to provide input
about flexitime from the manager's perspective. In answering the specific questions, *managers are to compare flexitime with the previous work-
hours system used.* For each question, ask the respondent to select one
answer only, and to place an *x* on the line adjacent to the answer
chosen.

THE FLEXITIME WORK-HOURS QUESTIONNAIRE
FOR MANAGERS

1. Travel time to work:

    _____ (a) Less time is required

    _____ (b) About the same as before

    _____ (c) More time is required

2. Travel time from work:

    _____ (a) Less time is required

    _____ (b) About the same as before

    _____ (c) More time is required

3. Arrival time at work:
   _____ (a) I usually arrive at work earlier under flexitime
   _____ (b) No change
   _____ (c) I usually arrive at work later under flexitime

4. Amount of time during the workweek for taking care of personal business:
   _____ (a) Significantly more
   _____ (b) A bit more
   _____ (c) No change
   _____ (d) A bit less
   _____ (e) Significantly less

5. Amount of time during the workweek for off-the-job recreational pursuits:
   _____ (a) Significantly more
   _____ (b) A bit more
   _____ (c) No change
   _____ (d) A bit less
   _____ (e) Significantly less

6. Amount of time to spend with family:
   _____ (a) Significantly more
   _____ (b) A bit more
   _____ (c) No change
   _____ (d) A bit less
   _____ (e) Significantly less

7. Amount of leisure time:
   _____ (a) Significantly more
   _____ (b) A bit more
   _____ (c) No change
   _____ (d) A bit less
   _____ (e) Significantly less

8. Job coverage by subordinates:
   _____ (a) Better job coverage under flexitime
   _____ (b) No difference in job coverage under flexitime
   _____ (c) Job coverage has deteriorated under flexitime

9. Internal communications within my department:
   _____ (a) Easier
   _____ (b) No apparent change
   _____ (c) More difficult

10. Communications (interfacing) with other departments:
    _____ (a) Easier
    _____ (b) No apparent change
    _____ (c) More difficult

11. External communications with other organizations:
    _____ (a) Easier
    _____ (b) No apparent change
    _____ (c) More difficult

12. Communications to locations in other time zones (via phone mainly):
    _____ (a) Easier
    _____ (b) No apparent change
    _____ (c) More difficult

13. Fatigue during work hours
    _____ (a) Less under flexitime
    _____ (b) No apparent change
    _____ (c) More under flexitime

14. Quick starts by subordinates on their arrival at work in the morning:
    _____ (a) More waiting around and a slower work start under flexitime
    _____ (b) No apparent change
    _____ (c) Less waiting around and a quicker work start under flexitime

15. Quantity or amount of work turned out by subordinates:
    _____ (a) More because of flexitime
    _____ (b) No perceived change
    _____ (c) Less because of flexitime

16. Quality of work produced by subordinates:
    _____ (a) Has deteriorated because of flexitime
    _____ (b) No perceived change
    _____ (c) Has improved because of flexitime

17. Efficiency and productivity of my work unit as a whole:
    _____ (a) Have increased under flexitime
    _____ (b) No apparent change
    _____ (c) Have decreased under flexitime

18. Opportunities for my own quiet time (periods during which even more concentration is possible):
    _____ (a) More under flexitime
    _____ (b) No apparent change
    _____ (c) Fewer under flexitime

19. Amount of cross-training (learning experiences that enable subordinates to perform a greater number of jobs):
    _____ (a) More under flexitime
    _____ (b) No apparent change
    _____ (c) Less under flexitime

20. Participation of subordinates in problem solving, and teamwork in decision making:
    _____ (a) More under flexitime
    _____ (b) No apparent change
    _____ (c) Less under flexitime

21. Organizational climate:
    _____ (a) Is more positive, open, and warm under flexitime
    _____ (b) No change
    _____ (c) Is more negative, closed, and cold under flexitime

22. Lateness among subordinates (arrival at work after core time begins):
    _____ (a) Significantly more
    _____ (b) A bit more
    _____ (c) No change
    _____ (d) A bit less
    _____ (e) Significantly less

23. Abuses of the system (taking unwarranted advantage of flexitime):
    _____ (a) Are extremely abundant
    _____ (b) Are moderately abundant
    _____ (c) Are about the same in number
    _____ (d) Occur infrequently
    _____ (e) Are nonexistent

24. Absence of subordinates from work because of sickness and other reasons:
    _____ (a) Significantly more
    _____ (b) A bit more
    _____ (c) No change
    _____ (d) A bit less
    _____ (e) Significantly less

25. Subordinates are available to me:
    _____ (a) More under flexitime
    _____ (b) No change
    _____ (c) Less under flexitime

26. The need to supervise subordinates has:
    _____ (a) Greatly decreased
    _____ (b) Moderately decreased
    _____ (c) Not changed
    _____ (d) Moderately increased
    _____ (e) Greatly increased

27. My need to plan, organize, and distribute work in advance to employees has:
    _____ (a) Increased under flexitime

_____ (b) Not changed
_____ (c) Decreased under flexitime

28. My work group meets deadlines:
_____ (a) More easily
_____ (b) The same as before
_____ (c) With more difficulty

29. Amount of overtime in my work group has:
_____ (a) Increased because of flexitime
_____ (b) Shown no change
_____ (c) Decreased because of flexitime

30. In my judgment, calling meetings is:
_____ (a) Less difficult under flexitime
_____ (b) Neither more nor less difficult
_____ (c) More difficult under flexitime

31. Turnover among my subordinates is:
_____ (a) Higher under flexitime
_____ (b) The same as before
_____ (c) Lower under flexitime

32. My professional status is:
_____ (a) Higher under flexitime
_____ (b) The same as before
_____ (c) Lower under flexitime

33. The time-recording system my department is now using under flexitime is:
_____ (a) Satisfactory—a completely different type of system is not needed
_____ (b) Unsatisfactory—a completely different type of system is needed

34. The morale of my subordinates (their group spirit, group resourcefulness, and commitment to employer goals) under flexitime has:
_____ (a) Greatly degenerated
_____ (b) Moderately degenerated
_____ (c) Shown no change
_____ (d) Moderately improved
_____ (e) Greatly improved

35. Overall, because of flexitime, the job satisfaction of most of my subordinates is:
_____ (a) Significantly lower
_____ (b) Somewhat lower
_____ (c) Not changed
_____ (d) Somewhat higher
_____ (e) Significantly higher

36. My job satisfaction as a result of flexitime is:
    _____ (a) Significantly lower
    _____ (b) Somewhat lower
    _____ (c) The same as before
    _____ (d) Somewhat higher
    _____ (e) Significantly higher

37. The feeling of most of my subordinates about working under flexitime is:
    _____ (a) They like it
    _____ (b) They're not sure
    _____ (c) They don't like it

38. My own feeling about working under flexitime is:
    _____ (a) I like it
    _____ (b) I'm not sure
    _____ (c) I don't like it

39. Our flexitime program leaves me feeling:
    _____ (a) Very satisfied
    _____ (b) In general, satisfied
    _____ (c) Uncertain
    _____ (d) In general, dissatisfied
    _____ (e) Very dissatisfied

40. Flexitime is beneficial to:
    _____ (a) The employee
    _____ (b) The organization
    _____ (c) Neither the employee nor the organization
    _____ (d) Both the employee and the organization

Obtain Objective Measurements of Productivity

Both of the above questionnaires are on the subjective side. Based on feelings, attitudes, perceptions, and behavioral tendencies, nonmanagers and managers state what they believe is a true picture of the flexitime system as compared with the system previously used. This type of information is helpful to an organization in evaluating results.

On the other hand, we know all too well that subjective evaluations frequently run counter to objective evaluations. Thus, in aiming to arrive at a more complete assessment of flexitime, it is also important to evaluate the system through hard objective data relating to productivity. This section is concerned mainly with that approach.

For the following factors, obtain objective measurements of productivity at least three different times during the first year of flexitime

operations: after three months, after six months, and after one full
year.

1. *Measure Employee Turnover*
   (a) Study the organization's records and measure employee
       turnover in departments where flexitime is in operation.
       Where possible, compute turnover rates for involuntary
       as well as voluntary separation.
   (b) Determine turnover during identical months over the
       three-year period immediately prior to installation of
       flexitime.
   (c) Compare the respective turnover data.
   (d) Where data show different turnover rates, determine to
       what extent, if at all, the rate differences are attributable
       to flexitime.

2. *Measure Absenteeism Rates*
   (a) Study the organization's records and measure absen-
       teeism in departments where flexitime is in operation.
       Where possible, compute the rates according to reason
       offered for absence.
   (b) Determine absence during identical months over the
       three-year period immediately prior to installation of
       flexitime.
   (c) Compare the respective absenteeism data. Where pos-
       sible, use the records of those employed over the past
       four years as a basis for comparison.
   (d) Where data show different absenteeism rates, determine
       to what extent, if at all, the rate differences are attributa-
       ble to flexitime.

3. *Measure Lateness Rates*
   (a) Study the organization's records and determine rates of
       late arrival at work in departments where flexitime is in
       operation.
   (b) Determine lateness rates during identical months over
       the three-year period immediately prior to installation of
       flexitime.
   (c) Compare the respective tardiness data. Where possible,
       use the records of those employed over the past four
       years as a basis for comparison.
   (d) Where data show different rates of punctual arrival at

work, determine to what extent, if at all, the rate differences are attributable to flexitime.

4. *Measure Amount of Overtime*
    (a) Study the organization's records and measure amount of overtime in departments where flexitime is in operation. Where possible, compute the rates on the basis of reasons for overtime use.
    (b) Determine amount of overtime during identical months over the three-year period immediately prior to installation of flexitime.
    (c) Compare the respective overtime data.
    (d) Where data show different amounts of overtime use, determine to what extent, if at all, the rate differences are attributable to flexitime.

5. *Measure Quantity of Work Produced*
    (a) Study the organization's records and determine the quantity of production in departments where flexitime is in operation.
    (b) Determine the quantity of production during identical months over the three-year period immediately prior to installation of flexitime.
    (c) Compare the respective data. Where possible, use the records of those employed over the past four years as a basis for comparison.
    (d) Where data show different production rates in terms of quantity, determine to what extent, if at all, the differences are attributable to flexitime.

6. *Measure Quality of Work Produced*
    (a) Study the organization's records and determine the quality of production in departments where flexitime is in operation.
    (b) Determine quality of production during identical months over the three-year period immediately prior to installation of flexitime.
    (c) Compare the respective data. Where possible, use the records of those employed over the past four years as a basis for comparison.
    (d) Where data show different production rates in terms of

quality, determine to what extent, if at all, the differences
are attributable to flexitime.

7. *Measure Productivity in Relation to Additional Criteria*
   (a) In relation to each additional criterion identified, study
       the organization's records and determine level of produc-
       tivity in departments where flexitime is in operation.
   (b) Determine productivity levels during identical months
       over the three-year period immediately prior to installa-
       tion of flexitime.
   (c) Compare the respective data. Where possible, use the rec-
       ords of those employed over the past four years as a basis
       for comparison.
   (d) With each criterion, where productivity levels show dif-
       ferent rates, determine to what extent, if at all, those
       differences are attributable to flexitime.

The information given in this chapter is useful to all organizations interested in setting up a flexitime program. To those organizations that carry out the procedure through the final phase — namely,
evaluating results of an expansive flexitime program — I submit these
suggestions. (1) Keep your objectives clearly in mind. In other words,
what did you hope to accomplish through flexitime? (2) Scrutinize the
data you obtained through the questionnaire surveys and objective
measurements so as to arrive at meaningful findings and results. (3)
Make an appropriate decision. If flexitime results do not approximate
the intentions and objectives originally established, the system should
be aborted. If, on the other hand, overall results are satisfactory, re-
tain the system and improve upon it.

Part III

Over the Horizon

11

Where do we go from here?

Part II unlocked the door leading into the world of flexible working hours. Explained and described were the alternative work schedules of staggered hours, flexitour, group flexibility, and flexitime. The reader was briefed on how gliding time innovations have worked in different types of organizations both inside and outside the United States. Attention was focused on both the drawbacks and the advantages of flexitime. Detailed information was provided on how to go about setting up a flexitime program.

Here, in Part III, my aim is to solidify the interrelationships between humanistic management and alternative work patterns. Chapter 11 first treats three prominent and vital issues which concern us now, and which will concern us in the future: work, leisure, and productivity. Interwoven amidst the discussion is the relevancy of flexitime. Concluding the chapter is a fourth and final topic entitled "A Point of View."

Work

In the dynamic and turbulent culture of the United States, predicting future events leaves one feeling as safe and confident as one would feel playing Russian roulette. We've often heard the statement: The only thing that's certain is uncertainty. Nevertheless, one can feel quite safe and confident in predicting that work is going to be with us for quite a while.

"To spend or use energy" is the definition of work given in Chapter 1. There are others: "Activities that produce things valued by the worker and/or by other people" and "What one is obligated to do." However work is defined, a lot of people are involved in it. More than 90 percent of all the men in the United States between ages 20 and 54 are either employed or actively seeking work. And in the United States, the civilian labor force is destined to exceed 100 million before the year 1985.

Many of the ancient Greeks detested work and relied on slaves to get things done. Aristotle declared: "All paid employments absorb and degrade the mind." Centuries ago many Hebrews saw work as punishment. And the first Christians did work as a penance. Perhaps St. Benedict should be credited (or blamed) for "inventing" the work ethic. In the sixth century he posted this rule for his monks: "Idleness is the enemy of the soul. And therefore, at fixed times, the brothers ought to be occupied in manual labor, and, again at fixed times, in sacred reading." Certainly, cultural imperatives are crucial both in kindling and in extinguishing the work ethic. Reference was made in Chapter 1 to the Tikopians of Oceania and the Siriono of the Amazon Basin, two tribes having different perspectives concerning work.

People work for various reasons. The money some of them earn from their work is enough to buy only the basic necessities of life: food, clothing, shelter. Most low-income earners are in this situation — although hardly by preference. Their endless chant is: "We go to work to get the dough to get the food to get the strength to go to work to get the dough to get the food to . . . ."

Besides working to survive and feel secure people work to satisfy their needs to associate with others and belong to groups. Such socializing provides empathy and sympathy and serves other supportive functions. Social psychologists in particular tend to emphasize the importance of these forms of human needs.

Third, many people perceive work as offering possibilities for attaining greater degrees of self-esteem and self-fulfillment. Elliot Jacques, an industrial social consultant, says: "Work does not satisfy material needs alone. In a very deep sense, it gives Man a measure of his sanity." Work offers many people pathways to responsibility and achievement. But as the authors of *Work in America* point out, if work is to provide esteem, it must be meaningful and dignified. Or, as the French philosopher Albert Camus phrased it: "Without work all life goes rotten; but when work is soulless, life stifles and dies."

In conjunction with our need for self-esteem, through work we gain a sense of competence and value. A job tells us we are needed, we have something to offer. Too often, however, how we rate at work is taken as an indication of how we rate as human beings. To "make it" in a job is to "make it" as a person. As psychoanalyst Erich Fromm explains: "Since modern man experiences himself both as the seller and as the commodity to be sold on the market, his self-esteem depends on conditions beyond his control. If he is successful, he is valuable; if he is not, he is worthless." This discussion of higher-level human needs conjures up yet another definition of work: "Providing human labor through the expenditure of physical, mental, and emotional energy in return for monetary and psychic rewards."

I recall a statement that has deeply impressed me: "The greatest reward for Man's toil is not what he gets for it, but what he becomes through it." This idea fits in with Abraham Maslow's assertion that growth and striving to actualize one's potential are manifestations of a healthy personality.

A fourth function of work is that it gives a worker a sense of identity. It is not by accident that when A meets B for the first time, "How do you do?" is usually closely followed by "What do you do?" Since most working people describe themselves by the organization to which they belong and by their work occupation, work makes them "somebody"; unemployed people become "nobodies."

Work also plays a significant role in determining the status of the employees and their families. What breadwinners do determines what they earn, and therefore where they are on the social ladder, where they and their families live, and who their friends are.

But even if work failed to provide belongingness, self-esteem, identity, or status, it would still fill another human need: that of bringing order to our lives. For many people, work is simply the best way to fill up a lot of time.

In addition to analyses of work based on fulfillment of needs, there is a closely related kind of analysis, namely, a psychological approach based on motivation theory. We have needs and wants. Needs and wants generate tension and motivation to act. These in turn cause us to establish target levels of performance or achievement. We demonstrate action-performance-achievement (behavior) to obtain rewards which, when perceived as equitable, result in satisfaction. And with satisfaction we come full circle. That is, when satisfaction is experienced, a corresponding need requirement is abated.

But human beings do not stand still for too long a time. Maslow puts it more formally: "A satisfied need is no longer a motivator of behavior." Because of the overwhelming pull of our aspirations and expectations, we reach out for and strive to attain what exists at present only in our imaginations.

What does all this mean? From many directions we arrive at a common ground of understanding, namely, that satisfaction is the end of the line. Whatever goals we set up and whatever means we take to achieve those goals, the needle on the compass points toward satisfaction. We strive to obtain rewards that bring greater satisfaction. To the psychologist, satisfaction is the ultimate purpose of our behavior (theologians and philosophers are more comfortable with the term "happiness").

In the view of most workers, obsession with work and work satisfaction is not what life is all about. Nevertheless, it is not a contradiction to say that most workers want greater job satisfaction. After all, the work arena is where people spend eight hours of most 24-hour periods. To say that on-the-job satisfaction is beside the point is to say that eight hours of life in each working day are not relevant to the pursuit of human satisfaction.

Present levels of affluence and satisfaction, the pressures of TV and other sophisticated mass communications media, and rising levels of formal education all nurture rising expectations. About 70 percent of the 1977 workforce had completed high school, compared with 43 percent in 1952. And more persons are in universities than ever before. This means that from the standpoint of persons achieving higher levels of informal and formal education, meaningful jobs do not exist in large enough quantities. As a former executive of AT&T, Bob Ford, describes the situation: "We have run out of dumb people to do dumb jobs."

In May 1976 *Business Week* carried an article entitled "Worker Unrest: Not Dead, But Playing Possum." As explained there, when the job security issue begins to fade as the economy recovers, employers and unions will be confronted once again by demands for more rapid change in the workplace. Essentially, young employees in particular want more satisfying jobs, less authoritarianism, and greater participation in making decisions that affect their working lives. Within a few years the postwar generation will make up a majority of the nation's workforce. The pressures for change may then become overwhelming unless organizations find ways to make work more meaningful and rewarding. As *Business Week* describes developments, despite the exaggeration of blue-collar and white-collar blues, worker dissatisfaction is a reality and the quality of working life must be improved.

What has all this got to do with the subject of flexible work hours? Everything! I talked about what people want in terms of need requirements. Some thoughts also were expressed about motivation theory, and about the views of young people. In applying the information to the work environment, all roads lead to hoped-for goal attainments of reductions in on-the-job dissatisfaction and increases in on-the-job satisfaction. On the basis of available information, organizations would do well to consider flexible working hours, and flexitime in particular. *In almost all cases where flexitime is incorporated, job satisfaction increases.*

Leisure

Reference was just made to the order that work brings to our lives. That is, for many people work is simply the best way to fill up a lot of time. As hectic as certain jobs are, some people find them positively orderly when compared with their activities after work hours. A philosopher once mused: "It takes a highly intelligent individual to enjoy leisure. Most of us had better count on working."

A considerable number of workers in the United States neither pursue nor enjoy leisure. One explanation is that these people find intrinsic satisfaction in working—for them, work is the whole ball game. It's where the action is.

A few years ago William A. Emerson, Jr., wrote a piece in *Newsweek* entitled "Punctuality Is the Thief of Time." He said in part:

> I respect time too much to waste it on punctuality.... Western man got hung up on punctuality when he set out to make a buck. It is the rallying cry of the industrial revolution, the soul of materialism, and the coldest virtue known to man. Punctuality is the underpinning of the Protestant work ethic—kick the habit and help bring on the postindustrial age. Just reflect on who is trying to get whom to the plant on time. Addiction to work is a national affliction, but it's no worse than addiction to booze or drugs. Finally, nobody can save you but yourself, so commute slow; hang in there tardy one day at a time. Before you know it you will have a new feeling of well-being.

There's no telling how many air crashes, train wrecks, and shootouts I've missed by being late. It makes me slow down when I think about them. Just a few months ago I was sauntering toward Grand Central Terminal in Manhattan, a minute and a half late for the 8:40 Stamford local. I was suddenly aware that the echoes of a fusillade of shots were dying out. I walked right past the door of a candy store where the cops in a police stakeout had just shot two robbers dead. Some seconds earlier a stream of bullets had crossed my path and chewed up a building. A more punctual man with a grip on logistics might have been cut in half. Better late than dead, I've always said.

I know that ultimately I will be completely freed from all aspects of time, including punctuality, so I'm going to try to loosen it up a little bit along the way. A friend once said, "We're going to be gone a lot longer than we are here." I try to appreciate this fact in stolen moments from somebody else's time. I know that I can't take it with me, so I think I'll spend it on myself before I go.*

Recently I was on a transcontinental trip by air across the United States. While searching for reading material I picked up the airline's monthly magazine and was particularly struck by an article in it written by a psychiatrist who teaches a popular course at Harvard University's Graduate School of Business Administration. Only husband and wife teams pursuing graduate study in the Master in Business Administration program are eligible to take the course. The course is aimed at instructing them on how to place work, home, and leisure in proper perspective.

According to the Harvard professor, many men who are outstanding managers on the job are miserable managers in both their home and their leisure environments. In verbalizing their aspirations and expectations in the classroom setting, these successful executives paint the following picture. The work arena is like a football field or a baseball diamond. It is *the* place where one experiences excitement, challenge, adventure, and action. Home is like a locker room, where one rests *briefly*—to gather strength before charging back into the work stadium and throwing oneself again into the exciting game of work. The resulting illiteracy in home-life and leisure-time management spells doom and catastrophe for many a marriage. Also, off-the-job problems do not remain off the job, but spill out over the desks and onto the floor of the work arena itself.

There are indeed many people who feel more at home when at work away from home. There is the stockbroker who takes his first vacation in five years, suffers two days on the beach, and is driven by anxiety back to his work world. There is the manager who feels guilty about "wasting" an afternoon watching a football game. Psychiatrist Francis L. Clark of Georgetown University views such people as victims of the American work ethic, which fails to take into account that leisure should complement work if one is to enjoy mental health and give full rein to one's creative impulses. For such individuals, work is their whole life and they cannot seem to enjoy anything else. They can no more give up work than an alcoholic can give up booze. In Clark's view, somewhere along the line Americans have lost something they had, instinctively, in childhood: a capacity for play, for fun, for engaging in pursuits that are ends in themselves and have no "practical" or "constructive" purpose.

Dr. Alexander Reid Martin, former chairman of the American Psychiatric Association's Standing Committee on Leisure Time and Its Uses, expresses it this way: "Leisure is not the inevitable result of spare time, a holiday, week end, or vacation. It is, in the first place, a particular state or condition of the mind and being—more specifically, an actively receptive condition of the whole personality." Martin further emphasizes that leisure is not the opposite of work, in the sense of being opposed to work. In work there is a focusing of energies, a contraction of faculties, and an acuteness of consciousness; during leisure there is an unfocusing of energies, relaxation of faculties, and a greater diffusion of consciousness. Psychiatrist Francis Clark says that creative growth depends on a work-leisure cycle; it is never achieved through leisure alone, but it is impossible without it.

Many thinkers have spoken about leisure. Said Socrates: "Leisure is the best of all possessions." In the words of Aristotle: "The goal of education is the wise use of leisure." Bertrand Russell said: "To be able to fill leisure intelligently is the last product of civilization." And Logan Piersall Smith commented: "If you are losing your leisure— look out, you may be losing your soul."

Attention has been drawn to workers who demonstrate a high resistance to leisure pursuits. What has been said applies to a number of people in the workforce, but the issue of resistance to leisure should be seen in its proper perspective. For workers who are devoted to their job, the pursuit of leisure is likely to be passive rather than active. But such an obsession with work is likely to be characteristic of a minority of people in the total workforce. Clearly, for many engineers and scientists and project managers working on Viking I and Viking II Mars missions in 1976, their work was probably the whole ball game. But when we talk about a total workforce that includes construction workers, bus drivers, assemblers, punch-press operators, office workers, and the millions of others doing routine work, we come up with a different conclusion. Most of these people demonstrate minimal resistance to leisure.

Whether or not people use leisure in an intelligent manner is another story. However, one thing remains incontrovertible: Most employees want more leisure time. They want to pursue off-the-job satisfactions—which means more vacation days and holidays and less overtime. Of course, there are also economic reasons why employees and unions push for reductions in the workweek. Making significant progress in reducing work hours means increasing job opportunities for unemployed persons. For example, during the fall of 1976, one of the demands made by United Auto Workers representatives in their contract negotiations with management was more time off the job. The union pushed the issue for at least three reasons: The work itself was not a source of satisfaction, union members wanted more leisure, and cutting work hours meant more jobs for the unemployed.

In reality, like it or not, we are headed toward more leisure—a trend some people perceive as unfortunate, yet one that most workers welcome. Max Kaplan, director of the University of South Florida's Leisure Studies Institute, reminds us that in little more than a century the workweek in the United States has been reduced from 70 hours to about 40 hours. The explosion of knowledge, computerization, advancing productivity, the pursuit of leisure, all mean further reductions in the workweek. We shall continue to make progress in this direction, and probably at an accelerated pace.

As illustrated throughout this book, *flexitime is compatible with a trend toward more leisure.* Use of the system opens the door to all kinds of off-the-job opportunities, including more time with family, more time for recreational pursuits, and more time for discharging off-the-job obligations of a personal nature. Flexitime also provides for a smoother alignment between job responsibilities and off-the-job interests. And, in all probability, as the system becomes more familiar, it will be supported enthusiastically by those psychiatrists who argue that "work freaks" must be brought face to face with the great big world of leisure out there eager to embrace them as members, a world they should actively participate in and enjoy.

Productivity

Work and leisure are like two sides of the same coin. Although only one side can "come up" at any given "flip of the coin," both are necessary to make the currency "legal." Feelings, attitudes, emotions, and learned behavior patterns are inextricably linked to work and leisure. The human being is the repository of all value — the "coin of the realm."

When productivity comes into the picture, relationships become scrambled and less clear. Work and leisure remain essentially related to one another, but no longer as the only repositories of value. In one view, leisure evolves into work, and work results in productivity. In another view, work results in productivity, and productivity enables workers to engage in leisure pursuits. A third view is that thoughts about productivity lead to work, and the aftereffect of work is leisure. Still another view is that, although people are essential contributors to it, productivity is mainly a matter of logic, hard facts, machinery, and quantifiable things. In this last view, people are of secondary importance.

My intention is not to separate the three elements from one another and rank them in order of merit. We can all agree that productivity is essential to the economic health of American society and, like work and leisure, is crucial to our discussion.

Productivity is often described in terms of output per worker-hour, which includes a particular standard of quality. Or, when calculated as the amount of goods produced per worker-hour, productivity rises whenever capital inputs, improved technology, and employee performance spur output increases without requiring expansion of the workforce. During the first half of 1976, for example, prices rose at an annual rate of about 4 percent, a vast improvement over the double-digit inflation rate prevailing in much of 1974 and 1975. Unfortunately, however, during the last months of 1976, prices rose at an annual rate of about 7 percent.

During the first half of 1976, productivity was 4.5 percent

higher than a year earlier, when the most recent economic recovery was beginning. By contrast, productivity rose only 2.1 percent during 1975. The recent 4.5 percent increase is high by almost any standard. It compares with an average annual rise of 2.6 percent since 1909 and 2.9 percent since World War II. In the first year of the last economic upturn, which ran from late 1970 to late 1973, productivity rose only 3.2 percent.

In addition to affecting prices, productivity also affects wages. A large productivity advance offsets the cost of a large pay increase. If a worker in an appliance factory wins a 7 percent hourly pay increase but also begins turning out 7 percent more applications per hour, the per-unit cost of his or her labor does not rise. Labor costs have been cited as a major source of inflationary pressure in recent years.

During the latter part of 1977, in making predictions for the four-year period 1978–1981, a number of economists were forecasting that the average annual inflation rate would be in the 5 to 6 percent range. For the same four-year span, after discounting the inflationary rise, less optimistic economists were predicting that the economy would show an average annual real growth rate of about 2 percent. However, some respected economists were predicting that the average annual growth rate would be 5 percent. In regard to unemployment, it appeared that the rate might not dip below 5 percent until 1981, at the earliest. Economic forecasting is a fragile business.

Between 1960 and 1974, productivity rose more rapidly in Japan, France, West Germany, and even economically troubled Britain than in the United States. More recently, however, the picture has changed considerably. For example, in 1975 productivity only inched ahead in West Germany, and declined substantially in Japan, France, and Britain. In 1976, of eight major countries in the industrial world — the United States, Japan, France, West Germany, Britain, Italy, the Netherlands, and Belgium — only one, West Germany, showed a lower inflation rate than the United States.

Looking far down the road, experts detect conflicting forces likely to affect U.S. productivity trends. There is a growing realization that the United States is undergoing major changes that in the aggregate could alter the structure of our society. Increasingly our economy is affected by developments taking place in world markets. From a former surplus of energy at bargain prices, the outlook now is for dearth and high costs. Where raw materials were once deemed in abundance, the outlook now is for relative scarcity and higher costs. Concerning humanistic management, the belief is growing that as people become better educated, they can expect more personal satisfaction and greater challenge from their working life than their parents experienced. Increasingly, our society is raising questions about whether there are more effective ways to sustain a high level of productivity growth and improve the quality of working life.

The more one considers questions of productivity, the greater the complexity of the subject becomes. Although some definitions of productivity are quite simple, multiple problems often arise when attempting to measure it. In recent testimony before the Senate Committee on Government Operations, Senator Charles Percy of Illinois said: "There is a myriad of approaches to the problem that not only involves the turnover of working capital. It involves the skill of the workers, the attitude of the workers, and such things as absenteeism, tardy workers, excessive scrap and rework, poor quality of work, [and] a poor attitude of people toward work."

The 94th Congress created "The National Center for Productivity and Quality of Working Life." It acts as an independent agency within the Executive Branch to promote America's continued productivity growth. The Center is a forum for the discussion of key policy issues by representatives of labor, business, government, and consumers. During 1976, then Vice President Nelson A. Rockefeller was chairman. In the following paragraphs I shall attempt to summarize a number of essential ideas offered by the Center.

Economists have endeavored continuously to arrive at a better measurement of productivity and what goes into it. They know that output per worker-hour is not a complete measure, particularly in work situations where the output cannot be counted in terms of number of units within a given time. As a result, the idea of "total-factor" productivity has been put forward. The total-factor view of productivity includes not only the cost of employee time but also such factors as capital investment, raw materials, energy use, and technology. In manufacturing industries, the costs and contributions of all these factors are difficult enough to identify and measure. Calculation becomes even more complex in the service industries, and there is a growing percentage of service-type jobs. On a production line, new machinery can often sharply raise workers' hourly output. In many service occupations, by contrast, it is difficult to estimate productivity gains precisely.

In looking carefully at total-factor productivity to see how productivity might be improved, it is imperative to acknowledge the increasing importance of the part played by people. The Center advances the following line of thought: "It is people, after all, who do the work, or make sure that machines are doing the work, or direct others to do the work, or decide about capital investment and technology needed to get work done, or determine what work practices will be used."

In an era in which technology and organizational practices associated with technology are undergoing changes of monumental proportions, organizations have devoted insufficient attention to how these changes in the work environment are affecting people. Various industries, including the service industries (banking, insurance, utilities, government, and so forth), are discovering that people can literally and figuratively throw a monkey wrench into electronic machinery. Paradoxically, in many industries the people part of productivity has become more important then ever *because of,* not in spite of, new technology and the new work routines it enforces on operations.

More capable and more highly motivated employees who will stay with the organization are essential for new technology to be productive enough to be worth what it costs. Turnover and recruiting are costly. Organizations must find and hold onto competent and motivated people, because it takes qualified personnel to maintain operations using sophisticated equipment. Given the demands and needs of the times, organizations have little choice but to give increased attention to the quality of their human resources, and to how these human resources can be wisely used.

Organizations have proved their innovative capabilities in introducing sophisticated physical technology. Just as they buy and install new equipment, they must invent and introduce humanistic innovations on the people side, and by deliberate design. Social and humanistic technologies offer ways to raise productivity levels while simultaneously improving the quality of working life.

The preceding paragraphs disclose major ideas advanced by The National Center for Productivity and Quality of Working Life. As suggested, to sustain and improve productivity, organizations need to introduce innovations in humanistic as well as physical technology, and by deliberate design. Does not a more vigorous application of flexible working hours fit the needs of the times? As documented throughout this book, where flexitime is used, *productivity levels are generally either sustained or raised.*

A Point of View

As mentioned previously, the 4-day, 40-hour workweek is mainly a product of the United States, whereas flexitime's origins are traced to Europe. Cultural mores in part explain why these relatively new working-time patterns grew initially on separate continents. Traditionally, European nations sprinkle numerous national and religious holidays over a calendar year, and often combine these with added time off the job to make longer vacation breaks. Also, lunch breaks of two and three hours are not uncommon.

I worked and lived in Europe and the Far East for nine years (as a university teacher with the overseas programs of the University of Maryland and Ball State University) and have firsthand knowledge of cultural differences. Especially in Italy and Spain, one should not plan to do much more than have lunch and rest during the midafternoon. When traveling by car in Italy, a driver should not plan to stop for gasoline between noon and 2:30, since service stations will read *chiuso* (closed) during at least that 2½-hour period in most cities and on most roads in that nation. I'm certain that many of my readers have similar travel memories. The point is that much of Europe traditionally views work and leisure in a reciprocal relationship, believing that work and leisure complement rather than contradict one another.

International interest in new working-time patterns led the Organization for Economic Cooperation and Development (OECD) to sponsor a conference in Paris in September 1972 " . . . to promote diversification and variability in the regulation and allocation of time for work, study, and leisure, under the highest possible freedom of individual choice." Delegates from the 23 OECD member countries were present. Heinz Allenspach, director of the Swiss Employers Association and a flexitime supporter, contended that flexible working time is in tune with modern society.

Some European delegates to the conference felt that the United States has bred a money-grubbing workforce interested in getting work out of the way — by compressing the workweek, if necessary —

rather than enjoying the more relaxed approach to work inherent in gliding time. In support of gliding time and in opposition to the 4-day workweek, Allenspach criticized compressed workweek formats as a reflection of the philosophy that work is a chore offering no prospect of on-the-job satisfaction. "Personally, I cannot get used to the idea that the worker must live for four whole days for work alone and for recuperating the strength he needs, while his cultural and social life, his human contacts in and outside the family, and his leisure time activities are pushed back and compressed into two weekdays and Sunday."

Clearly, flexible-working-hours systems will not solve all problems of morale, job satisfaction, work motivation, and productivity. But neither will a compressed workweek of 4 workdays and 10 work hours per day. The track record for the 4/40 compressed workweek is quite good. According to an American Management Associations report, one of every 12 organizations that tried the 4/40 plan dropped it. Many other organizations have found it a mixed blessing. John Roberts Inc. (a Texas company that manufactures school rings), Bergman Manufacturers (based in Texas), Fife Corporation (a company in Oklahoma City that makes industrial process controls), *Field & Stream* magazine, and Hon Industries (a metal-working firm in Iowa) are examples of firms that dropped the 4/40 system during the 1970s. Worker fatigue remains one of the big problems inherent in the 4/40 system. If the track record of the 4/40 system is quite good, flexitime's track record is very good. I'm aware of only one company where flexitime failed.

Earlier I spoke about the use of flexible hours in the U.S. Geological Survey. As the reader recalls, as part of a one-year experiment some 3,000 Geological Survey workers in the District of Columbia area went on flexible hours beginning in 1975. Among the agency's findings published in 1976 was the response to a question put to employees on the "All-Employees Questionnaire" following a trial experience with flexitime. Here's the question:

> Legislation is pending before Congress which would permit a four-day workweek (10-hour workdays) or a "broader" system of flexible hours (under this "broader" system of flexible hours, employees could vary the number of hours they worked each day, week, or pay period, provided that they worked the appropriate number of hours within a specified period—for example, any combination of hours per day equaling 40 hours per week; or any combination of hours per day or

per week provided they equal 80 hours per pay period, etc.). If this legislation were enacted and you had your choice, which *one* of the following would you favor?

Here are the selection alternatives and the respondents' choices:

Fixed hours	2%
Staggered hours	1%
Present flexitime	24%
Four-day week	39%
Broader flexitime	34%

The responses suggest a number of conclusions. (1) Not many
Geological Survey workers preferred fixed hours or staggered hours.
(2) The 4-day workweek received a substantial vote (39 percent). (3)
Some 58 percent favored a flexitime arrangement: either a flexitime
plan with more flexibility or the Geological Survey's flexitime plan as
operated at the time. Overall, therefore, both flexitime and the 4/40
system came out as big winners. (It should be noted, however, that
employees answering the questionnaire had not worked under the 4-
day arrangement.)

In 1974, I directed a study of flexible hours usage among nonmanagerial-level clerical workers in the banking industry. Colleague
Bruce M. Lieblich and I sought to survey the 300 largest banks in the
United States—ranked by total deposits held. Responding banks
numbered 160. We found that 10 percent of these banks had a formal
flexitime program in operation in 1973. For that calendar year, 88
percent of the user banks had either "very good results with flexitime" or "good results with flexitime," as compared with the previous
work system. The remaining 12 percent reported "no significant
change in results." No banks reported "poor results with flexitime" or
"very poor results with flexitime."

Of particular interest to the issue of flexible hours in the immediate future is another question explored in the bank study. Top
management at all 160 banks—both users and nonusers of flexitime
—responded to this question: "In comparison to 1973, in which direction will the banking industry as a whole move during the next seven
years (1974–1980)—in terms of the use of flexitime at the nonmanagerial level?" Seventy-six percent of the respondents projected
an "increasing rate of adoption," 22 percent forecast "no significant
change in rate of adoption," and 2 percent visualized a "decreasing

rate of adoption." In brief, more than three-fourths projected an increase in the use of flexitime in the immediate future.

What is the future of working-time patterns in the United States? Concerning the 4-day workweek, clearly the 4/40 arrangement will not thrive. Rather, workers would hope to see a 4-day workweek of 8 hours per day and 32 hours per week before the end of this century. Unions were not supportive of the 4/40 plan in 1977. In fact, most union leaders at the international level were vigorously directing efforts to bury the 4/40 concept.

John L. Zalusky, representing the AFL-CIO's research department, made these comments in a 1977 speech before the National Conference on Alternative Work Schedules:

> When we talk about the compressed workweek, we in the labor movement prefer to view it in a much broader context than has recently been the practice. The compressed workweek to us means shorter hours per day, per week, per year, and indeed a shorter working career at no loss in pay. However, to many outside the labor movement the compressed workweek . . . means something else — four 10-hour days, or in one case, three 12-hour days. This isn't more leisure; it is merely the same amount of time on the job packaged differently for marketing. With these programs we have serious problems. The 4-day, 40-hour week merely juggles the work schedule around. No additional time off the job is created; no new jobs are created; and there is, in fact, no reduction in the workweek. . . .
>
> Additionally, the 10-hour day does not fit into the social fabric of our country, unless the worker is childless and big on camping. Although workers have an additional day off to enjoy their leisure, in most cases their children or spouse do not enjoy the same free time. The worker, in fact, is away from home 12 to 13 hours a day rather than 10 or 11. Social functions they may otherwise engage in such as church activities, scouting, PTA, and others are well under way before they finish their evening meal. The end result would be the phenomenon sociologists describe as social isolation. . . .
>
> The idea of five 7-hour days (the 35-hour workweek) or four 8-hour days (the 4-day workweek) is our objective.

The hard winter of 1976–1977 — the coldest since Colonial days, we are told — and the consequent energy crunch got more people talking again about the 4-day workweek. But on examining the question at greater depth, most people in Washington and around the country came to realize the complexities involved in attempting to move to a 4-day workweek—whether 4 days of 10 work hours or 4 days of 8 work hours. Especially from an economic standpoint, the nation as a whole cannot shift overnight from a *standard* 5-day workweek to one of 4 days. The magnitude of such a sudden transition would be about as subtle as an earthquake measuring 7.00 on the Richter scale. For example, the United Auto Workers union has been pressing to make a 4-day, 32-hour workweek an industry standard. As explained in an article appearing in 1977 in *The Wall Street Journal,* if there were no operating efficiencies generated by a changeover, the automobile industry would need 25 percent more employees working 32 hours a week to accomplish the amount of work presently being done by the 40-hour-a-week workforce.

There are a number of objections to a 4-day, 32-hour workweek. Such an arrangement would do nothing to raise total output, the ultimate source of more jobs and more income. In fact, in many ways industry would probably be less efficient after sweeping changes had been made in long-established work practices. Less work for the same pay would also mean higher costs and strong upward pressures on prices. Real income might decline, as employees who were working fewer hours might discover that they also could purchase fewer goods and services with paychecks of the same amount. Some employees would use their new free time to moonlight, taking on part-time second jobs. The net result of a 4-day, 32-hour workweek, by itself, could easily be lower real income for the employed and fewer new jobs for the unemployed. Such a result is hardly desirable.

Through the Fair Labor Standards Act of 1938, Congress established the standard workweek of 40 hours, with time-and-a-half overtime pay for work in excess of 40 hours. The remarkable fact is that there has been almost no change in the average workweek since World War II. At least this tends to be true for most full-time workers.

When some unions use leverage to shorten the workweek with no reduction in pay, as the UAW did in 1976, workers naturally like the idea. But there is little indication that the vast majority of workers in the labor force are ready to exchange income for more leisure at the present time. Since World War II, various related factors have led most employees to prefer increased income. Immediately after the war, the entire population had a huge backlog of desires for goods— unfulfilled needs built up through 16 years of depression and war.

Consumers wanted boats, cars, houses, appliances, and many other things. And not long after the war the nation experienced a soaring birthrate. More dollars were required to raise children and send them to school and college.

It is of course impossible to say what the years ahead will bring. If the birthrate remains flat, if inflation pressures subside and the rate of inflation should drop to annual levels of about 4 percent, the result could be an increased demand for leisure and the resumption of a gradual shortening of the average workweek. Furthermore, if unemployment remains at dangerously high levels, the drive by major unions for a drastic cut in work hours, at no cut in pay, might win new converts. On the other hand, if the birthrate rises and the rate of inflation stays at high levels or accelerates, it is highly probable that most Americans will opt for increased income rather than increased leisure.* In an overall appraisal of the workweek issue, *The Wall Street Journal* commented in 1977: "The economy surely has its problems, but a 32-hour week by itself isn't the solution."

What, then, is the future of flexitime, staggered hours, flexitour, and group flexibility? Among these alternative work patterns, flexitime offers far more opportunities for employees and employers; consequently, it is likely to become by far the most popular schedule. But the staggered hours and flexitour schedules will have their role. Although not restricted to assembly-line operations and multiple shifts, the two schedules probably will find their greatest utilization in these circumstances. Concerning group flexibility, increased popularity and application are likely, especially in small organizations and in small work groups. And in regard to part-time employment that takes the form of job sharing ("twinning"), organizations will become increasingly aware of flexitime's merits.

The emphasis of this book is on flexitime. As of 1977 it appeared that the AFL-CIO leadership was in no mood to support flexitime debiting and crediting options, at least where arrangements would result in a weakening of overtime-pay requirements (this issue was discussed in Chapter 5). On the other hand, unions were in the process of further investigating the advantages built into the flexitime

---

*This possible development in no way contradicts what was said previously in the chapter, under the section entitled "Leisure." It was mentioned there that we are headed toward more leisure. That is, in the year 2000 the workweek will be significantly less than 40 hours; consequently, more leisure will be available. And in the year 2050, there will again be fewer work hours and more leisure hours.

concept. The Communications Workers of America is an example. CWA union members at General Telephone of California have worked under flexitime for the past few years. And provisions of 1977 contracts successfully negotiated between AT&T and CWA locals (states) called for flexitime work schedules at Pacific Bell, Mountain Bell, and Michigan Bell.

At the National Conference on Alternative Work Schedules held in Chicago in 1977, John L. Zalusky of the AFL-CIO said: "Labor unions and their members will welcome the opportunity to look at almost any alternative work-schedule proposal. Flexitime appears to be the most promising concept we have dealt with so far. The 10-hour, 4-day, 40-hour week offers very little; and job sharing offers even less. What we are looking for is the national recognition of the demise of the 40-hour workweek."

What final thoughts might be expressed about flexitime in relation to projected changes in the duration of the workday and the workweek? Within the 5-day-workweek format, in the years ahead we shall observe organizations move increasingly toward the 7½-hour workday (and a corresponding 37½-hour workweek), and subsequently toward a 7-hour workday (and a corresponding 35-hour workweek). In fact, a standard workweek of 32 hours by the year 2000 is not an impossibility. The closer we come to a standard workweek of 32 hours, the greater will be the proliferation of the 4-day workweek. It seems reasonable to assume that the transition will be evolutionary rather than revolutionary.

In an appropriate organizational setting, flexitime will be easily adaptable to a workweek of 37½ hours, 35 hours, 32 hours, or almost any workweek duration. Furthermore, whether organizations structure the total hours over 5 days, 4½ days, or 4 days, active consideration of flexitime will be appropriate. Flexitime is not a system that will soon pass into oblivion. Its popularity will grow. It is truly futuristic in design.

International management consultant John Diebold was asked recently to speculate on possible changes in work practices in the United States. He said: "I'm convinced that in the very near future it's going to be regarded as wrong that workers should be obliged to work only at times of the day and times of the year and times of their life that are most convenient for their employers." I subscribe to Diebold's point of view.

But what about the present moment? Some flexitime programs

already have a slice of the future built into them. For example, some organizations with flexitime are able to offer the option of borrowing and crediting work hours—without overtime-pay restrictions. Thus, in some respects, for the employees of these organizations, *the time of the 4½-day and 4-day workweek has already arrived.* For the fortunate few, the future is now.

Some employees are obsessed with work and have neither the interest nor the time to pursue off-the-job satisfactions. They are a minority in the workforce. By contrast, some employees are obsessed with pursuing off-the-job satisfactions; for them the job itself is neither meaningful nor pertinent as a source of satisfaction. They also are a minority in the workforce. In general, it is accurate to say that most persons in the labor force want additional on-the-job satisfactions *and* additional off-job satisfactions. It is not an either-or question for most workers. As stated in numerous ways throughout this book, flexitime enhances both on-the-job and off-the-job satisfactions. For reasons of economics as well as for humanistic reasons pertaining to the quality of work life in America, organizations must be more innovative and imaginative in applying flexitime.

I recently talked with a number of office workers employed at a downtown Los Angeles industrial supply firm. In one office the workforce consisted of a number of bookkeepers, all of whom were accountable to the same supervisor. Recording entries, processing accounts, and keeping accounts up to date were among the major functions performed in this particular office. At the end of each day the office manager laid out the accounts to be taken care of during the next workday. With one exception, the employees lived a considerable distance from downtown Los Angeles. As one bookkeeper remarked: "During rush hour it takes me an hour and forty-five minutes to drive to work. If I left home earlier in the morning, the drive would take only one hour, but the office doesn't open until 8:30."

This situation suggests the ultimate question managers must ask themselves. Is the working-time pattern in your firm based on a logical assessment of the firm's basic function, the nature of its business, societal needs, employee needs, and organizational climate? Or is it based primarily on tradition?

Index

DATE DUE

DEC 7 198			
GAYLORD			PRINTED IN U.S.A